FOOTBALL, SHE WROTE

FOOTBALL, SHE WROTE

AN ANTHOLOGY OF WOMEN'S WRITING ON THE GAME

Published by Floodlit Dreams Ltd, 2021.

Copyright © Floodlit Dreams and the authors.

Floodlit Dreams and the writers in this book have asserted their
rights under the Copyright, Design and Patents Act of 1988
to be identified as the authors of this work.

All rights reserved. No part of this publication may be reproduced,
stored in a retrieval system or transmitted in any form or by any means
electronic, mechanical, photocopying, recording or otherwise,
without the prior permission of both the copyright owner
and the above publisher of this book.

A CIP catalogue record for this book is available from the British Library.

ISBN: 9781838030025

Floodlit Dreams Ltd
5-6 George St
St Albans
Herts
United Kingdom
AL3 4ER

www.floodlitdreams.com

Cover design by Steve Leard
Picture editing by Alexandra Ridley
Printed through SS Media Ltd, Rickmansworth, Hertfordshire, WD3 1RE
Designed and set by seagulls.net

CONTENTS

FOREWORD — VIII
    Gabby Logan MBE

THE GIRLS OF '72 — 1
    Julie Welch

MY SEASON-TICKET FRIEND — 21
    Hayley Davinson

COOK WHO FOUND THE RIGHT RECIPE — 29
    Kate Battersby

TWO BLACK ROOKIES AND A MICROPHONE — 41
    Kehinde Adeogun

ESTATE OF MIND: THE MAKING OF EMMA HAYES — 51
    Suzanne Wrack

ANFIELD OF DREAMS — 63
    Cassie Whittell

WINNING AND LOSING — 73
    Molly Hudson

HIGHS AND LOWESTOFT — 85
    Ali Rampling

TAKE THREE WOMEN… — 95
    Isabelle Latifa Barker

WHAT IT COULD BE LIKE — 105
    Katie Mishner

GIRLS WILL BE BOYS — 117
    Fadumo Olow

A BUNCH OF FIVES	127
Jade Craddock	
STADIUMS OF LIGHT	141
Jane Purdon	
THE ACCIDENTAL GOALKEEPER	151
Julia West	
A CULTURE STILL CRYING OUT FOR CHANGE	159
Katie Whyatt	
GIANFRANCO WHO?	169
Renuka Odedra	
IS THIS THE REAL LIFE...?	177
Alison Bender	
MUMS UNITED	191
Christina Philippou	
AT THE COURT OF ST JAMES	201
Louise Taylor	
ALL INCLUSIVE	215
Tracy Light	
CONTRIBUTORS	227
ACKNOWLEDGEMENTS	232
Ian Ridley	

FOREWORD
BY GABBY LOGAN MBE

When I was a kid girls didn't play football, let alone grow up to write about it. When I say didn't, I mean couldn't. At my school there were probably six or seven of us who wanted to play in a five-a-side tournament. They, like me, were just the kind of girls who were in every sports team, the same kids putting their hands up for everything – the netball, the hockey.

My friend Basia, she was a really talented footballer. I always remember thinking how audacious she was, how ballsy and gutsy, muscling the ball off the boys at breaktime. We were thirteen years old then, the age you were expected to want to stand and flirt with boys, not tackle them. But with no football in our area, there were no female role models. So Basia – or any other girl who wanted to play – had nowhere to go with it. Missed opportunities for too many generations.

Instead, my world growing up was all about the men's game. Every weekend I was off to a match with my mum and my siblings, to watch my dad play. There were always women around, mainly afterwards in the players' lounge – and not just wives but fans too. But I don't recall many other girls going to games. They were not encouraged to, I suppose. At that time everything going wrong in society was being magnified on the football terraces. It wasn't the sort of place that you would want to bring your teenage daughter on a Saturday.

FOREWORD BY GABBY LOGAN MBE

I remember going to Leeds games and driving past all the away fans being frogmarched by police from the station. Or staring up at huge police horses when my dad was at Tottenham. There were often sirens and skirmishes. I used to feel a rush of adrenalin seeing that, that fight-or-flight reflex. Will it kick off? Will we be OK? I can't believe my mum carried on taking us, to be honest.

But once you were inside the ground, that's when the magic happened. The emotion of the victories and the defeats, the drama, the ebbs and flows. That highly compelling, unscripted reality that makes so many millions of people want to watch football.

I didn't ever think I might have a place in it, though. Not as a career. But I knew I wanted to work in broadcasting and so, after gymnastics, I was lucky enough to get an opening doing local sports radio in Newcastle.

It was the era of Warren Barton and David Ginola – and the absolute opposite of my experiences of going to Leeds in the 1980s. St James' Park was a citadel, this amazing place right in the middle of the city, a cathedral of joy. The whole city turns black and white on a Saturday. Everyone in their shirts, women included. To work in that environment was pure delight. No one batted an eyelid that I was a woman. It was the right place to cut my teeth.

I'll never forget my first big interview there. I was twenty-one years old and Darren Huckerby had just signed for Newcastle. There we both were, at St James' Park, and I think it was probably a first for the two of us because I asked him a load of questions and he nodded his head. For a radio interview.

Then Sky came calling, and a dream move to London to work in TV. At that time Sky wasn't putting women in serious positions for sports broadcasting; it was all reading autocue. But I desperately wanted to do live sport, so I knocked on the door of my boss every day until he eventually gave in… and sent me to the ice hockey. But Sky truly was an amazing place to learn because I was doing hours and hours of live TV. It was a bit gnarly at times, with old guys who could be hard and cutting.

You had to suck it up and get on with it. But there were other times, too, where they would show a human side and help you out.

In 1998, ITV got in touch and asked me to host *On the Ball* – the first female presenter to front a football show. Looking back at the young me now, I can't help thinking, *My God, you must have had some balls.* I can't believe I had the confidence to do it. I looked so comfortable. I didn't overthink it. But you know what helped me? Not having social media. I didn't see why I shouldn't be there. Whereas now, if you do anything pioneering or different, people decide to tell you what they think. Perhaps I wouldn't have been so happy and relaxed if every time I turned my phone on there were 300 people telling me I should get back in the kitchen. (And actually they did, when social media started. But by then I was older and wiser. I'd done my 10,000 hours. I wasn't going to listen to them.)

One person I did listen to was my boss at the time, Brian Barwick. On a Monday I'd go in and ask, 'What did you think of the show?' And he'd say, 'Look, Gabby, you don't need to load your questions with knowledge. I know you know your stuff.' The thing about football, though, is that there is this emphasis on knowledge. Stats and facts. And I was obsessed. Every week, the *On the Ball* team would do a weekly quiz. And I regularly got 10/10.

When I did *Final Score* for the BBC I would memorise the tables each week so that if you asked me who was tenth in League Two I would know the answer. Every Saturday morning, over breakfast, my husband Kenny would say, 'Right, I'm going to go from the bottom up,' and quiz me on it. But eventually I became more relaxed about it. I realised I didn't need to prove myself all the time. These days, being across three sports, my knowledge of the League Two table isn't quite what it was. And, to be honest, that's not a bad thing.

It was at the BBC that I made the documentary *Sexism in Football?* in 2011. It was an eye-opener, listening to the stories of women working in the industry. And it also made me reflect on my own experiences. I was twenty-seven and with my mum at a Premier League game when the fans first chanted at me. My mum thought they were asking to see my teeth. I

FOREWORD BY GABBY LOGAN MBE

said to her, 'No, Mum, they want to see my tits.' 'Oh,' she said. And she gave them a cross look.

It wasn't to be the only occasion. Covering Manchester United away to Sparta Prague in the Champions League, with Sir Bobby Robson and Ally McCoist in the studio, a small contingent of travelling fans began singing, 'Get your tits out for the lads.' Sir Bobby was looking ahead like he couldn't hear them, and I was looking at Ally and he was looking a bit embarrassed. I just felt embarrassed that this was all happening in front of Sir Bobby. And then, all of a sudden, he just opened his jacket as if he was getting his tits out and started shaking his chest about. It was so funny and unexpected; he completely defused the situation and made them look like idiots. Afterwards he turned and winked at me.

The next day when I was in the airport, a very hungover Man Utd fan came up to me and said, 'Er, I was one of the lads who was singing "get your tits out". I'm really sorry.' I said to him, 'You wouldn't sing that if your wife or sister were sat next to you, would you?' And he said, 'No.' So I said, 'Right, well, don't sing it again.' I felt quite powerful telling him off. But I don't think I would have done that without Sir Bobby's support the night before.

During the making of that documentary I met the late, great, football writer Vikki Orvice. Her voice in the film was so powerful because she really was at the coalface of women reporting on football – the first female staff football writer on a tabloid. She shared some shocking stories with me. But, despite all of the challenges, she carried on. She made me realise how fortunate I had been in many ways. More importantly, she gave me hope for the future because, in pursuing her path, she had ripped a massive hole in that press-pack bigotry. I experienced some of that myself, as an England reporter – the only woman among all those old-school newspaper correspondents. And she did it long before I ever did. All power and credit to her.

This anthology, of course, is inspired by Vikki. It is a really important and timely collection of work. While there are now so many women working across the industry in front of camera, as pundits and commentators – and that feels like a really powerful development – women writers still have less visibility and opportunities. So to curate a body of written work, by women, is a milestone that should be marked.

Of course, I want us to get to the point where we don't have to talk about being women. Where people don't say to me – which they do regularly – 'Oh, you're my favourite female presenter.' I've even had bosses say that to me. Can I just be a presenter? Not a female one? Evidently we need to keep pushing boundaries – and that is exactly why this book is important.

Gabby Logan was talking to Anna Kessel MBE, women's sports editor of the Telegraph *and co-founder, with Shelley Alexander, of Women in Football.*

THE GIRLS OF '72

The century-long struggle was arduous and tortuous. Victim of its own success, the women's game even endured a fifty-year ban. **Julie Welch** *charts the injustices and celebrates the Scotland v England game that heralded a new era.*

THE FOOTBALL ASSOCIATION
WOMEN'S FOOTBALL MATCHES
Decision of Council, 5 December 1921

The following resolution was adopted :—

'Complaints having been made as to football being played by women, the Council feel impelled to express their strong opinion that the game of football is quite unsuitable for females and ought not to be encouraged.

For this reason the Council request the Clubs belonging to the Association to refuse the use of their grounds for such matches.'

* * *

Scotland v England, 1972. The fuzzy analogue TV footage, the scratchy soundtrack on the radio, that Hampden roar. You can see the late-spring sunlight bounce off Alan Ball's hair, feel the studs go in as Norman Hunter and Billy Bremner hew lumps out of everybody, practically hear the sound of the ref scribbling in his notebook. Forty-six bookings in the first twenty-eight minutes – what a sensation. 'For a long time players seemed more intent on kicking each other than the ball,' tutted the *Sunday Express*. 'A disgrace,' thundered the President of the Scottish FA.

Except this wasn't the annual grudge match of the Home International Championships, which, in the words of the *Guardian*, 'for millions across both sides of the border… represents a chance for the ultimate victory over the enemy'. It wasn't May in Hampden Park but a bitterly cold November afternoon at the Ravenscraig Stadium, a council-run facility in Greenock, Renfrewshire. It wasn't the men's game, either. It was the women's, and it brought to an end half a century of hurt.

Come to think of it, make that nearly a whole century. If you're going to tell the story of how this colossal milestone came about – an achievement that owed almost everything to the determination of two single-minded young women, Patricia Gregory and Elsie Cook, to get to a point where the UK's first officially sanctioned women's international in modern times could take place – you need to go further back. Much further, all the way to spring 1881 and an encounter between women's teams from London and Glasgow.

That long-ago Scotland v England was played over two legs – one in Edinburgh, the other in Glasgow. We know where the players came from and what they wore – jerseys, knickerbockers, stockings, belts, high-heeled boots, neckties. What we'll never know is who they were really. These were false names on the team sheet. In the repressive atmosphere of Victorian society, it was too risky for them to reveal their true identities. Just as well. While the Edinburgh leg went off reasonably peacefully (it finished 3-0 to Scotland), the Glasgow tie was something else. A large proportion of the 5,000 spectators ('the absence of the fair sex was notable,' according to reports) forced the game to be abandoned ten minutes into the second half when they breached the ropes enclosing the pitch and chased the women back onto a horse-drawn omnibus. To add to the disaster, the gatekeeper made off with the proceeds. 'Probably the first and last exhibition of a female football match,' harrumphed the *Nottinghamshire Guardian*.

Not likely. In 1895, at Crouch End in London and to much hoopla, the pseudonymous Nettie J. Honeyball, pioneering founder of the British Ladies Football Club, staged what was de facto inaccurately called The First Ever Ladies Football Match. 'The first few minutes were sufficient to show that football by women is totally out of the question,' stated *The Sketch*. The *British Medical Journal* weighed in: 'We can in no way sanction the reckless exposure to violence of organs which the common experience of women has led them in every way to protect.'

It was never really about boobs, of course. Or skills. What horrified them was the female invasion of a male preserve in an era when the outside world belonged to men and the woman's role was to be the angel in the house. A fat lot of notice the girls took of that. The medical profession might have tried to clamp down on them, the gentlemen of the press might have taken a dim view, but the women carried on playing. And when the outbreak of the First World War meant the men's game was largely shut down, women's teams stepped up, playing to raise money for war charities.

Along the way, they proved as popular as the men's. Too popular. When the war ended, the men came home to discover women's matches were pulling in numbers some modern-day Championship sides would kill for. A fixture featuring Dick, Kerr Ladies and Newcastle United Ladies, played at St James' Park in September 1919, attracted a crowd of 35,000 people and raised £1,200 (a quarter of a million in today's terms). Most of the 35,000 had come to see the Megan Rapinoe of her era: the shocking, sweary, chain-smoking Lily Parr.

Dick, Kerr Ladies was a factory team, and Lily Parr the star attraction. She stood nearly six feet tall, smoked like the burning bush and had long, silky black hair that she stuffed under a beanie hat to keep out of her eyes when playing. In her first season with them, she scored forty-three goals. She could find the net from any point on the pitch. She earned enough from football to buy her own house, in which she lived with a special friend called Mary. Nobody in Lily's family thought anything of it. They were just accepted as Lily and Mary. But the powers that be hated Lily Parr like poison. A woman revelling in her own brilliance, not caring what men thought of her – whatever next? When 53,000 packed into Goodison to watch, they decided enough was enough. For men to be men, women had to be women – not occupying jobs or galloping around in shorts, covered in mud, with dirt under their fingernails and all their hair cut off. Our boys had fought and suffered for four years to preserve our way of life. Their reward had to be to come home and find that way of life waiting for them.

In 1921 all four Football Associations of Great Britain banned women's football as being 'quite unsuitable for females'. The medical profession was called upon once again to endorse the directive. One Dr Elizabeth Sloan Chesser said: 'They may receive injuries from which they may never recover.' Dr Mary Scharlieb of Harley Street added: 'I consider it a most unsuitable game, too much for a woman's physical frame.' It had to be women who delivered the stab in the back.

They were denied the use of pitches, and officials and clubs were warned that disciplinary action would result if they assisted the women's game in any way. And that's how it stayed. In 1947 the Kent County Football Association suspended a referee because he was working as a manager/trainer with Kent Ladies Football Club. It justified its decision with the comment that 'women's football brings the game into disrepute.'

The women didn't stop playing, not all of them. Clubs such as Dick, Kerr Ladies and Manchester Corinthians defied the ban, playing on public parks, company playing fields and municipal stadiums. The Manchester club toured South America, twice, where 80,000 people watched them. But the ban had effectively put the brakes on any progress. To all intents and purposes, women's football in Britain was outlawed. The old men in blazers, the medical profession, the anti-suffragists, the patriarchy had won.

* * *

Girls! Soccer needs you
20-year-old Patricia Gregory, of Mayfield Road, Hornsey, is interested in starting up a female football team locally. She recently wrote a letter to the 'Journal' about it, and would like to hear the

ideas and comments of any other local ladies. She also wonders whether there is already a female team in Hornsey but the 'Journal' does not know of one. Letters on the subject welcome.

The Hornsey Journal, 2 June 1967

By the time Patricia Gregory and Elsie Cook were in their teens, a cultural revolution was beginning. This was the Sixties, when the West erupted in a spectacular of music, fashion, gender-bending rock stars and footballers as the new pin-ups. We were the generation that fell in love with the beautiful game: with Pelé, who as a miraculous teenager had announced himself at the 1958 World Cup and who as children we found far more thrilling than *Blue Peter*; with Jimmy Greaves who scored goals by magic; with that elusive, tragic firefly George Best. We saw Bobby Moore lifting the Jules Rimet Trophy to become the most famous man in Britain, and for many of us that was the turning point. We weren't content just to look. We wanted to be part of it.

The fight for female equality that began in the US was taking root in Britain – slowly. For a young woman now it must be hard to fathom – well, looking back, it still baffles me – how many rules and conventions existed to ensure girls couldn't follow their dreams. Nowhere was this more evident than in sport, where clubs from cricket to golf to running – to name just a handful – were adamantly men-only, where female athletes weren't allowed to take part in the 10,000 metres, let alone the marathon ('They said our fannies would fall out, dear,' I was once told by a salty old lady athlete). As for football, it was tough enough getting to write about it, but when it came to playing it, where do you kick off?

One place might be Tottenham High Road, where in 1967 Patricia Gregory was standing in the crowd watching Tottenham Hotspur's open-top bus parade after their FA Cup victory over Chelsea.

'I suddenly thought, *Why don't women play football?*, so I wrote to the *Hornsey Journal*, asking if anyone was interested,' Patricia said. 'All these girls started writing back to me saying, "I want to join your team." I was no good at sport but I could swim, I played badminton and did ballet and tap – which I still do. I didn't play football. I didn't have a team. But we got together in my parents' living room and formed one.'

Patricia's team came from all sorts of backgrounds. There were students, secretaries, telephone-switchboard operators; she herself was secretary to Roger Fowler-Wright, sports editor of the *Sunday Telegraph*, a career that led ultimately to that of network sports coordinator for ITV. What they had in common was that none of them had ever played football. Nor did they have a trainer – they ended up teaching themselves – or indeed anywhere to train. The latter problem, at least, was solved when a men's team, White Star, invited them to share their training facilities. They also found a name.

'In the 1930s there was an amateur men's team, White Ribbon,' said Patricia. 'They used to train with Spurs, but they'd disbanded by the start of the Second World War. So we became White Ribbon.'

Now they needed opponents. That July, Patricia wrote to the Football Association, asking if there were any leagues for women. Its Secretary, Denis Follows, was swift to nip that outrageous concept in the bud, responding by return of post thus:

Dear Miss Gregory,

I enclose herewith for your information a copy of the Council decision of December, 1921, which decision was confirmed by the Council in December, 1962.

As the Football Association does not recognise ladies football teams, I am unable to inform you of any League to which you could apply for Membership.

No problem. Patricia advertised in football magazines for matches. They mostly ended up playing young men's sides, on their pitches, all over the south-east. 'Men v women – it was absolutely forbidden, but I never heard of anyone disciplined.' The crucial response, though, was from one Arthur Hobbs, a Kent-based carpenter who had set up a tournament for women's teams at the Betteshanger Colliery ground, which by 1968 had attracted thirty-three teams. Impressed by Patricia's competence and enthusiasm, Hobbs suggested they get together to fight against the 1921 ban.

'A MAN is leading the fight to get the Football Association to lift their ban on women's soccer,' boggled the *Daily Mirror* in November 1968, reporting that Hobbs had lobbied the Prime Minister and the Minister for Sport to force the FA to acknowledge the women's game. Back then, it seemed the only way to get the press to take notice. On the sports pages you were more likely to see a mention of cage tiddlywinks than a women's football match. Anyway, it worked. The ban was lifted in 1969 and the Ladies Football Association of Great Britain and Northern Ireland – mercifully soon shortened to the Women's Football Association – was formed. Hobbs became the Hon. Secretary and Patricia the Hon. Assistant Secretary, and forty-four clubs formally registered. Now, step by step, they could start planning the journey towards recognition by the FA. Which is where Elsie Cook – first Secretary of the Scottish Women's Football Association and the first manager of the Scotland women's team – enters the line-up.

I first met Elsie, now a grandmother, a couple of years back on a summer morning at Hampden Park, where in the bowels of the stadium the Scottish Football Museum was hosting an exhibition in honour of Stewarton Thistle. It's long gone now but this was the club that became the pre-eminent Scottish women's team of the 1960s, during which time it nurtured Rose Reilly, one of the greatest ever female footballers. To learn how all that came about, of course, you have to wind back the tape to 1961, where on a public park Stewarton Thistle Ladies Football Club met Holyrood Bumbees in a charity game held to raise funds for Freedom from Hunger.

Stewarton is a small town in Ayrshire, and Elsie's mother, Betty Bennett, was a netball coach. The team she assembled included thirteen-year-old Elsie, Elsie's two aunties and a gifted seventeen-year-old from nearby Kilmarnock, Susan Ferries, who was ten times better than all the boys and scored every goal in Thistle's 7-0 victory. Before kick-off, Elsie knew nothing about the playing side. By the time ninety minutes were up, an idea had planted itself: she was going to start her own football club.

Any female who played football in the 1960s will identify with Elsie's account of her years as player/manager of Stewarton Thistle. These were days of using fishing nets for goal nets, folded newspapers down the front of socks for shinpads, and first-aid kits consisting of sticking plasters and Sloan's horse liniment; blotting up puddles and marking out lines on muddy local parks with sawdust begged from the local timber yard (because heaven forfend that you'd be granted use of an actual pitch); arranging fixtures by post because not every household boasted a telephone.

'I'd queue at the phone box on the day of the game, waiting to confirm our fixture was definitely on,' said Elsie.

Then there were the church-mouse budgets. The United Free Church Women's Guild raised funds by running whist drives, bring-and-buy sales, and Daffodil Teas (a fancy name for a spring fête). Stewarton Thistle weren't alone in that.

'White Ribbon didn't have any money,' said Patricia Gregory. 'We had jumble sales. I went house to house to collect anything people didn't want. This family disappeared, came back with this bundle of clothing. It was warm. I thought, *Who did they make undress?*'

As for the lack of creature comforts, that too was a near-universal experience.

'It was Thame Utd against Foden's,' said the England centre-back Wendy Owen, 'and we had to play on the Thame recreation ground. There were no changing facilities and it was really muddy that day, no grass. We were all covered in the stuff and the Foden's girls had to travel back to Cheshire. So we walked back into town and got hosed down at the cattle market.'

The local press duly recorded that 'The ladies had to be led down like a herd of cows.'

This, of course, was all part of the fun, of feeling you were part of a female insurgency. But there were pains and frustrations too, not least the inevitable incredulity and ridicule from the more unreconstructed members of the male sex. The Scottish girls also had to contend with official indifference. Elsie Cook recalls a series of pleading but futile phone conversations with the Scottish Football Association.

'I'd tell them we couldnae get proper refs. If we had a game, the other team's manager had to referee, or someone passing through the park who looked as though they'd know what was going on. And though I could teach how to head the ball, tackle, organise the lines, and could get them fighting again, there were no proper coaches. All I ever wanted was for girls to be allowed to play football, to be coached properly.'

Lack of a coaching structure was a common theme. Girls learned by playing street football along with the boys, sometimes pretending to be boys themselves so they could get into a team. Then everything would stop at secondary-school age, when they had to settle for netball. Often it came down to where you lived. The England centre-forward Pat Davies grew up in the village of Netley Abbey, on the edge of Southampton, which was developing a network of women's teams. She'd been playing with local lads from the age of five when she was scouted, aged twelve, by Southampton. Two-footed, with close ball control and good heading ability, striker was the obvious choice of position for her, and she thrived. Plus she just loved scoring goals.

'The sound of the ball hitting the back of the net always gave me goosebumps,' she said. 'Still does after all these years.'

Another player whose start was playing alongside the boys was Wendy Owen. She grew up in Seton, Oxfordshire, in a council estate with a big green in the middle of which she was out day and night playing football with her brothers – 'I'd be Geoff Hurst or Martin Peters.' Then her brothers joined a team. Why couldn't she? 'I was told it wasn't allowed. I was devastated.' Her dad stepped up. A youth-club leader, he promptly rang round a load of other youth clubs: 'Any girls interested in playing football?' Not half. Later, Seton, the club he formed, played a fixture against Thame. 'They thrashed us but I was spotted by their manager.'

That was when things really took off. Her dad would take her to matches, and they'd play on all kinds of pitches – at factories, military bases, even hospitals – and she'd stay overnight with the manager's family. There's a great postscript to this, by the way. When she was a sixth-former, her dad had a phone call from her teacher, asking him to stop Wendy playing football because it wouldn't get her anywhere. Later on, as an England international, Wendy played and coached all over the world, and everywhere in the world she went she sent that teacher a postcard.

Wendy's dad might have been a hero, but not everyone's parents felt the same. Time and again I've heard stories from that era of mothers who didn't want their daughters playing football because it might put off prospective husbands, of girls from strict families who had to resort to subterfuge to play. One was so frightened of her father's reaction she stationed her boots at a friend's house and picked them up on the way to games, though if you think that's sad, you ain't heard nothing yet. At one stage, the devout Catholic family of the midfielder Paddy McGroarty were so against her playing football they packed her off to a convent in Ireland. There is, as it happens, a satisfactory ending to this. From there she left to join the Army and Thame Utd and, despite being so Scottish she was Paddy Crerand's cousin, was picked to play for England in the 1972 game.

When did the tide start to turn? For the WFA, 1971 was the breakthrough year when UEFA issued a directive to member countries to recognise women's football. This was key. This was what they'd worked for. They could stage the first Women's FA Cup. They could go from having their existence ignored to being recognised as a governing body, and an atmosphere in which the FA was almost falling over itself to help out. That's the impression, anyway, gained from the minutes of the WFA's executive meeting in April 1971, which records that the FA were 'most anxious to assist us with supplying qualified coaches, and a qualified person to lead and manage a national team, and generally wanted to help and guide us on this matter.'

While all that was going on, though, a storm had to be weathered. Within the preceding two years Harry Batt, a WFA committee member and manager of Chiltern Valley Ladies, had twice taken club teams on tour in Europe, where they were misleadingly called an England XI. His vision – of kickstarting a women's professional league in England similar to that already established in Italy – had already caused ructions with fellow committee members. His decision to take a team to represent England at an all-expenses-paid 'World Cup' in Mexico that summer was the straw that finally collapsed the camel. For the WFA the issue was clear-cut.

'You couldn't have anybody going rogue and taking a team, whatever the team was, and calling it something it wasn't entitled to be called,' said Patricia. 'It was the era of Do As You're Told, and the WFA did everything by the book. He wasn't taking an England team to Mexico; it was a club side, Chiltern Valley Ladies with a couple of additions. It wasn't England; it wasn't even Great Britain. Stop it. It wasn't fair to all the other players that we were trying to represent and look after.'

The Mexico trip did not end well. The young 'England' team, starry-eyed at making their first Transatlantic flight and playing at the Aztec Stadium, suffered drubbings and injuries at the hands of other, more experienced international sides and returned to unwelcome headlines such as 'Football mayhem as women are hurt' and 'Soccer girls limp home to a rumpus'. Batt was banned by the WFA, Chiltern Valley Ladies disbanded, and the girls who went out to Mexico dispersed into other teams. Many of them remain steadfastly loyal to the manager who had given them what had been, in spite of everything, the trip of a lifetime, but it was an unpleasant episode that reminds us that injuries in football are not only physical – what can hurt as much is the crushing of dreams.

* * *

FIRST IMPRESSIONS

By Eric Worthington

It is now about three months since I was offered and accepted the position of Team Manager to the England Team. My first impression of women's football was at the meeting I had with the International Committee and the then Assistant Secretary,

Pat Gregory. During the discussion, the thought came to me that perhaps what the Association needed most of all was a full time publicity manager rather than a team manager! I was more than a little surprised by what they told me about the developments and the amount of highly organised football, both in England and the rest of the world. Either I had read the wrong newspapers, or news about women's football has not been found to be acceptable by the sports reporters of the mass media.

Women's Football News,
Newsletter of the Women's Football Association

The FA staff coach Eric Worthington was a lecturer at Loughborough and a former player with Watford and Bradford City, and in a climate where most qualified male coaches would have regarded it as demeaning to manage a women's team, he comes over as definitely one of the good guys. He applauded what he saw as soon as he attended the Inter-League tournaments that doubled as England trials.

'I saw patterns of movement by individuals and groups of players that appeared to be identical with male players. In some cases they were obviously superior to those some men could perform.' There were, of course, caveats: 'Perhaps the weakest of the ball techniques was in passing, where much inaccuracy could be seen … the lack of cleverness off the ball … Many players are operating at a low level of understanding of how to support in attack and defence'. There was, it followed, work to be done. It was time to see who was serious about doing it.

That September, from the 200 players picked out at the Inter-League trials, twenty-five went to final trials at Loughborough, where the squad would be whittled down to fifteen. What followed was a day and a half's coaching, culminating with a Probables v Possibles at Leicester City's training ground. Wendy Owen was in the Possibles.

'We lost 7-1. I was very sporty and played netball for Bucks, and the next week I was going to start at Dartford PE College. I'd only just arrived at Dartford when I got a letter telling me I'd been selected. It was amazing.

I'd convinced myself I hadn't got a chance. Now I had to get permission to take a week's leave, from this glorified girls' boarding school.

'It had a pastoral system. Incoming pupils were given a second-year girl to mentor them – she was your College Mother – and a third-year girl to be your College Grandmother. I asked my College Mother, "How can I get this time off?" She told me I had to go to the Principal's house on campus, request an audience and plead my case. "And wear a skirt," she added. "If you fail to wear a skirt, you can forget it."'

In a skirt borrowed from her College Grandmother, Wendy entered the Principal's study.

'I blurted out to this grey-haired, middle-aged, married woman that I'd been picked for the England team, and she looked shocked. "Surely women playing football is just a joke," she said. I explained how it was a serious competitive game for females. She sent me away, saying she was going to have to put it to the college governor. Next thing I see is the Principal standing on the steps with a bloke in a suit. She beckons to me. The suit is the football-mad college governor. Who's dying to meet me! I thought, *Does that mean I can go?*'

Indeed it did. In the week leading up to the international, Wendy joined the rest of the squad for an exhibition match at the *Daily Express* five-a-side tournament at Empire Pool, Wembley. Contested by teams from the First Division and looked on back then as one of the big indoor events of the sporting calendar, this was big-time. First off was a photoshoot at the stadium itself. They changed into their strips in the sacred dressing rooms, where the *Daily Mail* photographer must have thought the god of snappers was smiling down on him in the form of an attractive eighteen-year-old with long blonde hair and a misplaced trust in the integrity of the journalistic profession.

'He produced this eye make-up and was looking for someone to put it on,' said Wendy Owen, 'and I said, "I'll do it!" because my mum and dad took the *Mail* and I thought, *They'll see me in the paper*. I never even opened the compact. But that photo's followed me throughout life. Just google "Wendy Owen football".

No matter. When it came to what happened next, everyone was ecstatic: they were allowed to walk on the *actual pitch*.

'We walked up that tunnel,' said Patricia Gregory. 'Onto that pitch. It was very exciting! This was the hallowed turf! It was just the magic – it was special.'

When it was time to leave, Wendy picked some blades of grass to keep for posterity.

After that they played an exhibition game at the Empire Pool. More excitement: the thrill of brushing knees with George Best on the way to their seats in the players' section; chatting to all the male players – Mick Channon, Geoff Hurst, the Derby County lads, all the stars. As Wendy was the sub, she was roped in to be interviewed on TV during the interval.

'I rang my dad to warn him. There were no video recorders back then so he filmed our television set with me on it with his cine camera.'

This was only the start. From there the squad travelled to the National Training Centre at Bisham Abbey for a day of training: attacking and defending strategies, set plays and, in the evening, film analysis. The next day they headed for Greenock. They were booked into a posh hotel nearby. On that topic, a letter from Pat to each team member had made one thing absolutely clear:

> I have been in contact with the gentleman who is arranging the hotel booking for us and he informs me that he has been requested by the hotel in Scotland to make our party aware of one or two points. The first and most important is that dresses (or skirts) will be worn in the hotel by the female members of our party. This does not only refer to meal times. I realise this will hit some of you quite hard in that you appear to have been born and bred in trousers! However, the hotel is large and caters for wedding receptions etc., and we do not want to upset anyone, least of all a bride. The other request is that you refrain from walking round the hotel in football kit. This is an unnecessary request as I am sure you would have the good manners not to walk into dinner in your muddy football gear.

You can laugh about that now, but what also strikes you is the attention to detail. Everything that could be done was done because everything had to be right. It was that important. As the established organisation, England's WFA were the trailblazers, and for Patricia Gregory this was the biggest test. Earlier that year Arthur Hobbs had stepped down through ill health. She was the Secretary now. This was all on her.

* * *

Four months before the international, Elsie Cook became the founding Secretary of the Women's Scottish Football Association. Unlike Patricia, she had no resources, no large pool of players to choose from and no help from the men's Football Association. Of thirty-three European countries, Scotland alone continued to refuse to recognise the women's game. In September 1972 she managed to fix up a meeting with Willie Allan, the SFA Secretary. Now that the Women's SFA was up and running, surely he would acknowledge their existence.

'I was dead excited. I thought he'd see how keen I was. How much it meant. There he was. A wee man behind a big mahogany desk. "Look," he said. "We cannae offer recognition. We don't think it's suitable."

'"Why, Willie? We've all got two feet. We've all got heads."

'"It's very physical," he said. "You could get damaged," and he patted his chest with both hands. He couldn't bring himself to say breasts, God love him. So I stood up and put my hands over my down-below.

'"What about the guys?" I said. "When there's a free-kick, they stand like this. What's the difference?" Which left him with his mouth hanging open.'

But the door was still firmly closed. Plus the international had been sprung on them. They had such limited time to prepare.

'England were so well set up, so well kitted out,' said Elsie. 'They had a top man as manager. They were organised. They'd been training for months. I'd brought in Rab Stewart as manager. He was a former player with Kilmarnock, a good guy and a friend, but he didn't know the girls. We did *not* have a goalkeeper. My first-choice goalkeeper turned up for the team photoshoot. Then nothing. Failed to turn up for training. Never apologised. So we went with Janey Houghton. She was well built, very quick, agile, fearless. She was Rab's choice. But far too wee. Lucky if she was five foot three.'

What they did have was the best Scottish woman player ever, someone with an unquenchable commitment to the game and a granite-hard desire to win. Rose Reilly got her first football at three and loved it so much she slept with it in her arms. One glimpse of what this seventeen-year-old could do and the opposition would be terrified. Here was a player who could raise an otherwise misfiring side to new heights – in today's terms a Gareth Bale, a Miguel Almirón, an Edinson Cavani.

'But though we had a great squad of girls, England had 200-plus to select from. We had eight teams in Scotland, maximum. It was David v Goliath.'

Even so, one thing could not be allowed to happen. Never again would a Scottish women's side let themselves be humiliated as it had been in the inaugural women's FA Cup the previous season.

Something of an explanation is needed here. Because there had been so few competitive teams north of the border, Stewarton Thistle along with Scotland's other big side, Aberdeen Prima Donnas, were incorporated into the English League. It followed, therefore, that they were eligible to take part in the competition. So far, so good.

'We put our closest rivals, Aberdeen Prima Donnas, out in the first round and before we knew it we were in the final against Southampton at Crystal Palace, beating sides 9-1, 11-0 on the way,' said Elsie Cook. 'Then the night before we travelled to London I had a phone call from Gladys Aitken, the Manchester Corinthians manager. All the big clubs were boycotting the final, she said, because Southampton had cheated. They'd formed themselves into a select XI chosen by trial from the twelve teams playing in the Southampton League, and calling themselves Southampton Ladies. They've been hauled up before the WFA, found guilty of misrepresentation and fined £25 but they're being allowed to play the final. I said, "Oh, Gladys, it's OK. We'll beat them anyway." We thought we were the bees' knees. We thought we were it. We lost 4-1.'

Stewarton shot themselves in the feet, mind. Not long back, they had played a friendly against a team of postmen and a week before the final Elsie brought in two of them to help with training.

'Tom thought he was God's gift. Willie was good at shouting at us,' she said. 'Then the night before the game they had the girls up drinking. There were only three of us on that pitch who hadn't taken part. Our goalie was hopeless. We lost two players in the last twenty minutes. I was left having to cover Sue Lopez, who was a greyhound – big, tall, blonde, strong. They hammered us.'

There were other ways in which the contrast between England and Scotland was stark. The FA provided the England girls with their kit. Scotland had to rely on Rose Reilly's dad, Hugh, who worked for the Provident loan company and got them to provide the money for a set of strips. Elsie paid for the Scotland badges and sewed them on by hand.

'My mum and her workmates at the knitwear factory attached the numbers. Can you imagine it? And here's one better. I'd arranged for a last squad get-together a week before the big game. It was going to be at Greenock, to introduce them to the pitch. Beth Smith of Motherwell says, "I've a friend with a minibus, I'll get them to take us."

'"Oh that's awfully good of you," I said. I'd been organising this all on my own. Now here was somebody helping me at last! So come the day and we're just standing outside the Anderson Cross bus station with sixteen girls and I say, "The time's getting on, Beth. Where's the minibus?"

'"What minibus?" she says. "Oh! I forgot!"

'I looked up at the heavens and then a bit lower down, at the Hielanman's Umbrella road tunnel, and saw this furniture van come through and stop at the lights. I did a 50-yard sprint across the traffic and knocked on the window. "I'll give ye thirty quid to take us to Greenock!" He and his mate started laughing: "Aye, job done." And we jumped into the van. We were sitting there, on armchairs and couches, surrounded by standard lamps and bric-a-brac. We laughed all the way. The Scotland team. Training for a blummin' big international match.'

* * *

Scotland's weather is capricious. Up till matchday, it had been fine. On 18 November, as the 2.15 kick-off approached, snow started falling on Ravenscraig Stadium and 'Scotland the Brave' rang out in a Christmas-card scene. Under the surface, the pitch was bone-hard with frost and ice. The men presided over an on-pitch discussion. They were amazed the women wanted to play at all. If it had been a men's game they would have called it off. But the girls had worked so hard and suffered so much to make this day a reality. If they gave in to the weather, would they ever get this opportunity again? No way were they going to back down now.

Once they were out there moving, it became clear that Scotland had the advantage, adapting quicker to the skating-rink conditions, Edna Neillis at inside-right dominating the attack. They were 1-0 up after twenty-two minutes, Neillis picking up possession and centring for Mary Carr to head into the far corner. Five minutes later, Rose Reilly bent an outrageous corner-kick into the net. But from experience, Elsie knew a 2-0 lead was never enough to relax. Fail to kill the game off and they'd be back. She was right. Coming up to twenty minutes before half-time, a Scotland attack broke down. Pat Davies, the young Southampton striker, picked up the ball near the right-hand touchline just inside the England half and spotted Sylvia Gore running, unmarked, onside through the middle. She released a superb pass that put Gore clean through to score: 2-1.

Now Scotland only had a one-goal cushion. As the second half got under way, they defended their lead the only way they knew: by attacking. England, in contrast, had rethought tactics. On that slippery surface the biggest trouble they'd had was turning with the ball. Now they were cutting out the midfield build-up, opting instead for the long ball from defence for the forwards to run on to. That plus putting Janet Bagguley in charge of neutralising Edna Neillis.

Pat Davies's passing was on fire. Midway inside the Scotland half, in the inside-right position, she spotted Lynda Hale flying down the right wing and slipped the ball in behind the full-back for her. She and Hale had made their debuts for Southampton on the same day, had been teammates ever since, and this was a move they'd played so many times it was almost automatic. Hale's powerful shot into the far corner was the equaliser. And then Davies was there again, on the edge of the penalty area as Jeannie Allott dribbled down the left wing and sent a ball looping in. As it bounced, Davies beat Janie Houghton to it, leaping high in front of her so Houghton couldn't get to it. The ground was so hard the ball bounced over the pair of them into the empty net.

That winning goal was given to Allott, but it was Davies who had made it happen. As she was sitting quietly on her own after the final whistle, Eric Worthington did a really nice thing.

'He came over and sat next to me,' she said. 'He asked how I thought I'd played and when I said I thought I'd done OK he just shook his head and said he thought I'd played exceptionally well. When I said, "But I didn't score," he just smiled and said, "Yes, but it was your name I was shouting after every goal."'

Those words, she said, would stay with her for ever.

* * *

Pioneering Scottish women footballers banned by SFA to be presented with caps by Nicola Sturgeon
The Scotsman, 27 May 2019

In 1974 Scotland fell in line with the rest of the enlightened world by recognising the women's game; Elsie Cook was appointed their first international manager. A nice coda is that, forty-seven years after playing at Greenock, the girls who represented their country that day were presented with their Scotland caps.

'I doubt that women's football in Scotland would have become established in the 1970s without Elsie,' said Patricia. 'She was tireless, and she took on the men and succeeded.'

In return, Elsie paid tribute to Patricia: 'She and I were from the same mould. She was meticulous, much cleverer than me but we both wanted to promote and progress the women's game.'

These two women were friends not rivals, let alone enemies. Together they had fought, and would continue to fight, for the right to play football. For Patricia, a single event summed it up. In November 2019, England v Germany at Wembley drew a 77,768 crowd – a record attendance for an England women's home fixture.

'You wouldn't have believed, fifty years ago, that it would come to this point,' said Patricia. 'From everything we had done fifty years ago we'd got to the point where England women played at Wembley.'

The sheer size of what these two young women had achieved boiled down to one simple thing – what it had been all about from the start: the battle for recognition. When I asked Elsie what it was like to lose to England, all she said was: 'It was actually nae problem. Because we just wanted a game of football.'

Read all about it:

A History of the Women's FA Cup Final by Chris Slegg and Patricia Gregory (The History Press, 2021)

Kicking Against Tradition: A Career in Women's Football by Wendy Owen (The History Press, 2005)

MY SEASON-TICKET FRIEND

The game can produce unique connections and bonds, as **Hayley Davinson** *found out so poignantly at Craven Cottage.*

It was a reference to Franz Kafka that made me realise that my friendship with Dom was pretty special. I wish I had written it down, as now I'd be able to remember it more accurately. It was around the time when we had a player at Fulham called Alex Kačaniklić. During one match, Dom suddenly referred to the player as 'Alex K', linking him (who knows how) to Josef K. and Kafka's book *The Trial*. Understanding the reference, I replied, keeping up the slow connections to Kafka's work, to which mid-match he delightedly exclaimed, 'Ah, you're a Kafka fan, Hayley!' and we continued to discuss our shared enjoyment of the great author.

Three things can be inferred from this exchange. First, you may be able to picture the quality of this Fulham team at home circa 2012, surviving comfortably in the Premiership but by no means setting it alight. Second, this is very 'Fulham'. We are sometimes mocked for precisely this kind of thing, but I love this uniqueness about our fans. Third, Dom and I were on a great level with each other.

We became friends purely by the anomaly of a computer. My friend Rob and I had recently acquired season tickets next to each other in H4 of the Hammersmith End and had extreme 'August' levels of excitement for the season ahead. A 1-0 win against Arsenal for our first home game of the season, bathed in glorious sunshine, had us dreaming big. To my right sat Rob, and to his right sat Dom. We were distinctly British about our first seating together, politely saying hello, not knowing if those around us were 'tourists' for the day, another newly moved season-ticket holder or, as it turned out, an already formed 'season-ticket bubble' to which we were the newbies.

More often than not, the season-ticket bubble, or STB, is a group formed from people who have been sitting across no more than about four rows, though not necessarily together, with enough regularity that they have formed a friendship group. They are usually of mixed age, background, political views – you name it, they are probably a varied group of 'it'. They are a strange mix from the outset, but over time a combination of perhaps a family, a couple, a few friends or a solo attendee have forged this group, and it has become a valuable asset to them all on matchday. The only parallel relationship I could draw for the uninitiated would be one where you get beyond the niceties with your neighbours or someone like your postman. They are not people you just say hello to; they are people you know, look forward to seeing, and end up learning about their family, health, and life circumstances. The bonus of the STB is that you all support the same team.

On that first meeting, Rob and I said hello to Dom but otherwise we spoke among ourselves. However, the power of the STB is strong, and during the next eighteen home games a friendship ensued between the three of us. This was buoyed, no doubt, by Fulham's impressive 2008/09 home record: undefeated in fourteen out of nineteen games that season, the backbone of us landing a now-infamous spot in the following season's Europa League.

By that point, Dom and I were firm friends. The discussions were mainly about football, of course, but slowly, over time, they began to expand. I'm not sure how it started, but post-match pub chat led to discovering our mutual love of a good old-fashioned boozer and cask ales, as well as a shared love of travel in the form of good away days and trips

MY SEASON-TICKET FRIEND

far beyond. I had to visit Budapest, he told me, 'The land where Zoltán Gera is the face of Pepsi. You have to see it, Hayley. Beautiful!'

It was all very trivial. But I guess that is the joy of the season-ticket friend. You intersperse chat about life with 'Oh what? What on earth is Johnson doing playing that ball?' Things never go too deep and can always be cut short if the ball reaches the attacking final third. But there is a genuine specialness to a friendship like this – the simple joy of chatting with someone you meet every other week. Often, there is also joy in the differences between you both. Dom and my worlds would have had slim chance of crossing in any other circumstance, and yet we had much in common. During a later period in our friendship, we would have differing views of Brexit. Did it matter? Of course not. He was someone whose opinion I trusted, though, so we could debate openly without it leading to anger or shouting. He was someone whose opinion opened up my own views. It didn't change them, but it made me consider things from another perspective instead of solely listening to an echo chamber.

Friendships such as these exist in stadiums around the country. Surely, in fact, the world. I imagine only people with a season ticket will have a proper awareness of them. The ecosystem of football grounds is unique, and these relationships are the reason such places thrive. They show the value of a single common interest as a starting place for people to develop connections. People may have different backgrounds, life views, opinions of the world, whatever. As long as they are keen to discuss their team's chance of making the play-offs, then a fellow fan will happily chat. Whether in one-off or more regular meetings, football is the conversational topic from which other strands quickly develop: it soon becomes easy to ask if a person is keeping well, to ask how work is currently, which quickly leads to knowing more about someone's family and background. This is more information than many of us will ever gain about some of our colleagues. The simplicity of this conversation is underrated. To me, these relationships are one of the unsung heroes of the sport. They are probably a large part of the reason people endure the hardships of football: bad weather, poor management or – the hardest one – terrible ownership.

You need something to look forward to that isn't reliant on three points or a good performance. Asking someone in your bubble how their mum is getting on and finding out she is on the mend is the sort of good news that can ever so slightly cushion a 0-1 defeat in the rain. Perhaps it puts some of the stress in perspective.

I suppose the difference between getting to know your postman well – even if it's very well – and your bubble is the fact that you've shared something with the people you sit near. Something that really matters. Shared values or a common purpose will often develop a thread in strong bases of community. Whether you are an LGBT+ group who has had to deal with homophobia together, or a group of local residents who campaigned to change the area for the better, among this togetherness lasting friendships will have been made. Of course I understand the stark differences between fighting to change laws or abject views and regularly attending football matches, but the parallel outcome is that something has bonded you together.

An example: the phrase 'that night in Hamburg' only makes sense to Fulham fans. But that sense is invaluable. (An abridged version of 'that night' is that, having reached the Europa League final after knocking out some major titans along the way, we lost the final in extra time.) For our fans, that final still means so much. From the people who flew across the world to be there, to the teachers who skipped school, to the planes, trains, minibuses and coaches that got people there, it was momentous. From the minute I woke up that morning in Berlin before catching a train, to crashing out in the hostel at an ungodly hour, the people I met, sang, danced and cried with that day will stay with me for ever. And yet now, it isn't just about them; it's about anyone who went. If I meet someone today who was there, it's about knowing that a person understands, went through the highs and the lows like I did. Best friends from school saw me a couple of days after that fateful Germany trip, and I'll never forget how grateful I was when they asked, 'Are you OK?', having fully expected them to shrug 'It's only a game.' Those best friends realised how important it was to me, but they hadn't gone through it. Only another fan who was there really knows what it felt like, or even what it feels like now – that we got that close but didn't get our fairy-tale ending – and it is with my STB that I know I can share this pain the most openly. Our bond may be a little odd, but it is very real.

Sometimes you are lucky enough to sit next to someone you connect with so well that the friendship extends beyond the stadium. Perhaps you find yourself swapping messages if someone misses a game, or you realise your chats within the ground are always a little short: either conversation broken up by the match itself or during fifteen minutes at half-time in which you attempt to speak at more length while also trying to squeeze in a pint. To anyone who has stood underneath the Hammersmith End, you'll know the impossibility of being able to achieve both successfully. It's nice to know a friendship has developed, though, and between you, it feels a perfect plan to meet without the stress of a match.

In our case, Rob and I began to arrange to meet up with Dom in the pub, alongside one of Dom's oldest friends, Mal, whom we had also got to know. This tended to happen for us during the close season, mainly because… well, we are football fans, and that is when we all know there is a void that needs filling. Times had turned quite dramatically at Fulham since our post-Hamburg high and nothing was quite so right ever again. The monotony of being mid-table created various levels of anger between the four of us. It's tough when your team is doing badly, as disagreements on whether or not it's time for a change of manager can be one of the few things to challenge an STB relationship. There can be stark differences between the 'Oh, give the manager time' view and the 'I give my money and this is what I get back' crowd. These things can get heated but, in the safety of a pub and a group whose values you know you trust, they can be discussed at length. You can refute, argue, analyse to your heart's content, all without any need to change the subject as you would when around those not quite so obsessed. You are not best friends, but these people play an important role in your life. Something you probably don't realise quite how much until you are informed that your pal has fallen ill, and it sucks.

I knew Dom had been sick via his friend Mal, but it was a chance meeting at a hospital between Rob and Dom that hammered it home. Rob reported back that Dom was on breathing apparatus and really in a bad way, and I was upset – more so than I would have expected, I suppose. That's when you really know a friendship, when its normality risks not continuing as it always has. It brings home to you what it means. But we continued to message, mainly via email. I was planning a trip to South America at the time, conveniently coinciding with the Brazilian World Cup, and Dom was beyond happy for me, telling me about some of his own escapades in some far-flung corners of the world. I wish I knew more now. My memory fails.

Having been concerned about him, though, it seemed all was OK: he made a good recovery and was back at Fulham games, and so life returned to normal. I was back from my travels with plenty of stories to share, from watching the England game in Manaus to managing to score a ticket for a match at La Bombonera. He was raspy sometimes, but our chats were precisely as they had always been. Post-travels, my season ticket moved and we were no longer seat buddies. It was fine – we still met for half-time beers, moaned about the manager and kept up the emails and close-season pub sessions. He was taking Spanish lessons at this point, and my rusty Spanish needed practice, so we'd attempt to discuss the current dire situation of the club with a mixture of our existing language skills and Google Translate.

But then, unfortunately, Dom got sicker. His breathing was struggling, and he was on an apparatus to support him, meaning no Fulham. If you know someone who is football-obsessed and a day comes when they are no longer able to attend matches regularly, it can be heart-breaking. Whether that person is ourselves or a parent, family member or friend, we know the routine of football, the rituals and the love of how clockwork it all is. We know that it could get taken away from us sometime before our final days – perhaps by distance or, in Dom's case, the incapacity to breathe freely.

Our email exchanges continued and, once he had some improved and more convenient apparatus, I went to meet him at a pub close to where he lived. It was a bit too modern for either of our likings, but the selection of beer on offer was of a high enough standard for us to enjoy. Dom was struggling more than I had envisaged from the tone of his emails, which of course had still sounded fuming and passionate, like all discussion between us was. His partner, Sue, and their dogs were his other passion in life. They were his kids and they'd just had pups. I insisted he send pictures of the puppies as soon as he was home. He dutifully did.

We continued emailing, though I was tardy, with my 'busy' life meaning it would be some time between replies. I have a draft of an email to him still in my inbox. I never completed it in time.

I would never want to glorify something as being more than it was. Dom and I never became best friends; we met only a handful of times beyond our designated slot of 3 p.m. on a Saturday (or as close to that as Sky will allow). But I truly valued all of it, I suppose because of its quirkiness and the fact it doesn't happen that often in the outside world. I still think of him often when Fulham are playing. He once told me José Mourinho said that only in England do the fans get so excited about a corner. I've no idea how true this is, but my mate regularly shouts, 'Only in England, Hayley, only in England!' when Fulham win a corner.

Just a few months after Dom's death, Fulham made it to the play-off final – our first time at Wembley since our FA Cup final defeat in 1975. It pisses me off sometimes that life didn't give him that before he had to go. He'd endured a lot, following Fulham in the 1980s and 1990s. But what can you do?

His funeral was lovely, with a brilliant eulogy from Mal that perfectly interweaved their friendship and a condensed version of Fulham's recent history (including Clint Dempsey's chip against Juventus that sent us through to the Europa League quarter-finals, naturally). But it was another part of the speech that really caught me out. Yes, Dom had mentioned his travels often, but it was only when it was too late that I discovered the scale of them. From extensive journeys in Eastern Europe before the fall of the Berlin Wall to completing trips on every single continent of the world, his travels put mine to shame. For all our time together, we'd not had the chance to get to that part of the discussion yet, and now I suddenly had so much to ask.

I'd do well to visit as many away matches as he and Mal did over the years, and I'll have achieved something if I get anywhere near his list of countries. But for now, I really should hurry up and book that trip to Budapest, making sure to raise a can of Pepsi to him and our Hungarian hero Zoltán, too.

COOK WHO FOUND THE RIGHT RECIPE

From a childhood of abuse via an eye-opening day at Manchester United to a top job with world football's governing body, the amazing but unsung Joyce Cook – passionate campaigner for disabled and gay rights – has quite a tale to tell, as **Kate Battersby** *discovers.*

The world is full of astonishingly resourceful people we have never heard of – individuals with personal stories of hardship and survival. But that pat little phrase reduces whole lives to a TV-movie-of-the-week, a series of cheaply packaged life lessons overlaid with soaring strings.

Joyce Cook's story is not easily condensed into oven-ready telling. At sixty-three, she knows too much about the words 'hardship' and 'survival'. You wouldn't guess it to look at her. On appearance, she seems… ordinary. Sensible. Easily overlooked. Central Casting wouldn't give her a second glance, more fool them. For in fact she is a dynamo of extraordinary achievement. Joyce Cook CBE OBE, football campaigner to improve disabled accessibility, is one of the world's leading voices on inclusion, anti-discrimination and sustainable development in sport and wider society.

An advocate for the LGBTIQ+ and disabled community, her role now as FIFA's Chief Education and Social Responsibility Officer did not exist before she became its first incumbent in 2019. With a department budget in the millions, she heads a staff overseeing human rights and anti-discrimination, sustainability and the environment, safeguarding and protection of children and vulnerable adults alike – matters that did not register in football a couple of decades ago. It is as if the sport itself was waiting for a person of Cook's energy and drive to show the game its wider responsibilities.

Hers is a many-chaptered story, all of which has informed the role she now holds. A childhood ravaged by abuse was followed by years closeted as a young gay woman, fearful of the professional consequences were she to come out. Having met the love of her life and created a career in medical sales at which she excelled, in her late thirties she developed a form of arthritis, requiring her to use a wheelchair. Forced to take early retirement on medical grounds, she was swamped by listless depression and could see no way forward.

Football was the conduit that allowed her to find herself again. Witnessing a single Manchester United match at Old Trafford in the autumn of 2000 was the first step on a long road of rediscovery.

'For two years I hadn't left the house,' she remembers. 'Needing to use a wheelchair was awful for me back then. Now, as a passionate independent disabled woman, I hate myself for saying that I really struggled with the wheelchair, the way people looked at me and the loss of control. But at that Man U game, I forgot how miserable I felt. Football gave me my life back.'

* * *

Cook is sitting at her desk at home in the airy duplex apartment south of Zurich that she shares with her wife, Rosie, who gave up her high-powered job in finance when Cook first came to work at FIFA at the end of 2016. The low-rise block where they live is a half-hour drive from the city headquarters of football's world governing body. Cook still marvels at the beauty of the snow-capped mountains and forests she passes on her commute to work (in non-Covid times). It is a long way from the couple's previous home on the northern outskirts of London, and a different planet from Cook's childhood.

Born to an eighteen-year-old single mother, she never knew her biological father. They lived blissfully with her grandparents until she was four, when her mother met her stepfather.

'It was an abusive childhood,' Cook says. 'I won't go into detail, but I look back and think, *My God, it was awful. Really awful.*'

Little Joyce always liked school because it was better than home. She laughs at remembering that her Hampshire convent education prompted her first ambition: to be a nun.

'Then I thought it would be cool to be a footballer, although that wasn't possible for girls back then. My family wasn't into the game at all, but I always loved it. A neighbour was a boy with muscular dystrophy, and I would kick the ball for him so he could kick it back. A couple of the local boys saw it and I started kickabouts with them, then played midfield in five-a-sides. I was better than most of the boys I was playing with.'

One local family of five brothers included her in their matches, and it was with them that eight-year-old Joyce spent the afternoon of 30 July 1966, feeding coins into the back of the meter fixed to the television set as they watched the World Cup final.

'I asked the others who the England player was with the straggly hair, and they said his name was Bobby Charlton. That's when I became a Man U fan, because of him. Afterwards we ran down to the local sweetshop to get another World Cup Willie badge. I still have it.'

At school she worked hard and enjoyed lessons. But her stepfather would exert pathetic cruelties to halt any enjoyment he could.

'I can remember when I was eleven, asking my mother why she never praised me when I did something good, and she said she couldn't because my stepfather would be jealous. He would ring the school before I was about to play in a hockey match to say I had to come home. When I was studying for my O Levels he would turn the lights off, telling me it was a waste of electricity.'

Her teachers and schoolmates arranged a party for her sixteenth birthday, ensuring she could attend by ringing her stepfather to say she had to stay behind for a lesson. But events were getting worse at home. She confided in no one about the abuse at the time – she would be in her thirties before speaking of it to another person. Her stepfather decided it was a waste of money to support her at home for her A Levels. She had to leave school, leave home and get a job. Her teachers helped her find work as a lab technician, going on day release to study at the local technical college. It wasn't easy.

'I could hardly afford to feed myself. Things were hard. I was a very young seventeen and I wasn't taking care of myself. It took me a long time to find my way.'

By this time, she was making other discoveries about herself.

'I first had a sense of my sexuality at school, although I didn't act on it and told no one,' she says. 'I didn't know anyone who was gay, and because my parents were strong Catholics, things like that were just taboo. I kept having very nice boyfriends who didn't work out. I was even engaged once to a nice man, but there was something deep-rooted that meant I couldn't have that love connection with a man.'

Four years on, she switched careers to nursing, ultimately specialising in coronary and intensive care.

'Nursing taught me about humanity, compassion, how quickly life can change, and those lessons have stayed with me,' muses Cook. She chose to nurse in Oman for five years, and on her return began carving out a new career in medical sales. The skills she acquired then – in decision-making and closing a deal – would eventually feed into her role at FIFA.

Meanwhile, her time in the Middle East yielded her first gay relationship and, having settled back home in Chester, she began going out on the local gay scene. Friends were relieved to hear her come out.

'A couple of them told me, "Thank God – it was obvious for ages,"' she smiles. In 1994, in her mid-thirties, she met Rosie at a quiz night.

'I first noticed her kindness, and her respect for other people. She had an aura about her. I knew it was different with her very early on – that she was a good person and wouldn't hurt me even if it didn't work out. She made me feel safe. It was the first time I really trusted someone.'

But at that time, Cook did not feel she could be open about her personal life at work.

'These days I own the fact that I'm a proud gay woman, but it was different when I was younger. I guarded everything I said for fear of revealing something. I'd excelled at the firm where I worked – they probably thought I was a workaholic with no life, because I never referred to a partner. I kept Rosie very secret. You're terrified that you'll say the wrong thing and give away that you're gay, or that you'll bump into someone when you're out and they'll realise. You didn't dare challenge a homophobic joke. It's a terrible burden for anyone to carry.'

Cook was so good at her job that she won an international award, the prize for which was a holiday for the winner and their partner. Exhausted by the secrecy, Cook told her employers she wanted to take Rosie.

'I was aghast by how bigoted some of the senior management were. They asked if we would behave, if we would snog on the dance floor. They were not prepared for her to go with me.' She took legal advice, and the company relented.

'When we got back I had a call from a Dutch colleague who thanked me. I was confused – for what? He said, "I've been with my partner for twenty years and I've never been able to take him with me. You've made a change now in the organisation that can't be turned back." That was the first time I realised what it means to stand up against discrimination.

'Ever since I took that step to come out, I've put my relationship on my CV because I decided I was never going back in the closet. In the role I have now, I feel a great responsibility to be public about it. It's hugely important that FIFA makes a safe space for people to come out if they wish to, or to keep their private life private if they wish – but to be their authentic selves without fear, because on the pitch or in the workplace people cannot perform to their best ability when they carry this awful burden of being in the closet.'

Cook's words raise natural questions about the 2022 World Cup in Qatar, where homosexuality is illegal. Amid all the other doubts about Qatar's suitability to host the jewel tournament in football's crown, here is yet another. Is it right that the tournament be held there?

'I've always believed we make change by going to places. It's never fast enough for me, but they are seismic changes. We've made a lot of progress together with the Qatari authorities, and we have to ensure it stays as a legacy. There's also a lot of work going on behind the scenes.

'I don't think there's been an occasion I've felt discrimination at FIFA for being a gay woman. I want to normalise it. I lead from the front. We have a zero-tolerance policy for any discrimination. It's a brave move to come out, and I wasn't famous or in the spotlight. Some of us are going to have to lead the way to normalise it across sport. I want to reach the point where we don't have to talk about it because it's just normal.'

In the late 1990s it seemed at last that Cook's life was entering calmer water. She and Rosie had bought a house together in Chester, had a busy social life and great jobs. So many tests were behind her. But she was about to face the biggest yet.

'I noticed that I struggled to straighten my knees after getting out of the car. When I came off the court after playing squash, it would feel as if someone had hit my knees with a hammer. Eventually I had it looked into, but for a long time the problem was misdiagnosed as mechanical. I started having surgery on my knees, even though my elbows and lower back were also painful, and sometimes my hips and hands. Everything continued to get worse for five years, so much so that I was advised to start using a wheelchair.'

Rarely in touch with her family, she received a letter from her mother describing the same symptoms in her younger half-sister, who had been diagnosed with psoriatic arthritis. Cook's doctors realised she had the same condition, and from there it caused such a deterioration in her health that she was forced to take retirement while still in her thirties.

'When we bought my first wheelchair it was a horrid moment,' remembers Cook. 'It was hard to know I had to rely on it. When we went out, it was like I didn't exist any more. Someone literally said to Rosie in front of me: "Does she take sugar?" I told Rosie I didn't want to go out any more. Friends came to us, but I wouldn't go out other than for doctor's appointments. I didn't realise how depressed I was. I'd lie in bed for hours, watching mind-numbing TV while Rosie was at work. My friends couldn't believe I had been this gregarious person, always out and about, the first to the party, travelling with my job and so on, and had changed so much.'

As Cook retreated into herself, so Rosie's concern naturally spiralled. It was many months before she hit on the idea that would prove the turning point for Cook: going to see her beloved Manchester United at Old Trafford, which she had never done previously. But making it happen was another matter, as there were 'obscenely few' tickets available.

And here's a strange twist. Neither Cook nor Rosie can remember which fixture they finally got to see. So overwrought was each of them by the meaning of that day in September 2000 that they recall nothing at all about the visiting team or the score – all the more remarkable when a bit of retrospective research reveals that it was probably United's 6-0 Premier League win over Bradford City.

'How could we not remember it?' marvels Cook. 'It's so strange, but for both of us the emotion of getting me there overwhelmed everything. I was so worried about going beforehand, but Rosie felt she had to get me to do it.

'I remember us driving down Matt Busby Way, and seeing lots of other disabled people parked in the same area. Everyone else seemed to know each other and I felt uncomfortable at being the odd one out. Rosie said she had been told there was a "disabled lounge" but it was really full and I didn't want to go in it because that was admitting I was disabled too. I was still in denial and hadn't come to terms with it. And then there was the match, which somehow I don't remember. Isn't that awful? But I remember the atmosphere. I hadn't been out for so long, it was scary. But I forgot that, forgot about the chair. I was shouting with the crowd, and I felt I belonged to something.'

That day, a tiny flame was lit. When Rosie went to work in the morning, Cook began getting up and finding hobbies. They gradually became more social again. Rosie started trying to get tickets for more games at Old Trafford, and rapidly discovered that without multiple phones there was no chance. But they did get to matches, including England's qualifying clincher against Greece for the 2002 World Cup, when David Beckham famously secured the necessary point by scoring in the third minute of stoppage time. Cook was subsequently invited to join the Manchester United Disabled Supporters Association (MUDSA).

'When I became disabled I realised how shit it was to go to a stadium as a disabled person. Man U used to say "we have the best facilities", but what they had was so limited as to be awful. If you were on the committee of MUDSA, you could get tickets to every game, unlike other disabled fans. It was elitism, excluding those we were meant to represent. To me, the existence of MUDSA was also a way for Man U to sanitise their situation and the disproportionate lack of seating back then. I didn't like the disabled fans' lounge either – I didn't want to be isolated or separate from other fans. So I was a bit problematic.'

Nonetheless, with her spirit of adventure restored, they booked for all England's matches in Portugal at Euro 2004.

'That was such a great time,' grins Cook. 'We hadn't had that much fun together since I'd become disabled. It was one big party even though the disabled fans' facilities were just awful. It was very common to have terrible sightlines where you just couldn't see. At one stadium they put the disabled fans on the roof. So we were in the blazing sun in the middle of the day, and the only accessible toilet was used by non-disabled fans too, who soiled it. Someone had defecated in the sink. It was vile and just not right.

'So when we got home I decided to write a report – no one commissioned it, but I delivered it to the disabled association at Man U, and I sent it to UEFA. By this time I was nearer to being my old self, and I would certainly have kept going until I got a response. It gave me something to get my teeth into.'

And respond UEFA did, deciding they would like some help reviewing it all. And so it began, with Cook being asked to meet the architects for Euro 2012 in Warsaw. As time passed, effectively she became a free consultant to UEFA until 2009, advising them on disabled fans' facilities at key stadia all over Europe, including Europa and Champions League fixtures.

The challenges were legion. When Liverpool's supporters flew into Istanbul for the 2007 Champions League final, they were initially herded into a tent without accessible toilet facilities. Some disabled fans were forced to soil themselves. Aghast, Cook recognised in herself a sense of mission and purpose.

Meanwhile, she had long since been invited to join the National Association of Disabled Supporters ('NADS! I never could believe that acronym'), later to become Level Playing Field, campaigning for disabled sports fans to have a positive inclusive experience.

'They'd have meetings and talk, but nothing much really changed. The Premier League, the FA and the Football League were avoiding us. The attitude towards converting facilities was always "it's too expensive, can't change, wish we could". I brought my business experience and persuaded NADS to do it differently. It was a well-intentioned group but frustrated and lacking the know-how to secure lasting change. There's an art to getting things changed, and I knew I would be good at it. Working as a nurse in intensive care you learn a lot about how to deal with people under stress. Then medical sales was a tough environment. I had a lot of skills. I knew how to negotiate and get what was needed from meetings with decision-makers.

'We had a meeting with the football authorities, where we met a mix of the patronising and the arrogant. I never felt patronised by anyone at UEFA, although I did in some early meetings with the authorities at home soon after Portugal 2004. I began building a network, meeting politicians and key people in the game.'

She was also invited to join Women in Football, becoming a founding board member of the organisation, lobbying to improve women's representation at all levels of the game, and joined the boards of the Sports Grounds Safety Authority and Football Against Racism in Europe. In 2009, she founded and led the Centre for Access to Football in Europe. Yet it wasn't until 2010 that she received any remuneration for any of this.

'I didn't like to ask,' she remembers diffidently, although at the time she was effectively working a seven-day week. The woman who had no trouble fronting up to all kinds of movers and shakers while campaigning for disabled facilities was apologetic when it came to being paid – and it didn't seem to occur to anyone that she should receive a salary.

'But I was on a journey back to who I used to be. I was on such a mission to change something diabolical that it didn't feel like a job. I had to pursue it. I still to this day think the least understood and most oppressed group are disabled people – and remember I speak as a gay woman. There's still such fear of disability. London 2012 did a lot of great stuff around that, although I hated Channel 4's 'Superhumans' advertising campaign for the Paralympics. To me, that campaign divided disabled people into two categories – you were either brave and bold and became an athlete, or you were a tragic disabled person. Patronising and divisive – Paralympians are supreme athletes but not superhumans.'

Cook's work was gaining ever-greater recognition. To her astonishment, she was awarded the OBE in 2012 ('the Queen reminded me of my nan') and made a CBE five years later. During the 2014 World Cup she supported FIFA's disabled accessibility measures and was involved in a project offering audio-descriptive commentary for partially sighted and blind fans. Then, after Sepp Blatter's benighted governance of FIFA collapsed, his successor Gianni Infantino harnessed Cook's abilities for the new era of leadership. In November 2016 she was appointed Chief Member Associations Officer, a senior management board position, to helm the FIFA Forward Programme for football development, supporting the 211 member associations and six confederations.

'I was gobsmacked but wowed to be approached,' says Cook frankly. 'Old FIFA was very arrogant. I'd been a critic, like so many, but I felt I should be part of the change if I could be. The job played to the relationships I'd built previously, although it was very evident there was a lot of work needed to put proper processes in places. By the time I arrived, this work had begun and there was a determination at FIFA to do it.'

But it was not immediately plain sailing.

'I was hurt to find out that some people thought I wasn't up to it. They weren't all male, and it makes me sad in my heart when women don't support other women. For me, that's unforgivable. It's so competitive out there that when you get somewhere as a woman, it's because you've worked damn hard. We should be paving the way for others because we know how tough it is to be taken seriously. There are times when it's still tough now.'

In fact, more than 40 per cent of FIFA's employees are female, including Secretary General Fatma Samoura, the first holder of the post to be female or black or Muslim – she is all three. Cook is the only senior staffer with a visible disability (hidden disability being that which is not immediately obvious, such as Crohn's disease or mental ill health). Meanwhile, her professional value was so apparent that in late 2019 came her current role, as FIFA's first ever Chief Social Responsibility and Education Officer. Infantino hailed her appointment thus: 'While Joyce Cook is already a key element of the FIFA administration, I find it very fitting that she takes over a role that capitalises on her invaluable expertise of finding effective ways to contribute to the improvement of society – in particular of those who need it the most.'

To say Cook relishes the ground-breaking role is an understatement.

'It's exciting and dynamic – we're moving fast,' she says. 'We're finding our way as an organisation going through seismic change. Some people don't like change but I thrive on it. I can get things done. FIFA is committed to driving through ideas, for example on safeguarding and child protection, putting in place measures to prevent harm, harassment and abuse. In sport, these can range from a child or adult being over-exercised, bullied, verbally abused or threatened, or a victim of severe sexual abuse.

'I'm proud to have led the creation of the FIFA Guardians programme with the help of a dedicated expert team. As well as putting measures in place to prevent abuse, FIFA is also investigating reports of abuse such as those in Afghanistan and Haiti. We're having to do this without always being able to rely on local statutory agencies. In some cases we are providing victims with safe refuge and a package of care support.'

Measures being worked on include the creation of an international safe sport entity, with trusted reporting lines, to investigate abuse cases. It will make the victims the absolute priority, to help ensure they feel safe to come forward in the first place. The ambitious plan is fully supported by the FIFA President and a multitude of stakeholders.

'FIFA, like all sports and indeed society in general, were late to the table with this. None of this work happened before. We're now writing the script. In the past twenty years sport and society have made great improvements in human rights and inclusivity but it's still a work in progress. Will we ever finish the job? I doubt it. But we're putting a lot of effort in at FIFA.'

Throughout all this time, Cook's health has remained perpetually challenging. She mentions her 2014 breast cancer and radical mastectomy as a verbal footnote, and even now is in the midst of yet more operations on her knees, having long since lost count of the tally.

'I'm a terrible patient. I didn't tell most people about the cancer because I didn't want to be taking endless well-meaning calls from people. I just wanted to take care of Rosie and me. I suppose I was frightened, but I went back to work as soon as possible because I wanted to get it done and be back to normal.'

Then as now, her working hours are 'pretty bonkers'. But the job enthrals her. Football changed Cook's life, and now at FIFA she is changing the lives of others.

'I'm ambitious and honest, with a lot of integrity and passion for the things I do. I don't see it as work. A long time ago I gave up for two years, and a game of football gave me my life back. I don't know if I can ever repay my debt to football, but I'll give it my best shot.'

So here she is, Mrs Joyce Cook ('I correct people who don't call me Mrs,' she says happily), the ordinariness of whose very name could be mistaken for the winner of best Victoria sponge at the Smalltown Women's Institute – although she would chide that idea by saying, 'There's nothing wrong with being that person.' In fact, you could justifiably call her superwoman, except she wouldn't set great store by that either. Maybe it boils down to this: she does what she can. For many, that wouldn't amount to much. But in her case, it's a mind-boggling pledge.

Life has done its best to place limits on her. Life chose the wrong person. Joyce Cook is doing what she can, and very little can stand in her way.

TWO BLACK ROOKIES AND A MICROPHONE

Showing huge ingenuity and resourcefulness, **Kehinde Adeogun** *and her sister Taiwo persuaded the BBC World Service to allow them to cover the African teams at the Women's World Cup of 2007 in China. It proved to be quite some adventure.*

On 20 September 2007, how did we – two Black, female, football-loving twins with a sense of adventure – end up in a city that was being evacuated because the mother of all typhoons was heading our way? We looked around, wondering how we'd ask for help in a country where the language was so different, and all we could do was laugh out loud at the ridiculousness of the situation.

Well, it all started with a call to the BBC earlier that year. I'd just finished listening to a news piece about the two African women's teams that had qualified to represent the Confederation of African Football (CAF) at the 2007 Women's World Cup in China between 10 and 30 September. The ever-present powerhouse Nigeria had qualified, and they were to be joined by Ghana. The women's game didn't have the global reach or publicity that it has now, but – thanks to the BBC World Service and its dedicated African sports programme, *Fast Track* – it was possible to listen to African sports and, in particular, details of African women's football on the radio.

I called Bush House and asked to be put through to Farayi Mungazi at *Fast Track*. I told him I was a fan of the show and had a simple question: was *Fast Track* sending a sports reporter to cover the African women's teams at the World Cup? Farayi said they weren't as they didn't have the funds. I don't know what possessed me but, without hesitation, I said that my sister Taiwo and I were going to the tournament and we'd cover it for the show. (England had qualified in one of the five UEFA spots and knowing that England were managed by our long-time friend Hope Powell made the trip a no-brainer.) Unbelievably, my suggestion wasn't dismissed out of hand.

I must admit, when I broke the news to Taiwo, we did panic a bit. Did we have any experience of broadcasting? No. Did we know what it would entail? No. Did we love football? Yes. Well, that was enough for us; we'd find a way...

It wasn't just that we didn't want to let anybody down; we also didn't want to make ourselves look foolish or over-promise what we could do – and, let's face it, neither of us knew what the front end of a microphone looked like, let alone how to use one properly. But as luck would have it, that spring Morley Adult Education College in south London was running a short course on radio journalism, so we enrolled on it and quickly learned the basics.

Over the summer Bush House felt like a second home. We had meetings with members of the *Fast Track* team – a great bunch of people who just loved sport, like we did. We got to know a bit about what freelancers would be expected to provide out on location, about audio of interviews, opinion pieces for the web, match reports and – most daunting – about being available to take part live in the show's news programmes.

At the beginning of September we collected a Marantz recorder from Bush House. Farayi and his colleagues were so trusting, and we really appreciated the faith they had in us. But now everything was real. Suddenly, we were two rookies with a mic on a mission: to get interviews and match reports to BBC World Service *Fast Track* and the BBC African Sports website.

The start of the adventure saw us board a flight from Heathrow on 8 September 2007, landing in Shanghai the next day with a copy of *Lonely Planet: China* held tightly in our eager hands. There was no point at all in taking a phrase book. I mean, have you seen written Mandarin? It really is a foreign language. It was a strange thing for us as, no matter where we had travelled in the world before, we had always been able to make out the relevant parts of a language and try – albeit with a ridiculous accent – to at least exchange a hello or goodbye. This time, however, we decided before we left England that no amount of goodwill on our part would make us able to converse even at a basic level.

On 9 September our work began. We were to take part in a two-way preview piece setting the scene. Thankfully, it was to be recorded, so it wouldn't go out live. Instead, we'd get a call at a specific time to our hotel from one of the *Fast Track* producers in London. We didn't mess it up, which was thrilling but frightening at the same time. Because at the end of that call we were given instructions for the following day – the first day of the 2007 FIFA Women's World Cup.

We agreed to get audio from the stadium at the opening ceremony and to do a two-way interview looking ahead to the Nigeria v Sweden game on 11 September in Chengdu. We were to take part in a live debate ('Have your say: is women's football taken seriously?'), and we also agreed to send in two 400-word pieces on Ghana and Nigeria for the website. Talk about jumping in at the deep end, but we were determined to swim.

Entering the Hongkou Football Stadium Shanghai on 10 September for the opening ceremony and the first game of the tournament, we felt a mixture of excitement and relief. When the final whistle blew, we felt sad that the result – a thumping 11-0 win for Germany, the reigning world champions, over Argentina – would taint the tournament, making people think women's football wasn't worth watching. The result was not that surprising as Argentina had only arrived in the country three days before the game and so had had no time to acclimatise or prepare. They hadn't stood a chance. We couldn't dwell on the result, though, as we had to get some rest ahead of an early internal flight to Chengdu, where we would report on Nigeria's opening game against Sweden.

Although Nigeria had been CAF's representative at every World Cup since the first FIFA Women's World Cup in 1991, they had only ever progressed out of the group stage once before (at the 1999 tournament). Football wasn't as organised on the African continent, with no established leagues running regularly like in Europe or North America. In addition, opportunities for national teams to camp and play were few and far between (and still are) as, because of the FIFA ranking structure, most high-ranked teams only want to play friendlies against those in and around them in the rankings. Lower-ranked opposition offer no benefit in terms of tournament preparation. At the 2007 World Cup, Ghana's Black Queens were the lowest-ranked team at the tournament, at 47 in the world. Nigeria was the second-lowest ranked team, at 24. For African teams, previous international competition had been limited to regional tournaments between national associations within the CAF regions or at the African Women's Cup of Nations. In fact, the first time an African women's national team played in a friendly international tournament outside of Africa was when South Africa's Banyana Banyana was invited to the 2009 Cyprus Cup. Not experiencing playing against teams from other Confederations put the World Cup's African teams at a disadvantage, as they weren't used to different playing styles or tactics or adjusting to different climates, all of which impacted on performance. But none of this stopped us enjoying watching the teams play and sharing their exploits with football fans back home.

As freelancers for the BBC, we had BBC media accreditation rather than FIFA media accreditation. That meant we didn't have easy access to players or to pitch side or the mixed zone or media centre for the pre- or post-match press conferences. Strangely, though, we weren't daunted. We knew that the only way to get into official press conferences was by blagging our way in, and so we used the guile of a Nigerian reporter who left a door open for us to access the media centre for Nigeria's first game. We never knew his name but called him Black Angel. (This would never happen today with access accreditation scanned and triple-checked and security at a premium.) Gaining access to the media zone meant we had the FIFA technical team sheets before the start of the match and then stats at half-time and full-time. That information meant we could quickly identify a starting XI, when goals were scored or subs made, rather than having to decipher the tannoy announcements or try to find a match programme.

Watching Nigeria's opening group game against Sweden was exhilarating. Despite the lack of regular competitive international experience, the Super Falcons gained a valuable point with a 1-1 draw, meaning their World Cup journey had started with points on the board. However much we dreamed about following the Super Falcons and Black Queens to the final game on 30 September, we knew that the teams would be striking gold just by advancing out of their respective group. That would put the players in the shop window and could lead to transfers to professional leagues abroad. We kept our fingers crossed in hope.

Getting back to our hotel that night late after the game, our fatigue and hunger were all-consuming, so we cursed when we discovered the hotel restaurant was closed. Somehow, through truly embarrassing sign language, we were able to let the staff know that we needed to eat. A waiter opened the cavernous restaurant and motioned for us to sit at a huge banqueting table. Ever since we'd arrived in China, we'd found that trying to order food in restaurants or takeaway venues was a difficult experience. We soon realised that we needed to forget what our mother had taught us about pointing being rude. Trust us, this was the only way to try to establish what to eat from a menu. (Thank God for pictures, that's what we said.) The hotel restaurant's waiter handed us the menu with the ever-present pictures of the dishes that could be ordered, some of which we thought we could identify but weren't too sure. One picture looked like bear claws and other parts of animals that our palates just weren't accustomed to eating. We finally settled on the only things that we could confidently identify: boiled rice and steamed cabbage. Ordinarily that would not be our first choice, but at least we'd go to sleep with full bellies.

After the waiter had gone, the two of us just sat for an age at the table. Had we been wrong to assume he'd understood that we actually wanted to eat? Had our menu selection not been clear? Just as we were deciding whether we should give up and go to our room, the waiter appeared and put a bowl of steaming rice and an aromatic bowl full of cabbage in front of us. We were so grateful, saying thank you and nodding numerous times before we started to eat. The waiter left… but only to stand behind a curtain at the side of the restaurant, where he was joined by what looked like the chef and lots of other workers from the hotel. And there they all stood, popping their heads around the curtain and watching us eat. We didn't care, though – we were hungry. It wasn't the first time we'd felt like exhibits at a museum, and it wouldn't be the last.

In the morning we checked out of the hotel and travelled to Hangzhou to watch and report on Ghana's opening game against Australia. Having booked into our hotel for the night, we took a taxi to the Yellow Dragon Stadium in Hangzhou. It didn't take us long to learn that if we wanted to travel in the city, the best thing we could do was find an English-speaking hotel concierge and ask them to write on a piece of paper in Mandarin where we wanted to go. Some hotels actually had ready-printed cards with destinations, which guests could then hand to a taxi driver. Bitter experience had taught us that telling a taxi driver 'the Shanghai Hilton' just wouldn't wash. Non-Mandarin words were unrecognisable – even those we'd assumed wouldn't need to be translated because they were international brands. Often all we could do was pray that the written translation from the hotel concierge was correct.

When we got out of a taxi at a destination, we had to remember that there were no rules for crossing multiple lanes of traffic. Even when the lights were flashing green for pedestrians to cross, cars, lorries, bikes – in fact, anything that moved – just kept moving. Apart from putting our hands over our eyes, all we could do was make sure we were sandwiched between local pedestrians, the logic being that they must know what they were doing. Fortunately they did: there was method in their madness, and we lived to tell the tale.

Arriving at the stadium, we were surprised to see a large contingent of Black men and women draped in Ghana flags and wearing T-shirts with 'Official Ghana Supporters Club' written on them. They told us that the Ghana FA and the government had funded dozens of fans to travel to China to support the team. It was brilliant to see them at the stadium, playing their djembe drums and cheering the Black Queens on. Their support was in sharp contrast to the bizarre sight of regimented rows of Chinese supporters at games. In front of these local fans, in the rows closest to the pitch, were what can only be described as conductors who held up placards with symbols for clapping or shouting. It was so obvious that these 'fans' had no idea about how to react to what was going on on the pitch. We hadn't seen anything like it before at a football match – or since.

Despite the 1-4 loss suffered by Ghana, it was great to see another African team with skilful players on the world stage. We managed to get a recorded interview with Graham Potter, the Technical Director of the Ghana team at the tournament, and were unsurprised by his take that African women footballers had all the skill but, due to a lack of playing opportunity, that skill didn't translate into success at national level in international tournaments.

The next morning, we travelled back to Shanghai as we wanted to be at England's second group game, against Germany on 14 September. We were also shattered from all the travelling we had already done and couldn't face the time or expense of a plane trip to get to Chengdu for the group game between North Korea and Nigeria. But when we got to our hotel in Shanghai late that evening, we found our reservation at the Crowne Plaza, where a number of England supporters were staying, hadn't gone through. More to the point, there were no rooms available for us to book into. It was late, we were tired, and we had no idea what to do. Some England fans we knew had said we could kip on the floor in their room, but we'd made a bit of commotion about the lack of reservation, so we weren't exactly inconspicuous and we didn't think we'd get away with sneaking into the lift and up to rooms that weren't ours. We called a few hotels but had no luck. Then one of the concierges at the Crowne

Plaza said he knew a friend who worked at another hotel not far away, so he'd call him and see if there were any rooms for the night. Luckily, there were and it was just a short taxi ride away – we were so happy! It looked a bit run-down and had corridors that seemed strange and uninviting and wound around the building like it was a rabbit warren. But at least it was a place we could lay our heads for the night. It wasn't until the next day, after not much sleep, that we discovered it was a pay-by-the-hour hotel, which explained the noisy toing and froing that had gone on all night from gentlemen making visits to rooms along the corridor.

In spite of the difficult night, it was a thrill to relax for a day and truly enjoy watching a match as full-on spectators. A point and a clean sheet for England against the defending world champions was brilliant, and England supporters began to get carried away with how far the team could go in the tournament.

The World Cup was played across five cities in China: Shanghai and Hangzhou were pretty close to each other, but Chengdu, Wuhan and Tianjin were some distance away in different directions. We meticulously mapped out our routes and modes of public transport to get to the stadiums across the country, and were pleasantly surprised by the clean and air-conditioned trains and subway system. That is, when you could get on them. We learned the hard way that – no different to lots of other places in the world – queueing wasn't part of social norms. So the best way to get to the ticket counter or on a train, bus or plane was for us to hold our hands on our hips with our elbows at a 45-degree angle to prevent anybody getting in front of us. It was difficult with bags and a camera but, believe me, we soon got the hang of it and travelled like seasoned professionals.

Unfortunately, it didn't always work. A train delay meant we arrived at Ghana's second group game against Canada, on 15 September in Hangzhou, about twenty minutes before the full-time whistle was blown. We were so stressed as we'd agreed to get match reports and an audio interview to *Fast Track*. Even though we'd travelled for ages to get a report, we decided there was no point trying to get into the stadium and so we collared Ghana fans for their take on the game as they exited the ground. Despite the 4-0 loss, the fans were exuberant, and we got a real buzz talking with them. We got the match report in, too – job done!

Thankfully there were a few days off before the next group games. Hanging out in Shanghai with supporters from different teams was fun, and everybody had a story or two to tell about how Chinese culture differed from where they lived in the world. For us, we experienced first-hand how Chinese people reacted to us, two Black women. It didn't matter where we were; the response was the same: we were greeted with open-mouthed awe and wonderment. Regularly we noticed cameras being produced and surreptitious photos being taken, but sometimes parents brazenly pushed their children to stand next to us while they happily snapped away. In one supermarket during a last-minute, late-night shop, we were followed around by an ever-increasing line of shoppers and it felt like we were the pied piper. It was annoying and interesting at the same time and it made us realise how closed a society it was. We did have our fun, though, walking up and down and around the same aisles while those watching us were trying hard but unsuccessfully not to catch our eye. We laughed because most of the shoppers watching us were dressed in pyjamas and dressing gowns and so, to be honest, we thought the sight of them was more interesting.

The easiest way for us to get our pre- and post-match interviews from players and staff was to go to the team hotels. The opportunity to interact with players was much more relaxed than it is now. One standout memory was us waiting to get an interview in a hotel lobby with Perpetua Nkwocha and Stella Mbachu – two icons of Nigerian women's football – before their last group game against the USA on 18 September. Stella was playing her club football in China for Tianjin Teda, and her Chinese club coach had travelled to Shanghai to see her. It was wonderful to watch him advising them both about the game they'd just played against North Korea. He had sheets of paper with diagrams indicating positioning and runs that could have been made. Apart from the odd Mandarin phrase, the predominant language spoken between the three of them was 'football'.

What a game that was. A narrow 1-0 loss for the Super Falcons meant their tournament had come to an end. Ghana's last group game, against Norway, was to be played in Shanghai the following day and, no matter the result, they would not advance to the knockout stage either. The match was to be a celebration, though. Lots of Ghana fans were looking forward to sending their team home with a fitting fanfare, proud that they had made it to the tournament.

Sadly, Typhoon Wipha put paid to those ideas. It was forecast to be one of the most ferocious typhoons to hit Shanghai and the surrounding area for decades. FIFA made a decision to relocate and reschedule the game. Instead of being played in Shanghai, the game was to take place the next day in Hangzhou. We were able to get return train tickets to Hangzhou and watch the game, but it was an unsettling time for players and supporters alike as everyone's match preparation and travel had been disrupted. It was not surprising when the Black Queens went down to their heaviest defeat of the tournament: a 7-2 loss.

That night, we travelled back to Shanghai with the rain pouring and wind swirling around us. Our sports reporting for the BBC World Service on the Super Falcons and Black Queens had come to an end. We turned to each other and laughed out loud. It had been an exhausting and often bewildering adventure, but we wouldn't have changed a single second.

ESTATE OF MIND: THE MAKING OF EMMA HAYES

Suzanne Wrack *goes in search of the places that made the charismatic and successful Chelsea manager, and talks to the people who know Hayes best.*

'She's not ashamed of who she is and where she's come from,' says former Arsenal and Chelsea star Katie Chapman of her friend and former manager Emma Hayes. 'Where she's come from is what's made her who she is. She's not ashamed about coming from Camden from a council estate and she talks about it all the time. Sometimes that's really nice for people to hear.'

It is. When I sat down to write a profile on manager Emma Hayes for the *Guardian* before her Chelsea team took on Barcelona in a first Champions League final for the south London side, I did not expect to feel such an overwhelming affinity with her. Yet, having spoken to the family, friends, players and coaches who know Emma best, the love I felt and feel for the council estate where I grew up – that was such a critical part of forming who I am – washed over me. Emma and those closest to her credit much of who she is as a person and manager to her council-estate roots, and their words chimed vividly with my own feelings. Where Emma grew up on the Curnock Street Estate in Camden, I grew up on the Hobbs Place Estate in Hoxton. I loved it and I feel defensive of it.

'It's key to know who you are,' Emma's older sister Victoria tells me. 'We grew up on that council estate with the biggest mixtures of every culture and different types of nationality and you have nothing to do but play. It was great. It was concrete. I remember that we had a slide and, in the winter when it froze and had ice on it, we used to go around Tesco's and get their bread boxes and then go down the slide on them and skid across the playground. You cannot replicate it. Brilliant days.'

It would be wrong to completely romanticise life on a council estate in north London in the 1980s (in Emma's case) and the 1990s (in mine). To get to my family's fourth-floor, two-bed flat you had to navigate the piss-stinking lift – if it was working – or the badly lit, grey, concrete staircase that was used as a toilet or quiet corner for drug deals. In those days there was no key-fob entry to blocks. There were floods when neighbours' washing machines would break. We had gates on the windows to prevent break-ins. There was never enough space.

But we're all too used to those narratives of council-estate living, and council housing, being a negative, and to grey concrete blocks being used in films and TV to show poverty and crime. What you rarely see are the vibrant, colourful and protective communities that live within them, and you rarely hear from the people who love or loved living as part of those communities. I remember trying to target water bombs at friends from the balcony; old ladies allowing us to feed our string and cup telephones across their balconies; being able to go and play with other kids from the estate in the concrete playground without my parents because all the blocks faced it; dropping my mum's drying bra into the neighbour's garden below and them hanging it on their fence for me to pop down and collect it. I could walk to the corner shop to pick up the Sunday papers for my dad without crossing a road. It was an area I knew every inch of, one I could duck and dive my way through with confidence to lose a man who had followed me home from school when I was ten years old.

Then there was football. On a hot day, with the balcony doors open, you could hear the cheers from Highbury when Arsenal scored. During major tournaments you felt like you were in every front room as celebrations echoed from most flats. The whole estate would be buzzing. How could you not be sucked in? How could you not be drawn towards a sport that united everyone around you? I would spend hours with my football in the playground, picking a brick on a wall and trying to hit the same one over and over, or weaving it around climbing frames and swings, crazy-golf style obstacles on our rough pitch, in matches with friends.

Emma's story is similar. 'She played with all the boys [on the estate]. It didn't matter what age she was, she just played; there wasn't a question as to whether she would or she wouldn't. She was accepted in that environment. You played football until Mum called you in and then you went indoors and you watched it. That's what happened,' says Victoria.

'We're a total football family,' says Rebecca, Emma's other sister. 'I shared a room with her, so I'd have to watch *Match of the Day*, even if I didn't want to watch it. She was very into international football. We'd go on holiday and, without fail, I'd pick up a doll and she'd pick up the Inter Milan shirt, the Barcelona shirt, whatever the local shirt was. I've still got them up in my loft now.'

'Emma is a great football fan,' adds Victoria. 'The players and managers that inspire her, certainly up there, are Maradona, Gazza and Lineker… Gary Lineker's legs, she used to love those! In his little shorts!' she says with a laugh. 'By the time Emma was about ten, it was the World Cup in 1986 when Diego landed on this earth and we watched every single game. The time difference meant that we might have been up a hell of a lot later than we should have been as kids, but we lived for those days. They were the best days. Diego Maradona was just God. He might have had the hand of God but he was the person she replicated when she played football.'

Emma was the only girl to play in her primary school, and a teacher referred her to a club in Holborn called Mary Ward. 'How can I describe that team?' says Rebecca, who also joined. 'It was the best in all the London boroughs. We used to beat everyone. We used to go to the Met Police finals. Emma was always the star of the show in terms of her football. She was a creative, tricky player, the goalscorer.'

'They won everything,' Victoria tells me. 'Whatever they turned up to they won. My mum had a corner cupboard in the front room that was filled with so many trophies you couldn't get any more in there. It was ridiculous. I think that's where she got her winning mentality from, thinking about it. It was that team; it was her mates. She had a team that played for one another, and she learned the true spirit of teams working together. If they all worked together as friends and worked hard, they won. She was great at it as well – an amazing left foot, great crosser of the ball.'

Arsenal manager Vic Akers would link up with Mary Ward, which became an unofficial feeder team, wearing the Arsenal kit but with the Mary Ward name. Once they were in secondary school, on Tuesdays and Fridays Emma and Rebecca would head to training at the JVC centre. At weekends they would travel up and down the country playing eleven-a-side. At seventeen, though, the dream died. Emma injured her ankle on a ski trip and was told she would never play again.

'It was a cartilage injury,' says Victoria. 'She was heartbroken. Just inconsolable. It was the end of the world. She was told she's not supposed to kick a ball. You still see her do it in training with the players today and I think, *Oh, Em, what you doing? You're going to end up with arthritis.* She's also had knee-ligament tears, which also hinders her. But that injury changed her.'

With a career in football ruled out, Emma went to Liverpool Hope University and studied European Studies, Spanish and Sociology. Her intention was to become a spy. She went to Salford University to do her masters in Intelligence and International Affairs. During the holidays, she would travel back and work in the various businesses her dad, Sid, was involved in.

'She would get up at five o'clock in the morning, come down to one business and bake bread. She would go there on her own and cook 2,000 baguettes,' says Sid. 'She's capable of doing a day's work. She shows that in what she's doing now – she works very, very hard at it. I can't say enough about her.'

Unable to pull herself away from the game, she played for the university team in Liverpool, but she also started to pick up coaching badges, not just in football but in anything and everything, from swimming to table tennis. After dropping the James Bond fantasy, she worked in sports development for Camden Council, but there was an itch that needed scratching.

'I remember her laying in the bath – that's how close we are; one would be on the toilet and one would be in the bath,' said Rebecca with a laugh. 'She was like: "This is my time to change. I need to go where the elite is in this sport, where it's the most professional, where I'm going to learn, where I'm going to grow, and it's going to be America." And as much as that was devastating for me because it was like taking my other arm off, she was so determined. She just hated the culture, the hurdles, the politics in this country. She just wanted away from it all and wanted to go learn it from a different perspective, because the game out in America was the best of the best.'

Victoria and Rebecca drove her to the airport. She had bought a one-way ticket, had a backpack of clothes and $1,000 on her, and a job at Major League Soccer boys' camps on Long Island waiting for her.

'I remember stopping at the Tesco garage in a Harrow back road somewhere,' says Victoria. 'Me, Emma and Bec are sat in the car sobbing, but she was adamant. We were always very good in our household at supporting anyone who wants to do whatever it is you want to do. So if Emma wants to go to America: "I'm going to go to America, and I'm going to go and learn how I can change the game. I need to change the game," then: "All right, Em, whatever." I didn't doubt for one moment that she was going to do that.'

In 2001 she would become the youngest ever head coach in W-League (a predecessor to the National Women's Soccer League in the US) when she was put in charge of the Long Island Lady Riders. The following year she was named national coach of the year, aged just twenty-five. She then took charge of the women's team at Iona College in New York, where she met Amanda Vandervort, head coach at NYU at the time.

'My assistant coach was friends with her,' says Vandervort. 'We didn't really know each other that well until a couple of months later, when I was going on a recruiting trip to Providence, Rhode Island. Emma didn't have much of a budget at Iona College so I invited her to share my room at this tournament and we car-pooled up and went recruiting together. Emma and I went out that night, and when we came back the room had been destroyed by my two black Labrador retrievers. I'd forgotten my contacts solution, so I took them out and I put them in a glass in water next to the sink and Emma woke up in the middle of the night and drank my cup of contacts. This was our first time spending time together,' she laughs. 'We would go recruiting all over the place together. We were recruiting a different profile of player so it just worked.'

At Iona, in 2004, she would be named the Metro Atlantic Athletic Conference coach of the year. Former Wales international Eleri Earnshaw, who is now a coach herself, was her captain and says Emma instilled a sense of belief in the whole Iona group.

'We weren't Chelsea; we weren't the best team,' Earnshaw tells me, 'but she demanded the highest standards when it came to work rate and things that we could control, like how we responded to adversity. Because of that, we went into every game, rightly or wrongly, thinking that we could win, because of how hard we worked and how tenacious we were. We didn't have the most money in the conference, we didn't have the same amount of scholarships as everyone else, which obviously limits the talent that you can bring in, and we carried this underdog mentality with us. She really played on that and used it to our advantage massively.'

One of the things Emma did at Iona was have motivational sayings printed on the back of the training shirts, as Earnshaw recalls: 'In my first year the saying was [Mark Twain's]: "It's not the size of the dog in the fight, it's the size of the fight in the dog." It wasn't really until I left I realised how prominent a part of our mentality that was.'

She also put an emphasis on leadership and player decision-making.

'She put a lot of trust in myself and the other captain, Sarah,' says Earnshaw. 'She let us in a fair bit, which some managers don't do – there's a big barrier sometimes between managers and players – but it was very open, very open communication, a lot of honesty.

'I remember it was one of my roommates' twenty-first birthday coming up. It was midweek and obviously they wanted to go out, but we had a massive game coming up on Friday. So myself and the other captain approached Emma and said, "What are you going to do about it?" And she goes, "What are *you* going to do about it?" She put those tough decisions on me and the other captain, knowing what decision we would make, but she wanted us to be the ones to make it and us to be the ones to communicate it.'

Anson Dorrance, the head coach at the University of North Carolina and the mastermind of the US women's national team's first World Cup win in 1991, met Emma when he was on the coaching staff for the National Soccer Coaches Association of America. Emma had signed up for a course that would travel to the city of Curitiba in Brazil. At that point, Curitiba had 'sent more Brazilians to sign contracts in Europe than any football player-development platform in the world,' Dorrance explains. 'In most American coaching courses you don't have a lot of references when you're trying to teach the coaches. Why? Because they don't really know the game because the coaches don't watch the game. All of a sudden I'm listening to this woman – and obviously I love having any woman on these courses because of my background – and I'm thinking, *Holy crap, her references are better than mine.* Here I am, teaching the course, and this little snot had better references for the game at the highest level than I did. So I immediately took to her, immediately completely supported her and I became a fan from then on.'

Years later she recommended he attend the summer school of Dutch coach Raymond Verheijen. 'I loved it,' says Dorrance. 'One of the problems I have is if I walk into a room I'm the expert and so I rarely learn anything. If you have a reputation, you're almost not allowed to listen to anyone else speak. Emma brought me into this Verheijen philosophy of player development that was absolutely fantastic. She was sort of my North Star pupil in Curitiba and then all of a sudden she pays me back by inviting me into this.'

Having followed her career, Dorrance has seen Emma go 'from confident to commanding,' he says. 'This is a critical quality. She is openly ambitious. The trouble with the way we raise our girls and young women is we teach them to basically genuflect. She was confident back then and I was completely impressed, but now she's commanding. Amanda [Vandervort] is the same way. These are wonderfully ambitious women. We praise men for having this quality and yet we seem to excoriate women for it.' He believes Emma's biggest takeaway from her time in the US was not tactics or methodology but attitude. 'In our country, the women's game is respected, partly due to Title IX. And women in these positions are respected and the players are respected. The teeth of the patriarchy in sport in our country aren't as sharp.'

Vandervort says Emma learned how to recruit in the States. 'In the college recruiting system you're dealing with intense competition. You have to try and convince players to come to your school when you have no budget, no money, no scholarship. You have to work out what it takes to get a player to commit to come and play for you. Emma proved time and time again that caring for somebody and demonstrating how you want to see their success and development and growth made people want to be a part of what she was doing. She got players to come to Iona that were offered full-ride scholarships with other schools but they wanted to come to Iona because they wanted to come to a winning programme and they wanted to play for Emma.'

'She likes to have good personalities,' says Katie Chapman, who played under Emma in Chicago as well as at Arsenal and Chelsea. 'You can't always give someone that. You can give them the rest of it – you can give them help with their technical ability and that sort of stuff – but to have a good person who you can trust and is going to fight for you, I think that's harder to find. That's something that in her recruitment process she really digs into. She really gets to know someone before she makes that decision. Her recruitment process will be over a long period of time. Building a culture and a nice environment to be in – they're the things she prides herself on. When you create that, that's when you build success, because everyone's on the same page, everyone wants to do the same thing and everyone wants to play for the club and you. That is massive.'

On returning to England in 2006, Emma worked as academy director for Arsenal Ladies and assistant coach to Vic Akers.

'If anyone knows Vic personally,' says Rebecca, 'they know he would never let anybody in that door. Assistant coaches? Never, no one. No one was allowed to touch his players. He was the only coach. But he let Emma in the door. She was allowed to come in and give two training sessions. After that… well, it was game over – they won the quadruple after that season of her coaching. She was a massive influence and part of that quadruple.'

'That year at Arsenal was fantastic for everyone there,' says Chapman.

A year later Emma upped sticks again, with the launch of the new professional league luring her back Stateside. Akers says he was 'disappointed, obviously,' when Emma chose to go to America but that he 'understood, deep down, what path she wanted to follow. That was, at the time, the best league in the world and the finances were massive there.'

Emma signed Karen Carney to the newly launched Chicago Red Stars. She was a big fan of a young Portland College forward whom she would later select as the second overall pick in the 2009 draft: a certain Megan Rapinoe. Carli Lloyd, Ella Masar and Brazilian forward Cristiane were just some of the star names in the squad. The following year, additions included Chapman, Anita Asante, Formiga and Jess McDonald. Then she was fired, five games into her second season.

'I was standing in Kentish Town when she called me. She'd just got the call, like five minutes before that, and she was heartbroken, absolutely devastated,' says Rebecca. 'That was the biggest learning curve of her life. And that's when she stepped back from football.'

'She learned so much about the way things could be,' says Victoria. 'She also learned about failure there. We never look at failure as failing. Failure is a first attempt at learning, and that was her first attempt at learning to build a team.'

'I remember her saying, "You know what? I'm going to self-reflect,"' recalls Chapman. 'It was never about [blaming] anybody else. It was always about her – what she needed to do better and how she was going to progress from there.'

After a stint as a consultant for a Washington Freedom team that included US stars Abby Wambach, Ashlyn Harris, Allie Long, Briana Scurry and Becky Sauerbrunn, to name a few, Emma flew back to London and worked for the family business.

'She needed something mundane, to come away from it, see if [coaching] is really what she wanted to do,' says Rebecca. 'People were phoning her, wanting her involved in different clubs, but she needed that time out to assess, review and just enjoy growing something for the family.'

She did keep her toe in the water football-wise, working remotely from London as technical director for Western New York Flash, where she advised on transfers, helping to put together a team that would win the Women's Professional Soccer championship in 2011.

Not long after that, sitting next to Emma at Wembley for the 2012 London Olympics final, Sid realised just how good his daughter was.

'There was the ceremony on the pitch where the three teams [USA, Japan and Canada] collected their medals,' he says. 'I think there were around fifty players queuing up for their medals. When they're collecting the medals, Emma said: "Dad, you see those fifty people out there? I've coached forty of them." I thought, *Wow, but you're sitting here unemployed?* It was time to come back. Whatever happened in America, it was time for her to get out there.' That month, August 2012, she took the job at Chelsea.

'At Chelsea she's built absolutely everything,' says Chapman. 'She's fought for every little thing there – from having the kit washed to having food, to having our own building, to having our own training and pitches. Now it's an absolute professional set-up.'

Emma has been at Chelsea since 2012, gradually expanding the facilities from one chair in a shared building at the back of Cobham (Chelsea's training ground) until the women's set-up occupied the entire building, and guiding the team through to professionalism. In 2014 she won her first trophy, the FA Cup, and in 2015 she led the team to the first of four league titles. They have since picked up a second FA Cup, back-to-back League Cups in 2020 and 2021, and reached a first Champions League final in 2021. Of her 260 games as Chelsea manager, she has won 157. It is a remarkable record.

Emma's family have been critical to her success, a support network through the good and the bad, much in the same way the estate is a support network. She had to lean heavily on her family when, at twenty-eight weeks pregnant in 2018, she lost one of the twins she was carrying. It was 'terrible, awful, so traumatic,' says Rebecca. 'I went on every one of the visits to the hospital. She knew she needed to keep that away from the players [who were getting ready to play in the FA Cup final]. She doesn't want attention on her for that sort of stuff because nobody can take that pain away from her. She kind of pushed that aside a little bit.' Her family were desperate for her to take a step back, recalls Rebecca, 'but there was no stopping her. No stopping her whatsoever. The last game of the season, against Liverpool in May 2018, she literally had to get pinned down: "You can't go, you're due any day. You can't go." My mum very much supported her in all of it. She travelled to Wolfsburg the month before, went on 10 million trains with her, and then we had to get our cousin who was a midwife to take her on another journey when it got really close because of the complications. The doctors were advising her not to do it, but she did it. Nothing would stop her, not even her own health at that point. It's all about the team; she'd do anything for winning. Remember, that's her ultimate goal. She never gets bored of it.'

Chapman says it is the mentality drummed into her by Sid that keeps her wanting more. 'He's her hardest critic. He doesn't let her get away with anything. That's what drives her.'

'With us at work, with Emma, he always wants more,' says Rebecca. 'You're never ever awarded with a "well done" for anything. It's just, "You've done that, what's next?" It's just more more more, there's no praise whatsoever. You have to ask him: 'Dad, any chance? Well done?" He'll say, "Well, you know that, go on."'

Yet Sid does say he's proud – unprompted – when he remembers seeing Emma's impact at coaching conventions in the US over the years:

'This little girl from Camden teaching all these international coaches [at] the biggest coaches' convention in the world, wow… She has a presence, Emma, at these places. I'm well proud of her, obviously. She's got a skill, a skill you can't buy.'

Sid feels it, the emotion of seeing the kid from the north London estate, on top of the world, shining as a coach, as a pundit and as a force for good. I do too. Emma is not just from the estate; she has taken all the positive experiences and values of estate life – the atmosphere of unity, diversity and togetherness – into every team she has built and it is a key part of her success. These are the estate stories people need to hear.

ANFIELD OF DREAMS

Football was a foreign land to **Cassie Whittell**. *And so she created her own map showing how to get there.*

'All right, call me a tomboy. Tomboys get medals. Tomboys win championships. Tomboys can fly. Oh, and tomboys aren't boys.' *Julie Foudy, two-time World Cup winner and Olympic gold medallist*

1978

I am standing at the end of the line of boys, as befits my status in the gang: the lone girl, the outlier. I don't mind being last. It gives me a chance to hear which teams the boys are picking. I want to be different, special. I don't want to be like the rest of them. I want to be the one who stands out from the crowd, when I'm seven, a talent I wish I could have held onto as I got older.

'Go on, then. Who you support?' The eternal question among seven-year-olds. The way to gain social acceptance, kudos, points. Supporting someone 'crap' (our local team, Reading, for example) was a one-way ticket to social oblivion in the primary school playground.

'Nottingham Forest.'

'Yeah, Forest.'

'Got to be Forest.'

'Man U.'

'Man United.'

'Forest.'

Down the line the team names come – Forest, Man U, Forest, Man U. Just two teams left before me. Arsenal or Liverpool. I know Michael Sadler, standing next to me, will pick one of them – he's no Man U fan, can't stand Forest. Whichever team he picks, I think, I will pick the other. If he says Arsenal, I'll say Liverpool. If he says Liverpool, I'll say Arsenal. Decided on this course of action, I close my eyes, cross my fingers. I want Liverpool very badly. I want to be part of Kenny Dalglish's gang.

'Go on then, Mike. Who do you support?'

I hold my breath. Mike Sadler scuffs his Clarks in the playground dust. Looks around.

'Ars'nal.' He says it quietly and my heart soars. That means…

'Candice Whittell, who you supporting, then?' Someone sniggers. I stick my chest out proudly.

'Liverpool Football Club.' I let the words flow smoothly off my tongue. 'I support Liverpool.'

There's a respectful silence. I've done the unthinkable – gone against the grain – and am now feted as the only Liverpool fan in the class. I'm allowed to take free-kicks against the wall at break and be the first to pick sides for matches. I am asked my opinion on upcoming matches, who will win. When I come to school with a red plastic LFC kit bag, people crowd around to touch and admire it. I am the hero of the hour.

I do not reach such dizzy footballing heights again for a very long time.

1980

Our school has set up a five-a-side football tournament for all the years. Whether you're six or eleven, if you can form a squad, you can take part in the tournament. There is high excitement. Who will be in your squad? Who are you going to play with? What's your team name? Who's your striker?

I'm annoyed that no one has asked me to be part of their team. So I grab four of my girlfriends and ask them if they want to make up a squad.

Everyone I ask wants to take part. We've never played football before but with me coaching them – I've never done that before either, but no one is to know – and with my dad designing our team kit, we're ready to play. We call ourselves The Flamethrowers and all five of us proudly wear our hand-drawn kit T-shirts to school on the first day of the tournament.

I boldly go up to our PE teacher, who is organising things.

'We'd like to register for the football tournament.'

He looks at me, surprised. 'You would? Who's in your team?'

'Me, Kirsty, Emma, Rachel and Audrey.'

'But you're girls.'

I wait patiently. Yes, I know that. I also know we're the only girls brave enough to form a team to play in the tournament. Despite the jeers and sneers of the boys around us.

'Girls can't play football.'

This is the first I've heard of it.

'Why not?'

'You don't play football,' he says, dismissive. 'Go and ask Miss Simpkins to put on a netball tournament for you instead.'

I am furious. My dad complains to the headteacher – to no avail. Girls can't play football at our school. The Flamethrowers are disbanded before we ever kick a ball in competitive anger. There's no place for us girls in the tournament. There's no place for us in football, is how it feels.

1986

We are in Sheffield at my nan's council house – a two-up two-down with an outside loo in the yard still – and there is World Cup football on the telly. I am sat at my uncle Pete's feet, half-watching the screen – England v Argentina, a crucial match – half-watching the men around me, sat on the settee, perched on arms of chairs, Tetley beer cans in hand, cigarettes smouldering between their rough fingers. They all seem to have a language that is unknown to me. I am watching them, trying to copy them. This is the language of football. At fourteen years old, I very much want to learn how to speak it.

'Ref! Ref – fuck's sake, what was that?'

'Christ, these are shit. What's he playing at?'

'You see that offside? Lino needs glasses.'

These words have no real meaning – I have never been to a football match in my life and don't really understand their anger, their dismissive comments – but I want to be part of it; I want to swear and shout at the telly too. I want to know why 'lino' needs glasses. My uncle tries to explain the offside rule to me in between sips of beer and puffs on his cig. I breathe in the acrid smoke as it curls around me, nod my head, pretend I understand.

Something happens on the screen – a jumping figure in blue, the outstretched hands of the goalkeeper, a contentious goal – and roars of fury, of 'cheating bastard', fill the room. My uncle Dave, ex-Army, ex-Falklands, is incensed, howling at the screen, 'You fucking, fucking cheat.'

'What, what is it?' I cry, but I am drowned out and my auntie Maureen comes into the room, takes my hand, leads me out.

'It's not for you, love,' she says, smoothing my hair down, kissing my cheek. 'Leave the men to it.'

1987

My first proper boyfriend is the son of my mum and dad's mates, who live in Muswell Hill. When I go over there, I'm allowed to go up to his room, to watch football on his portable black-and-white telly. He is a Tottenham Hotspur fan. His room is decked out in blue and white, and he likes Glenn Hoddle the best.

We snog, all clashing teeth and soggy fumblings, and he tells me we can't go all the way because I'm not Jewish like he is. If we go all the way, we might have to get married and he can't marry me because I'm not in his faith. I'm sixteen years old. I tell him I don't want to get married to him, not even if he has a Spurs season ticket.

'You'll regret it,' he says, laughing.

I don't think I will.

1990

I am trying to decide who I fancy more, Gary Lineker or Paul Gascoigne. In truth, I prefer David Platt, but this is not an acceptable answer for my girlfriends, who are watching a World Cup match while piled onto our friend Jo's bunkbeds.

In the end they get bored and go out to the dark summer garden, leaving me to witness Platt's sublime goal against Belgium in the dying seconds of the game. It is the best goal I've ever seen and I think my heart will burst from the joy of it. Platty wheels away, arms uplifted and a smile on his face. I wonder how he feels in that moment. I can't imagine it.

'Are you still watching this crap?' Jo comes back up to her room, peers at me curiously. 'I don't know why you bother with it, it's so boring.'

'It's great.' I jump down from the top bunk, land gracelessly on the floor. I can hear the others out in the garden, talking about A Level results. 'It's a laugh.'

'It doesn't mean boys will like you,' Jo says drily.

'I know that.' I'm eighteen years old and boys tend not to like me anyway, because I can quote stats about football and know about the offside rule.

'So why do you care?'

'Because…' I pause. How can I explain it to her, that watching football – when I get the chance to watch it, which isn't often – is like watching the best play ever written or hearing the sweetest song? That seeing a perfect goal – like Platty's, like just now – is the finest feeling in the universe, a concrete coming-together of science and art, nature and physics?

'Because it's a laugh,' I say lamely.

Jo shakes her head. 'Come on, then. I've nicked a bottle of Lambrusco from my mum. Want some?'

Yeah, I guess I do.

1993

There is a man a couple of feet away from me and he is monotonously chanting 'Wanker. Wanker. Wanker,' every time Blackburn Rovers touch the ball.

This is my first time at an actual football match – an *actual match* – and I am entranced by Blackburn's Alan Shearer. He is shining strangely brightly among the dark lines and walls of Bramall Lane, a player so good that even the Sheffield United fans around us have to admit he has something classy about him.

'Not bad, that Shearer.'

'Aye, he's all right.'

He puts two past United, and the Rovers fans whoop and holler from the away end while we look on, miserable. Genius has touched the Arnold Laver Stand and, sadly, it is not from one of our own. I have never known such an outpouring of derision in my life. These are Sheffield United fans talking about their own team as if they hate them.

'They are shite!'

'Aren't they. Fuck sake, don't know why I bother.'

'Did you enjoy it?' asks my boyfriend afterwards. He has organised this trip to football, has negotiated the tricky tasks of buying tickets and Bovrils and knowing where to stand and sit and keep out of trouble. He has drawn a mental map for me, which I am eagerly trying to follow without getting too lost.

'I loved it,' I say. 'Can we go again?'

1994

I am amazed at my own daring. It is a weeknight match and I am on my own at Rotherham United's Millmoor Ground. There aren't too many people here, or that is how it feels to me. I am rigid with fright in case someone asks me what I'm doing on the terraces by myself. I pretend to read the programme, worry about walking back to my car, parked a couple of streets away. Try to look casual, comfortable, like I've done this a million times.

There doesn't seem to be another woman here. Groups of men stand chatting, companionable, cups of tea and snouts in hand. A couple of old lads, dogs at their heels. The floodlights seem to fizz and sputter in the damp night air. I can hear the M1 motorway, flat out there in the darkness, whizzing people away from this small South Yorkshire town, towards another world.

'Here we go!' The teams stride out onto the pitch and I can forget all about feeling anxious and alone. I can just watch the match and cheer and shout, and bay for blood, with no one caring what I say or do. I'm free from all the rules that I normally follow in my life as a shy 22-year-old: don't take up too much space, don't make trouble, don't make a noise, be quiet, be good, behave, do what the others do, don't rock the boat. Whatever you do, don't rock the boat.

Here at Millmoor, I can be… me. Just me, raw and bold, whooping when Rotherham score, groaning when they concede. I can feel free.

'You enjoyed that!' says one old fella, leading his terrier past me at the final whistle. 'It does you good, doesn't it?'

It does. It really does.

2000

'You know quite a lot about football.' This from a beefy colleague of mine in sales, who likes to come in on a Monday morning with his takeaway coffee and a bacon roll and rehash West Ham matches loudly over his desk with his office pals. I've chipped in with a couple of comments, just a handful of times, and have now got his attention. He's a big lad, blonde, eyes like currants pricked into his doughy face. He looks at me, unsure.

'Thanks so much,' I say, trying not to be smug.

'For a girl,' he continues with a knowing smirk. 'Your boyfriend a fan?'

2004

I am not a fan of going to Old Trafford particularly. Old Trafford for me is anathema – home of the awful and detestable Manchester United – but what I do like is going with my husband and his mates for the Boxing Day match, the one that means people turn up in Santa hats and Christmas jumpers, still shiny-full from their turkey and Christmas pud the day before, showing off their new phones and watches, faces pink from all the festive good cheer.

It is the pure ritual I like. I want to get to the pub, have a glass of wine and a packet of crisps, listen to the football banter from men who have been watching this team all their lives. When Dave turns up – he's a City fan, which is a horror – we all get to tease him. I am mildly ribbed for my Liverpool tendencies. We have a couple of drinks then walk up the road to Old Trafford, streaming along the bypass with the other devotees, tiny particles in a bigger sea, a sea of red and black. I can get lost in this ocean of people. I don't have to talk; I can just be, silent and small, one of a hundred thousand others who make up this noisy, bubbling crowd.

'You don't have to come,' my husband says to me, the last year I'm married to him. 'I know you don't like Man U.'

'It's fine,' I say casually. 'I only go to see you lose.'

2010

Thirty years after that playground line-up left me a Liverpool fan, I finally get to go to Anfield. I have watched the team many times – on TV, at other grounds – but I've never seen them at home, at the stadium in Liverpool, until now.

There's nothing special about Anfield, apart from the fact it's home, and it's always been home. I've never actually been there before, but I've been there so many times in my imagination, on TV, in photos, that it's like I've always been there. And that makes it the most welcoming place on earth. I walk over Stanley Park, see the stands and the crest and the lights and the Shankly Gates, and I'm so quiet my partner asks me if I'm OK. I'm overwhelmed, I say. I've not been here before and it's just… wonderful.

We watch a shitty 0-0 draw with Swansea but I'm not bothered. I've sung 'You'll Never Walk Alone' and meant it. I've seen the team on the glorious pitch. I'm at Anfield and it's all I've wanted since I was seven. I'm here. I am here. I want to scream it to the rooftops and yell it from the bottom of my lungs. I want Anfield to hear my voice, my own true sound, from the seven-year-old me to the woman I am today. I roar on the team. I am shouting so loud my throat hurts afterwards and I can barely speak above a whisper. It feels good to give voice to all my football frustrations. I hope it's not long until I can do it again.

2017

'You can work in football… like, a job?'

'Yes, of course.' The man I'm having coffee with about a volunteer role at a not-for-profit football tournament is amused by my bemusement. 'There are loads of jobs in football.'

'But I don't play. Or coach,' I add hastily, in case he has misunderstood.

'But you can write. And organise things.' He puts his coffee cup down, nods to the little portfolio of writing work I've brought along to show him. 'Come and do some writing for the tournament.'

I end up doing more than just writing at this football tournament. I run press conferences, organise journalists and interviews. Put together rotas for match coverage. Manage a pool of writers and photographers. Write social media posts, create videos. It's hectic. I love it. I'm working in football! No one can believe I've never done this before. You're a natural, they say.

It's all the times I've been told 'no, this isn't for you' that makes me confident now. I know I can do this. I know it's my time. I can write about a football match because I've watched so many. I can tell a story because I know how it feels to not speak my own truths, with my own voice. It's an exhilaration to realise that the sport I've loved for so long is something I'm now a tiny part of. I'm thrilled. I don't ever want this feeling to end.

2019

After volunteering, I start work for a football organisation, and one of the scary, wonderful things I sometimes get to do is talk about football. For the Women's Football Weekend, I am asked to give a quick interview for the club TV channel before a WSL match, talking about the organisation I'm working for and why women's voices in football are important. Why our stories need to be heard. Why we need to be confident about telling them, about making a platform, about not being put off by those men who see football as theirs. It's not theirs, of course, but we need to be able to speak up, to claim the sport as ours as well. Like it's always been, for me. I just had to find out how to forge my place in the sport I've loved for so long. To fight for my place. I hope my fight will make it easier for the women and girls who come after me, who follow my dogged trail, spot the signs I've left out for them along the way.

The interview is brief – two or three minutes – and it's over before I've even had time to think about what I'm saying. I chat to the interviewer afterwards as we wait for kick-off, and she's friendly and charming, as so many women working in football are. As we say goodbye, she nudges my arm, smiles.

'You're ever so good, talking about football,' she says. 'You must love it a lot.'

'I do,' I say. 'My whole life. I've loved it my whole life.'

WINNING AND LOSING

In the midst of victory, loss has a habit of reappearing and reminding. **Molly Hudson** *considers her bond of grief with the Chelsea and England player Fran Kirby following the deaths of their mothers.*

Football is the most important of the least important things. For many it is the soundtrack to our lives. From children's football kits to season tickets, people's lives can be defined by their love of the game. It's the indescribable feeling of joy at watching your team score a last-minute winner. It's the heartbreak of conceding a last-minute goal. But most of all it is the feeling as you step inside that football stadium. For you, and for the nameless person a few seats away who you see every week and who for ninety minutes lives and breathes everything that you do, it is togetherness and hope. It is nothing, and yet it is everything.

Grief is, in many ways, the antithesis of football. It is bleak, lonely and devoid of joy. Nagging at every happiness, it pours scorn on something as meaningless as football against a backdrop of such emotion.

We proudly display our footballing colours, yet grief is hiding in plain sight among us all – it is, simply, part of life. Those footballers who provide us with such escapism are often suffering too.

This is the story of Fran Kirby – an extraordinary footballer, with an extraordinary story, whose refreshing honesty in her struggles after losing her mother at the age of fourteen gave comfort to me and many others in similar circumstances.

For both Kirby and I, 14 March 2021 was the day that grief and football aligned. The Continental Cup final – the women's League Cup equivalent – coincided with Mother's Day. When you have lost someone, it feels as though the Days should be capitalised, because they become a series of named events to hate. To bring anxiety and loathing and a guaranteed wave of grief. The first birthday without them, the first Christmas, Mother's Day, their own birthday. After the first, comes the second, no easier. With that wave of grief come your own personalised coping mechanisms.

Since my mum died in January 2020, mine has always been to allow myself to feel the sense of loss on that day, to try not to fight it, for it would be in vain. Book the day off. Wallow. Tomorrow will be better, easier somehow. But this year the Continental Cup final coincided with Mother's Day. 'It's OK,' I told myself. 'Get a lift with a close friend and colleague who knows the situation, easily able to distract me with small talk. Sit in the press box. File the report. Go home.' Easy, right?

As I began to get dressed and face the world, I thought about Kirby. About how she might be feeling as she began her own day – she did not have the luxury of the relative anonymity I had in a press box. She would be on Watford's Vicarage Road pitch, front and centre as she took to the field with her Chelsea teammates for the final against Bristol City, her openness in her mother's loss meaning it was what we were all thinking, writing, commentating as the game began. By the time the clock ticked onto thirty minutes, Kirby had already provided two assists for her teammate Sam Kerr, and this time she had found the net herself.

She looked to the sky, fingers pointing upwards, wearing the number 14 shirt to mark 14 June, her mother's birthday. In that moment, the world was watching and appreciating her greatness, and yet she had only one supporter on her mind: Denise, her mother, the one who had believed in her more than any other. By the time she was withdrawn in the sixty-first minute, Kirby had scored twice and provided four assists, a direct hand in each of the six unanswered Chelsea goals that saw them thrash Bristol City and lift the Cup.

To understand Kirby's story we must rewind thirteen years, to Kirby at the age of fourteen, when she was already a clearly gifted footballer – Denise had written in a birthday card that her daughter would one day play in a World Cup. Having joined the Reading academy at the age of seven, Kirby and her mother were attending a regular feedback session with a coach in 2008. Denise put her head on the table and passed out. She had suffered a brain haemorrhage, from which she would not recover.

Kirby reflects that the full force of her grief was not immediately evident. A strange quirk of grief is that, while your world grinds to a painful, immediate halt, the rest of the world continues spinning on its axis, unaware. So Kirby carried on playing football, progressing at Reading, playing for England youth teams. 'It was great really; it was kind of just like nothing had really happened,' she reflects. She readily admits her family did not speak about her mother or their loss. Anyone who has experienced grief will know that this is not sustainable – eventually that wall you have built between your feelings and reality, simply to function daily, will begin to crumble, and you cannot run from the reality for ever.

Ironically it was at an England camp when Kirby's wall eventually came down. 'I turned very introverted, when I was fifteen, because I was going through this dark phase. I wasn't there; I was a zombie,' she told the *Players' Tribune* in an emotional video describing her grief with the intention of helping others going through similar tragedies.

'It was probably when I went away on an England camp that I realised, *OK, something is not right here*. I went up to Manchester and I remember sitting in a room with Mo Marley [former England youth coach], who ended up managing me in the seniors eventually. I remember sitting in the room with Mo and I just said, "I want to go home." I was like, "I don't want to do this any more." She said, "What do you mean?" And I feel so embarrassed about saying this now, but I remember sitting there and crying and I said, "I miss my mom." I remember just sitting there and I was just crying, crying, crying, and she actually said to me, "OK, we're not going to come to you. You need to tell us when you're ready to come back into this environment again.'"

Sometimes you need to reach rock bottom before you can rise again, and this was Kirby's rock bottom. Enveloped in the tentacles of depression, she quit the game she loved, for it simply did not bring her the joy it once had.

That is the 'problem' with grief and loss. You could build a thousand-piece jigsaw puzzle that has taken hours of your time, but if there was one piece missing, the 999 others would be totally irrelevant. It would never be complete. Without that missing piece – the person you love – it can feel as though there is no point to anything, even the things that make you the happiest. If that sounds depressing, stark, it's because it is. Grief, depression and other forms of mental illness go hand in hand, as Kirby would discover. There would be days Kirby could not get out of bed, go to college or do any work. Some days she would get as far as the bus stop before grief overcame her and she had to go home.

'I was just trying to find myself again and allow myself to have that grief, just to get it out of my system and go again. It was a real whirlwind few years definitely, from believing that nothing happened to then just the world coming down.'

One of the cruel realities of grief is that life has been taken away from someone so desperate to live it, which then impacts upon the life that you are still able to enjoy. It created a nagging feeling for Kirby that, although her mother wasn't able to be alongside her on every step of her footballing career, should she waste the opportunity and talent that she clearly had?

A friend invited her to a local Sunday amateur league, with the promise that she could turn up, play and go home. There would be no pressure or expectation that she had experienced even at such a tender age. It was a turning point of sorts – Kirby's love for the game returned, having stripped professional sport back to the bare bones, the joy of playing for fun that makes football the most popular sport in the world.

Four years after her mother's passing, she felt prepared to return to Reading's academy. Over the course of the next three years, she made her professional debut for the club at sixteen and was included in the 2015 Women's World Cup squad. This spell at Reading would be the one where she caught the eye of Emma Hayes, her future manager at Chelsea. It is remarkable to watch the footage of Kirby from May 2014, flummoxing Kinga, a World Cup winner, with such ease, knowing how much she had already overcome in her young life.

'I just remember watching a moment when she pirouetted on the ball against Kinga at Arsenal and blew past her, and I thought, *Wow, that's unbelievable*,' Hayes remembers.

The 2015 World Cup saw Kirby's talent showcased to an entirely new audience, many watching the Lionesses for the first time and experiencing the nation's heartbreak as Laura Bassett's own goal against Japan at the semi-final stage ended their hopes of lifting the title (although the team still went on to make history by winning the bronze medal).

At just twenty-one, Kirby was drawing comparisons with Lionel Messi, who many consider to be the greatest male footballer of all time. Mark Sampson, the England manager at that time, labelled Kirby 'mini Messi' after she had scored the opening goal in a group-stage victory over Mexico. 'We had to stay patient. We had to wait for our moment to score and then our little mini Messi, Fran Kirby, found a way to put the ball in the back of the net,' Sampson said.

Although the nickname was not one Kirby particularly enjoyed, the lofty comparison showed just how highly thought of she was. The image of Kirby – short-haired, seemingly running at a speed of thought and feet way beyond the opposition, first at Reading but more so in that tournament – is the one I first remember, my first true women's football idol. As a seventeen-year-old young carer (my mum had suffered complications from an operation when I was fourteen), I remember sitting with Mum downstairs in a makeshift bed, both of us glued to the television in the small hours as England played in Canada, shedding tears as Bassett's unfortunate own goal ended their dreams, and ours.

Players from that team now reflect it was a breakthrough moment of sorts for the women's game – perhaps the first time people truly cared about the result of a women's game on a mainstream level. That wider impact was a macrocosm of the feelings in my household. Men's football was our first love, and the one that would go on to spark an interest – or obsession, depending who you ask – in football that would fuel not just a hobby but a career. The men's FA Cup final was a tradition in our household like many others, with cheese and pineapple on sticks a vital staple of the buffet that would magically appear moments before kick-off.

Living in the Fens, in Cambridgeshire, opportunities to actually play girls' football were largely out of reach – non-existent in any education setting bar the school playground at lunch break, while the one club was too expensive to join for a child who relied on free school meals. Thankfully the game is far more accessible now than it was even a decade ago.

It was narratives like that of Chelsea striker Didier Drogba in the men's Champions League final of 2012 that had attracted me to the prospect of writing about the game – moments of history and pure emotion that Bassett also evoked, albeit in less joyous circumstances. Since the 2015 World Cup, I had been a women's football fan, but two years later I was attending my first Women's Super League game for *The Times*, having stumbled upon the opportunity through a guest lecturer at Staffordshire University where I was beginning the second year of my sports journalism degree. And as women's football began to grow, so too did the coverage. A short round-up in a national newspaper had blossomed into coverage of the England team and regular interviews – and, unexpectedly, my love of women's football had grown into my dream career.

Having watched that tournament in 2015 and received my first newspaper by-line in 2017, my aim was to work at the next World Cup, in 2019 in France. But while my professional life was going from strength to strength, my personal life began to fall apart. In April 2019, after several months of deteriorating symptoms, my mum was diagnosed with bowel cancer. The initial prognosis was reasonably bright: the tumour was operable and, though it was a major operation, there was a high chance that she would be able to return to health.

A month later, an attempt to operate had failed and the prognosis was terminal, three to six weeks the estimate of how much time we would have left. As her condition deteriorated, the World Cup was put on the back burner; the timeline was simply impossible. Then, as though it was meant to be, the day I travelled into London to meet with my sports editor and officially cancel all travel plans, Mum's specialist offered renewed hope. The diagnosis was still terminal but she may have months not weeks.

Mum was, as she would often sign off messages, my 'biggest supporter'. Her worst nightmare was for her illness to have affected my future career and so, with her blessing and with the full support of *The Times* that I could come home whenever needed, plans began in earnest for the tournament.

The tournament itself was surreal. I watched and interviewed an England team – many of whom had been my idols – while learning and improving as a journalist and seemingly living the dream. But in the quiet moments, before and after the matches in the confines of an Airbnb or a hotel room, reality would set in: my mum was dying. There began a pattern, which I would not identify until several years later, of using work as a distraction from grief. At times it was the greatest tonic – ask journalists and they will tell you little can replicate the adrenalin rush of a live report on deadline – but it did not paper over the cracks entirely.

My admiration of Kirby grew – not just for the exceptional player she was, but for what she had gone through in her personal life. Shortly after Mum had received her terminal diagnosis, I tweeted about my circumstances. A couple of days later I received a direct message from Kirby, whom I had interviewed but did not know personally. It read:

Hi Molly

Just wanted to send a message regarding your post with your mum. I didn't want to message on the day and wanted to give it a while because I know something like that can be very emotional.

I'm sure she's so proud of you, and you doing that will be the most important thing to her. It's always a challenge to accept and overcome any form of illness, but please know you're not alone and you can talk about it whenever you feel like. I know obviously I don't know you, but I know you're a massive part of women's football so even if you need to rant to me about anything, I'm only a DM away. Keep killing it, I'm sure you already do but she will be the best motivation you will ever have! Take care,

Fran

As my journey in France came to an end, so too did the short hiatus from reality. A terminal cancer diagnosis eventually, cruelly, strips both the patient and their loved ones of hope. When I received the news that I had earned a full-time job with *The Times*, the person I wanted to celebrate with knew she would not see my career unfurl. There was an unspoken rule that whenever I made my regular trips from London to Peterborough, we would not discuss the elephant in the room, instead relaying my week, the games and places I had been to.

By Christmas of 2019 it was evident that the mum I knew had gone, both in a physical and mental sense. There was a sense of foreboding as others celebrated the New Year – I knew what was coming. Then, as the clock struck midnight on 15 January, Mum succumbed to the cancer.

Luckily – or perhaps unluckily, given what I was about to encounter – I had never experienced grief before, nor death at such close quarters. It is depicted in books and film, but it is no wonder the brain struggles to process something so stark in its reality. A person you have known – in my case for twenty-two years – is still in front of you seemingly the same, and yet in that moment you will never converse with them again. The finality is crushing, but more so is the wave of other emotions. For me initially there was relief, a perverse emotion in the circumstances but relatable to anyone who has ever lost a loved one to a terminal illness; finally their suffering ends. But even that too is bewildering: why was I unable to cry while people who had known Mum a fraction of my life were easily shedding tears?

The month that followed before her funeral would feel like an endless pit of darkness. I had used work as a distraction and was now on compassionate leave. The constant background to any part of my life – and even more so in the year of her illness – had always been Mum, and it was now echoingly empty. Seconds, minutes, hours and days passed as I sat in my shared flat in London. Time was merely a concept without Mum. What was the point in life? In speaking to those worried about me? In simply getting out of bed in the morning?

You can have the greatest support network – and I am thankful for those who have been there for me throughout, many of whom I have formed close relationships with from journalism – but grief is, and was, in my experience, lonely. *But do you really understand? Have you felt what I am feeling?* I would think, as the latest well-meaning friend told me things would get better with time.

Somewhere in that period of despondency, and on my search to understand what grief actually was, I found a diagram – which also appears in Ian Ridley's excellent book *The Breath of Sadness* and is as good a depiction of grief as I have seen – known as 'the box and the ball'. Imagine your life is a box and the grief you feel is a ball inside the box. Also inside the box is a pain button. In the beginning, when your loss is so fresh and new, the grief that many people feel is overwhelming and large. It's so large that every time you move the box – moving through your everyday life – the grief ball can't help but hit the pain button. Over time the ball shrinks; the box doesn't change, nor does the size of the pain button. Whenever the ball hits, it is as painful as ever, but gradually it happens less often. It never disappears.

While still at the stage of the ball being unbearably large, it seems strange to say there was no better time to fly across the world to cover a football tournament, and yet so it proved. The 2020 SheBelieves Cup began on 5 March, three weeks after Mum's funeral. A first trip to America was, for much of the tournament, a useful distraction. A scroll through my camera roll from that period would find trips to Disneyland and selfies in Times Square sandwiched between three matches in three different states, as I watched some of the best players in the world. Disneyland in particular was a bittersweet moment – picking a Betty Boop lanyard that was Mum's favourite character, and visiting Disneyland something on her bucket list that she would never be able to tick off.

At times the ball would hit the pain button and it would be almost unbearable. One particular moment stands out for its utter bleakness: shortly before landing in New Jersey, the towering skyline visible as small as Lego blocks in the distance. While sharing a flight with the entire Lionesses team just seats away, I quietly sobbed at the unfairness of being unable to share this moment with Mum, who had been desperate for me to travel and see the world in a way she never had.

It felt cruel that, in the moments I was supposed to be the happiest, I felt such intense loss. Grief is not talked about nearly enough, and I had never read about this particularly unnerving symptom until I heard about Kirby's story. It is why she was crying on the Chelsea team coach in May 2018 while her teammates were singing and celebrating winning the Women's Super League that day, as well as the FA Cup. Kirby had won two individual awards and been shortlisted for the Ballon d'Or in a stellar season.

'I realise now how weird it must have looked,' Kirby wrote in the *Players' Tribune*. 'My teammates were probably thinking, "Why is she crying? We've just won the double." But all I wanted to do was make a call. There was only one person that I wanted to share that moment with. And I knew I couldn't.'

As Kirby has grown older and begun to understand more about the relationship between grief and mental health, it is something she has been keen to explain to others – that it is not just the tough times that prove difficult for those suffering.

'I think people think that sometimes people struggle with their mental health when things are going bad,' Kirby told the *Equalizer* a few days ahead of the Women's Champions League final. 'But for me, I feel more emotional when things are going well, because [of] all the things you've had to overcome, and people who maybe aren't here who would be proud of me.

'It's quite an interesting one, because everyone is always asking, "What triggers you? What makes you sad?" For me, people never realize the emotion of winning, and I think that is a really important element. Just because things are great, I can still be quite emotional. Even though we won the league last weekend, I can still be quite emotional about something like that.'

Crucially, Chelsea has become a home where she is able to share these emotions, primarily with manager Hayes, who has been a constant support for the past six years, including during the period where the rare condition pericarditis – inflammation of the sac around the heart – threatened Kirby's career. When asked how she approached their relationship, Hayes highlighted the missing maternal figure in Kirby's life.

'I don't think you can underestimate the impact of losing a mum at that age,' Hayes said. 'Being in a household of boys, I have always felt the one thing Fran needed from me, rightly or wrongly, was the maternal eye, and that was the commitment I made to myself about what I was going to do for her.'

That perception of her players' needs far beyond the confines of the pitch is one of Hayes's best attributes as a coach, and was on show once again in the build-up to the Continental Cup final. She had written a card to every Chelsea player to mark Mother's Day. Both Kirby and Carly Telford, the substitute Chelsea goalkeeper, have spoken openly about their bereavements and its impact on them, both personally and professionally.

'It's pertinent to mention how difficult it must have been for them and how thoroughly professional they were, even though it could be a difficult day,' Hayes said.

I wrote in *The Times* after Kirby's masterclass: 'Those who have suffered loss will know grief can be harder to comprehend in the good times than it is in the bad. Long after the trophy lift and the gold streamers, at some point Kirby will be alone with her emotions. She will undoubtedly feel sad, but she should be proud, with her strength and talent the perfect tribute to her mother's memory.'

Perhaps I was writing those words as much to myself as to Kirby. I have learned, and continue to learn, that there is no quick fix for grief, no solution or user guide. Recovery is not linear; there will be highs and lows, and sometimes it is enough to make it through the day.

Kirby has picked herself up from that teenager who gave up the game, and has gone on to flourish into the footballer her mother predicted she would be. Her achievements do not need to be viewed through a lens of grief to be appreciated, for she is simply one of the world's best. But, for those who have felt loss or even those trying to understand it for a loved one, her strength is perhaps even more admirable than her astonishing footballing talents.

HIGHS AND LOWESTOFT

__Ali Rampling__ delves into the remarkable story of the small club who won the Women's FA Cup – and were forced to disband six months later.

A small seaside settlement in Suffolk, Lowestoft is famed for being the most easterly town in the UK rather than a place renowned for sporting pedigree. In May 1982, however, this little pocket of East Anglia became home to the winners of the most prestigious cup competition in English football when Lowestoft Ladies beat Cleveland Spartans 2-0 in the final of the WFA Cup. It was a victory that should have etched their name into footballing immortality and been the catalyst for years of success, but the cup-winning team would never play another season together, let alone have the opportunity to defend their crown.

This was women's football, and this was the 1980s. The game was still reeling from the fifty-year ban that had decimated the sport in 1921. Lowestoft were a victim of the game's fragility and instability, and within six months of lifting the WFA Cup, the team had disbanded.

Despite the modest stature of the town, Lowestoft's cup win was no plucky underdog story. Throughout the 1970s and early 1980s Lowestoft were one of the most ambitious, well-run and forward-thinking women's teams in the country. They produced numerous England internationals, travelled abroad to play in tournaments and boasted a set-up that many clubs today would be proud of. Yet, while Doncaster Belles and Southampton WFC – and Dick, Kerr Ladies before them – are now celebrated for the trail they blazed, the name Lowestoft Ladies has faded from history.

Fittingly, this unique football team stemmed from unconventional beginnings. In 1970, the town of Lowestoft competed in *It's a Knockout*, a BBC gameshow that pitted towns and cities against one another in a series of daft, 'adult sports day' challenges. Water and fancy dress were non-negotiable ingredients. In the breaks between the absurdity, male competitors from the Lowestoft team would have a kickabout. The women joined in, caught the bug and asked Geoff Frost – a former Fulham footballer and organiser of the *It's a Knockout* team – if he could start a ladies football club. Frost obliged and the Waves, as they became affectionately known, formed in 1971.

Attitudes ranged from the supportive to the sexist; onlookers were either surprised by the standard or merrily making remarks about swapping shirts at full-time.

'It was funny because you didn't tell people that you played football,' says left-back Jackie Slack. 'You were like, "Oh, we're a netball team," because people looked down on it. But we played because we loved it.'

'It was a little bit of a joke,' adds Mike Pearce, club secretary between 1971 and 1978. 'But we turned it round and showed them what could be done.'

Lowestoft soon became a force to be reckoned with. They cruised to three successive East Anglian Women's Football League titles and, having outgrown their local division, were sweet-talked into the South East of England Football League by team manager Joe Annis. Lowestoft promptly won this three years on the bounce. They regularly found the net more that a hundred times per season, despite never playing more than twenty league games.

'You'd usually jump all over each other when you score, but with Lowestoft it was like, "Oh, it's just another goal",' recalls Maureen Martin (formally Reynolds), who captained Lowestoft between 1976 and 1981.

'Everyone used to just walk back to the middle. It was just a matter of fact that we'd score.'

Martin remains a scholar of the game, owning everything from 1970s *Lowestoft Journal* match reports to the latest edition of *She Kicks*, and an England cap is afforded pride of place in her front room. The defender was one of countless players who earned international recognition while at Lowestoft. ('Playing for your country is a lot harder than people think,' she says. 'People are criticising this player and that player and it isn't as easy as it looks… Mind you, I don't think Steph Houghton should have taken that penalty.') Striker Julia Manning was the first Waves player to be called up to the national side in 1972, followed by winger Angie Poppy in 1975.

Poppy had signed for the club ahead of the 1974/75 campaign after turning in an eye-catching performance against Lowestoft the previous season for Middleton. Blessed with searing pace that remains legendary to this day, the Lowestoft contingent nicknamed her 'the Middleton Wonder Girl'.

'My football hero as I was starting playing was Angie Poppy,' says England right-back Vicky Johnson, who joined Lowestoft from Spurs Ladies in 1981. 'I'd never seen a woman run so fast down the wing. It was like, "*What?* Did I just see that?" She'd leave everybody standing still. It was awe-inspiring. My second game [for Spurs] was Lowestoft and I remember thinking, *Wow, I didn't know women could play football like this.*'

In September 1976, the Waves beat West Ham 27-0. Linda Curl scored fourteen times and earned her first England call-up that year, aged fourteen.

'Linda Curl was an exceptional player, she really was,' says Martin. 'She was *class*. Brilliant, skilful, fast. A fitness fanatic. She should have been a boy, really; she'd have made it in professional football.'

From the start of the 1977/78 season, Stewart Reynolds, a former semi-professional with the Lowestoft men's side, joined the Waves' coaching team. Reynolds later took over as first-team manager, and his tactical nous, knowledge and experience were a further injection of quality.

'He knew what training to do,' explains Slack. 'With a lot of the teams back then there wasn't a lot of coaching going on. A lot of the people involved in women's football weren't qualified; it was just, "Oh, my dad will do it." Teams didn't always have the coaching available to them, whereas we were lucky because Stewart was really good. Stewart taught football; we had a passing game and he had tactics. He was playing wing-backs back then. It's a "new thing" now, isn't it? But it wasn't, he was playing wing-backs then.'

Key to Lowestoft's success was their efficient set-up. They played at Crown Meadow – home to the Lowestoft men's side – drummed up attention in the local press and attracted a strong following in the community. Home crowds of 200–300 spectators sometimes exceeded that of the men's side, and the loyal band of supporters would hire a coach to away matches and follow the Waves across the country.

'We always had a full 52-seater supporters' coach,' says goalkeeper Rita Fossey. 'People like [former England centre-back] Terry Butcher's grandparents were huge supporters of Lowestoft Ladies; they used to go everywhere. If they missed a match – including the away ones – they were not happy at all. We were, without a doubt, the best supported. Everybody knew each other. In the early days a lot of them were from fishermen's families and there were some quite dreadful times if a trawler went down, that would be affecting someone in the community. They'd all still come and they'd all support one another because that was just what happened.'

'In the East Anglian League there was hardly anyone watching,' adds Martin. 'Just people whistling and making remarks about women in short shorts. But Lowestoft Ladies had a good crowd come and watch us. That was a professional club really as far as women's football goes.'

Lowestoft were a family club, with a backbone of volunteers helping to run the side. Such is the town's geographic isolation, they estimate it cost them £7,000 a year in travel in order to get to away matches in London, Aylesbury and Luton. The team funded themselves to tour abroad, playing tournaments in the Netherlands, the South of France, Malta and Sweden (where they won the Gothia Cup). Volunteers Terry and Jackie Borrett fundraised ferociously, selling Christmas cards to help to cover the travel costs and chasing sponsorship to fund new training kit. It was a community effort.

'We were travelling on a Sunday, and then we were getting home really late on a Sunday night and getting up for work because we couldn't afford not to work,' recalls Fossey. 'My mum used to wash all the kit. And I used to iron it all.'

'Now you know how she got in the team,' manager Reynolds chimes in with a chuckle.

With no centralised National League until 1991, and certainly no Women's Super League, the only way to stake a claim as the best women's football team in the country was to win the WFA Cup (which became the FA Cup in 1993). The Waves reached the WFA Cup final in 1979, but not even a player-of-the-match performance from Fossey in the Lowestoft goal could prevent them suffering a 1-0 loss to six-time champions Southampton.

'We got murdered 1-0,' Poppy recalls grimly.

'They were huge favourites,' says Pearce. 'I don't think anyone expected us to win it.'

'They were the top team back then,' adds Slack. 'We were definite underdogs and we looked it.'

Defeat would spur Lowestoft on.

The Waves had forged a reputation locally as the team to play for, seducing the very best talent from across East Anglia and beyond. After two uncharacteristically barren seasons, Lowestoft signed Johnson from Spurs and fellow England international Debbie Bampton from Maidstone ahead of the 1981/82 season.

'Debbie Bampton, when she wanted to come to Lowestoft – can you remember her coming?' asks assistant manager Terry Borrett.

'Can I remember her coming? Course I remember her coming! *Dame* Debbie Bampton,' laughs Reynolds. 'We had an exceptional team, and she just made it that bit more exceptional.'

The additions gave the Waves a new lease of life and they raced to another South East Regional League title. But it was the WFA Cup the club really wanted. However, their hopes were dented when the quarter-finals saw them drawn against Doncaster Belles, the side widely regarded as England's finest. The Waves were on the cusp of a last-eight exit when they found themselves 2-0 down at half-time, with sixteen-year-old defender Sallie Jackson in tears after conceding the penalty that led to the Belles' opening goal.

'I remember we went into the dressing room at half-time – well, outside, we didn't have a dressing room. At Doncaster, in the middle of the race course,' says Reynolds, 'Sallie was crying at half-time and I said, "It should be me who should be crying – get out there!"'

Eight minutes into the second half, the Waves were level thanks to goals from Johnson and striker Shirley Jones, who was forced off fifteen minutes from time after suffering a double fracture to her collarbone following a clash with the Doncaster goalkeeper. Poppy then won the ball inside her own half, raced through and netted the winner to send the Waves into the semis. The competition became theirs to lose.

'I can remember that vividly because I was so, so angry,' recalls Poppy, whose son would also go on to play for Lowestoft. 'I really, really was angry. That was the only thing that kept me going. Because the pitch was so heavy it was like a bog. Sheer determination.'

The Waves beat Maidstone in the semi-finals in front of a 2,000-strong crowd to book their place in the final. In preparation for the showpiece event at Loftus Road, Ipswich Town manager Bobby Robson opened up the club's training ground for three Friday nights for Lowestoft Ladies to use.

Two coaches packed with Lowestoft supporters made the 280-mile round trip to west London for the match. Having been restricted to a cameo from the bench in the 1979 final, Slack led Lowestoft out as captain at Loftus Road three years later. She had only taken up football when, nursing a badminton injury at college, she saw an advertisement for Lowestoft Ladies in the local paper and suggested in jest she switch sports.

'I jokingly said, "Oh, I think I'll go and play football instead," she explains. 'So one of my friends said, 'Go on, I dare you." So I did.'

Slack would go on to win thirty-two caps for England.

The final against Cleveland Spartans was played ahead of QPR's Division Two fixture with Bolton, with fans gradually pouring into the stadium to take in the Cup final – the first time many had ever seen women play football – prior to the men's match.

'I can remember a supporter of QPR said it was the first time he'd ever been to a game and fallen in love with the left-back,' laughs Reynolds.

Curl, who was working as a police officer in those days, opened the scoring for the Waves in the first half before a stunning 57th-minute solo effort from Poppy confirmed Lowestoft Ladies as WFA Cup champions.

'Curley passed it to me from somewhere and I got it on the edge of the box on the left-hand side and curled it into the top right-hand corner,' Poppy recalls.

'We were in the dugout, and [former QPR forward] Mike Flanagan was stood next to me,' adds Reynolds. 'He turned to me and went, "Blooming heck, I'd have been really proud of that one!" After the game they had it on the news and they said, "You won't see a better goal in the whole of the English First Division this year."'

Slack had the honour of hoisting the trophy aloft in front of a crowd of over 1,000, with future England boss Terry Venables among them.

'Amazing,' the former Lowestoft skipper laughs. 'I sound like Beckham now, don't I? *Amazing*. It was brilliant. *Everybody* wanted to win the FA Cup. Apart from playing for England, that was the one thing everybody wanted.'

The celebrations commenced but, with the 140-mile coach journey back to East Anglia looming, they could not be too indulgent.

'We sang "We Are the Champions", drank bottles of straight champagne and then we went to a Greek restaurant,' says Johnson. 'And that was it because we had to get the coach back. It wasn't like staying in a four-star hotel; some of us had to go to work the next day.'

The brief festivities were somehow fitting. Before the cup had arrived in Lowestoft, there were rumblings that the club's future was in jeopardy. Various teams were dropping out of Lowestoft's South East Regional

League and the division soon folded. Being the best side in the country and the most easterly town in the UK would be the club's downfall: Lowestoft were too good for local leagues and too far away for those of a suitable standard. Five divisions – the Home Counties, Nottingham, Midland, Chiltern and Hounslow leagues – rejected the Waves as teams could not afford to travel to a far-flung corner of East Anglia for a game of football.

'Our nearest away game was London, so that puts it into perspective really,' says Poppy. 'And they are complaining about one game in Lowestoft.'

'That was what made it so hard for all of us, that a team wouldn't come down and play us once a year. They just didn't take into account all our expense,' adds Fossey. 'We never moaned once about it. Yet they just let us basically disappear.'

Reynolds attended a meeting with the WFA in Birmingham in an attempt to save the club. The WFA offered Lowestoft a place in a small, local division, but the Waves would have racked up a cricket score against such a calibre of opposition.

'It was just an insult,' says Reynolds. 'It would be like asking Liverpool now to go and play in Non-League.'

'And the teams we would have been playing and annihilating wouldn't have been very happy,' notes Fossey. 'You'd also got several England players, and it wouldn't have done them any good. They'd have lost their places eventually.'

By the end of October 1982, less than six months after winning the WFA Cup, with no division to play in, the spine of the Waves' first team were forced to depart for clubs who could guarantee them a league match. A reserve team was put up to defend the cup, consisting of players as young as twelve years old. Less than a year after their Loftus Road triumph, the Waves' star-studded first team had been dismantled and the club was forced to fold.

'It felt quite frustrating, and let down by the WFA, because you've just won the cup and you're now technically "unemployed", for want of a better word,' says Johnson. 'You've got so many internationals in this team and there's nowhere for them to go. It was so sad about Lowestoft because they could have gone on to do amazing things. With that calibre of player today you'd go on to play in Europe, but it just wasn't available back then.'

'At least we finished at the top,' Poppy reflects. 'But we were at our peak. We could have gone on and run the next two or three years. You've just won the biggest trophy there is in women's football, only then to be told, "Never mind, nobody wants you."'

'It was just awful,' adds Fossey. 'And there was nothing we could do about it. We finished at the ultimate high. There was no one else to touch us. That makes it even harder when you see what they've got now. We weren't even asking for that; we were just asking to play. It was heartbreaking, to be honest. But I feel immensely proud to be part of it and always will be.'

'I haven't watched a women's football game since,' says Reynolds. 'I refuse to. It made me so angry, that we fought to get that far and then nothing. To just get discarded.'

So just how good were the Waves? In 1995, the FA Cup-winning team came out of retirement to play a charity match against the Lowestoft Women's first team. It was a fit, amateur, weekly Sunday-league side in their twenties against a team in their late thirties and early forties who had not played together for thirteen years.

'Stewart came back and managed us, and one of the key things he said was, "You're not going to be as fit and everything else but you've not lost your football brain. So don't try and run them off the park, just play them off the park,"' says Fossey. 'We beat them 8-0 and they were devastated. I think that showed the skill that that team had. When I watch football now and I think back to the skill level of Lowestoft at its peak… So much of it was also the personal determination. And that pure desire to play. We had to work for everything we got.'

Today, the opportunities for a side of Lowestoft's quality would know no bounds. From Champions League football to lucrative sponsorship deals, Panini stickers to matches being broadcasted on terrestrial television to audiences of millions. Instead, the majority of the Lowestoft Ladies

WFA Cup-winning side do not even have their own Wikipedia page. But the Waves simply played for the sheer joy that football brings.

'I wouldn't change a thing,' says Johnson. 'It was a fantastic time to play. It was just unfortunate that we didn't have the sponsors and the opportunities that girls have today. But it's people like our generation that have carved the way for youngsters today.'

'I'd still love to play. I never wanted to give up,' adds Martin. 'If I could play now, I'd like to play for Man United. To be honest, I wouldn't have minded managing Man United.'

'Course, I'd love to be earning a living doing something I love, but it just wasn't to be,' reflects Slack. 'That's just the way it was and you have to accept that. But being with everyone – the team, the camaraderie – it was just special.'

TAKE THREE WOMEN...

In August 2019, **Isabelle Latifa Barker** *won the first Vikki Orvice Scholarship and a two-year contract to work on the sports desk of* The Sun. *Here she tells of her early experiences in covering football and meets two exceptional media professionals in Carrie Brown and Jacqui Oatley to hear how it was, and is, for them.*

As a young writer your success often boils down to one simple thing: hard work. But I've found a gentle nudge from some great people in the industry has helped too. Just over a year into my job on *The Sun*'s sports desk, I received support from a male ally. It may come as a shock to some that this ally was hard-nosed English football boss Sam Allardyce.

With nearly twenty years as a player under his belt – plus almost thirty years as a coach and boss – Big Sam is one of the most recognisable faces of British football. He was known as a robust defensive general throughout the 1970s and 1980s, and an imposing touchline presence as a gaffer since 1994. Over the years, he has seen it all, so when I wandered into one of his press conferences for the first time in January 2021, I thought he wouldn't take much notice of me. I was twenty-three years old and, as you can probably imagine, I was nervous.

A few weeks previously, Allardyce had been summoned from the managerial antechamber by West Bromwich Albion after two years out of the game. Now West Brom were preparing to play an FA Cup third-round tie against Blackpool – Allardyce's first permanent job in management, where he was ruthlessly axed after just two years in charge despite leading the club to the brink of promotion in 1996.

The reporters in the tight-knit Brummie press pack took turns to ask their questions. They laughed and joked with Allardyce, who seemed to know them all on a first-name basis. I guess his large frame and gruff voice have made it easy for some to characterise him as a brute rather than a successful manager who has lifted himself through sheer hard work and bloody-mindedness. Maybe that's the assumption I also made when he greeted me with ''Ello, love.'

I cleared my throat and said: 'It seemed a bit of a blessing in disguise when Blackpool sacked you. You took the club to the play-offs and moved them forward quite rapidly. I guess there wasn't much loyalty shown back to you. What has that taught you about management?' There was a moment of silence before a large intake of breath. Big Sam replied: 'Do you know you've just pulled off the best question of this afternoon? It teaches you there can be no loyalty both ways. Sometimes it doesn't matter how much time, effort or what you do for a football club, within a short space of time your moment can be up. That experience at Blackpool gave me a big insight into the ruthlessness of football if you're a manager.'

When it came to the reporter after me, Allardyce said, 'Are you going to ask a question that good?'

I was chuffed because one of football's most no-nonsense managers had given me a helping hand. He saw that I was the only woman in the room that day and, although he didn't have to support me in front of everyone, he did. Not all heroes wear capes and not all male allies are protesting outside Parliament with a picket for women's rights. *The Sun*'s sport editor, Shaun Custis, was an incredible support to Vikki Orvice (who worked at *The Sun* for twenty-four years and was the first staff female football writer on a UK tabloid newspaper) and always has been to me too, even though his own career began in the smoke-filled, hyper-masculine newsrooms of the 1980s and 1990s.

The work of male allies is something Carrie Brown, senior correspondent at BeIN Sports and first female chair of the Football Writers' Association, has opened my eyes to.

'We hear a lot about the battles that women have but it's so important to celebrate the male allies,' Brown tells me. 'We often hear about women coming into the industry, their struggles and the #MeToo generation. However, the reality is that when many of us women came in, there were only men in the industry and lots of them helped us greatly.'

Cotswolds-born Brown went from farm girl to reporter after she started with a bang on the ITV sports desk post-university in 1996. Her hard work, perseverance and passion meant it didn't take long for her to be flying at the top of the industry. But she credits one of football's most famous faces, Manchester United legend Sir Alex Ferguson, for helping her meteoric rise.

Fergie, like Allardyce, is someone who played his football and began coaching during an era when the sport was very much 'a man's game'. It is worth remembering that as recently as 2017 David Moyes, as Sunderland boss, told the BBC's Vicki Sparks she might get 'a slap' after she'd asked him if the presence of owner Ellis Short put extra pressure on him following his side's 0-0 draw with Burnley. It's shocking moments like this that make the support Allardyce gave to me, and Fergie to Brown, so important when old-school, default sexism continues to lurk beneath the shiny, superficially sanitised and outwardly politically correct surface.

Despite Fergie's famous dressing-room temper, Brown somehow won the Scotsman over during a stint as a Eurosport reporter covering the Champions League from 2002 to 2005. In those days you couldn't just saunter into one of Fergie's elusive press conferences; getting into one was like getting onto the VIP list at the Mayfair Club.

'I was asked to get an interview every week from each British club that was in Europe at the time,' says Brown. 'Manchester United were the biggest club in the world and at the height of their fame. But the club's press officer, Di Law, explained that it's a bit of a tradition for United to only allow in certain recognised and local media – normally people the manager knows really closely. The following week I rang Di again and asked how I could possibly get in. She said, "It has to be someone Sir Alex knows." I don't know what came over me but at the height of my youth and cheekiness I said, "Well, can I have an interview with him then, so he can get to know me and trust me?" Di just laughed and said, "We'll see."'

Bold as brass, Brown didn't know at the time quite how ludicrous her question had sounded. But to the astonishment of her terrified bosses, when she returned to her desk the following week, there was a phone call awaiting her from Manchester United.

'Di rang and said, "Interview. Sir Alex Ferguson. Next week," before putting down the phone. I couldn't believe it, but what was even more unbelievable was the reaction from friends and colleagues and first of all from my frightened boss, who said, "Just don't get banned."'

Sir Alex had not given interviews to the BBC since their 2004 documentary made allegations about his son, Jason. The year before, Sky Sports had been banned for several weeks after Ferguson was doorstepped by one of their reporters. He was also once caught on microphone asking a club press officer to ban a journalist who had asked a question about Ryan Giggs. It's no surprise Brown had sleepless nights in the build-up to the interview.

'Sir Alex liked short interviews, didn't like to be asked anything too controversial, and he loved Darren Fletcher,' says Brown. 'I just went in and kept it super short, asking seven questions. It was probably the shortest interview I've ever done. The press officer had her face stuck to the door the whole time, before Sir Alex walked out and just said, "She can come back again."

'When I finally got into his press conference I just sat there, very aware that I was there and it was unusual for someone to be there. I sat very quietly, didn't ask a question. When I got up and left, Ferguson said, "If you're going to come, ask a question next time." For me it was that nudge, him saying, "You've got here now, come on." It was great to have that support as there were some really tough moments.'

Despite some of his explosive tirades, Brown caught glimpses of a softer side to Fergie that contrasted the macho and blokey football bosses of the time.

'There was also a lovely moment with Sir Alex when I dislocated my knee after going down a waterslide at a friend's wedding,' she tells me. 'When I came back from the wedding, the hospital scanned it and told me I hadn't dislocated it. A few days later Rio Ferdinand saw me in the tunnel at Old Trafford and he instantly went: "That's not right. You need to get some more medical advice." They were all so concerned, and I was on crutches. I nearly fell over and Sir Alex grabbed my arm and said: "Don't worry, I'll be your crotch," and Karen the press officer said: "You meant crutch!" He said: "Didn't I say that?" Then there was just this wonderful moment of Sir Alex holding me up by one arm during the post-match interview.

'He won't be the first big man in the industry that was really supportive and kind to women, but you almost don't notice when a male ally is at work.'

Now when Brown is in a press conference, she follows Fergie's advice and always tries to ask a question. 'It's one of the things he instilled in me,' she says, 'and it was just a really big show of faith.'

Maybe as women in the industry we take particular notice of male allies because thankfully there is already a supportive band of women in football holding one another up. This is something I, and other women who have just stepped into journalism, have the likes of Brown and Vikki Orvice to thank for.

'A really strong network of women in football have helped me,' Brown says, 'like Vikki was such a big support. It took me ages to go up to her because I didn't want to assume she would support me just because I was another woman. But I wish I hadn't waited so long to approach her and get to know her because I didn't know that I'd been dealing with so much on my own.

'Don't do what I did with Vikki,' she advises me. 'If you see another woman anywhere just grab them; they will always be happy to help. Make sure you're allies and that you never see another woman as your rival.'

Jacqui Oatley's metaphorical trophy cabinet is as glittering as the many football trophies she's seen lifted. She went from intellectual property sales and marketing manager to pioneering sports broadcaster after swapping careers in her late twenties – and she has continued to break ground ever since.

Oatley started covering and commentating on non-League football for local radio before moving to BBC Radio 5 Live and eventually television. She is best known for being the first female commentator on *Match of the Day* and anchoring ITV's coverage of Professional Darts Corporation tournaments. Her efforts to champion the role of women working in football as well as banging the drum for women's football led to an MBE in the New Year's Honours List in 2015. But two of Oatley's proudest achievements will always be bringing up her daughter Phoebe, born in 2011, and son Max, born three years later.

Oatley was five months pregnant when she got her first shift as a sports news television presenter for the BBC. Pregnancy can be so special for expectant parents, but it can also be a worrying time for some.

'There was nobody I talked to about becoming a mum and working in this industry,' Oatley says. 'That's why I'm so passionate now about trying to help women wherever possible – and men too – because I felt I didn't have anyone to go to that I could discuss it with. I would have loved to have had somebody on the end of a phone or WhatsApp to just say, "Oh my gosh, this is hard, juggling parenthood with constant prep. What do I do?" I had to work it out as I went along.'

As a Women in Football ambassador, Oatley leads seminars to give new and prospective mums advice and confidence in returning to work. Having covered the Women's FA Cup final in 2014 just six weeks after a Caesarean section with her second child, she knows first-hand how hard it can be going back to the day job. For some women, breastfeeding is easy, convenient and wonderful. For others, it is frustrating, painful and debilitating. These struggles can all be made worse when mums make their way back to work.

'I think the worst thing you can do,' she says, 'is pile too much pressure on yourself and do what I did when I drove up to Milton Keynes to host the Women's FA Cup final. I'd planned to take baby Max with me, but my husband felt it would be better to keep him at home with our toddler. I wanted them to be settled so I went along with it. I was still breastfeeding, and I had real issues with it. It was utterly horrendous.

'I was running late for the production meeting for the Cup final and I had planned to stop and pump milk on the way. I was on the M1 and… put it this way: I had to pump while I was driving. I remember overtaking a lorry. I had both hands on the steering wheel, but I had the pump under my top and I was thinking, *If that driver knew what I was doing!* This pump was attached to my boob, trying to get some milk out while I was going around the roundabouts. I made it to the production meeting and all I could think about was when I could next pump as the whole experience was so sore. I thought, *What the hell am I doing?* Baby Max was happy and I saw the funny side. It was just so difficult to make it all work.'

In 2018 an image went viral of the athlete Sophie Power feeding her three-month-old son on one breast while pumping milk from the other at a rest stop during the 105-mile Ultra-Trail du Mont Blanc race. In 2019 another ultrarunner, Jasmin Paris, stopped along the 268-mile Montane Spine race – which she won with hours to spare – to express milk for her fourteen-month-old daughter. Oatley may not have pumped while performing such heroics, but she did it in hair and make-up before the Women's FA Cup final that day so that she could conduct post-match interviews. She has proved that pregnancy didn't mean her title switched from 'sports presenter' to 'mother' and, although the two titles didn't necessarily always coexist in perfect harmony, she navigated the minefield of motherhood while continuing to do what she loved.

'I was praying there wouldn't be extra time at the Women's FA Cup final,' she says, 'because my boobs filled up with milk and it was agony. We did the match, and the post-match coverage all worked fine. When it was all done I went into the studio to pump and I had all this lovely milk in the fridge for the baby at home. But when I went to get it from the fridge I said to the make-up artist: "It's a bit warm in here," and she said: "Oh my God, sorry, I unplugged it for the hair straighteners!" All this precious milk I'd really struggled with over the past few weeks had to go down the sink. I was devastated. I just remember thinking, *You absolute idiot, making it so hard for yourself.* I love my job, I loved covering women's football. I wanted to do the Cup final because I felt I could and was emotionally fine, but the logistics made it so complicated.'

Oatley is all too aware of the feeling of guilt mixed with concern when returning to work, having missed countless school collections, her daughter's sports days and her son's first football match. Yet she knows to keep it in check.

'I missed some of my daughter's sports days due to live shows and some mums would absolutely draw the line at that but the sort of jobs I've been doing are not your regular day shifts. I finally made one of my daughter's sports days and I had arranged for Chelsea Women goalkeeper at the time, Hedvig Lindahl, to come along as well and meet the kids, but somehow I ended up missing all my daughter's races while hosting the Q&A session. I was thinking, *What kind of parent am I?*, although she didn't notice and my husband was there to watch her. But what's important is that, while you look at yourself and think "that's terrible" missing three sports days in a row, the issue is actually our own guilt. My daughter was oblivious to the fact that I didn't see her races!'

The unsociable hours of sports journalism mean new mums in the industry have to juggle hectic hours with childcare. Not all parents have Oatley's work hours, given she swapped the school run for Saint Petersburg during the five-week Russia World Cup in 2018. But lots of parents can relate to the struggles of finding the perfect childminder, no matter what industry they're in.

'I'm really keen to share how I went about finding childcare for ad hoc work hours,' she says. 'I found it hard to work out solutions as we didn't have any family nearby to help out. Having found my own way, I now try to help other women so that they don't feel completely at sea. Speaking to neighbours and local friends was how I discovered an amazing lady called Frida who was doing school pick-ups and post-school childcare, but was prepared to become Ofsted registered and look after my kids as and when I needed her. Hallelujah!

'I became much better at planning childcare, lifts to kids' clubs, parties, etc. – reciprocating lifts and play dates with friends is a good option and I manage my time much better now, although it's still a challenge.'

As a young woman coming into the industry, the thought never crossed my mind that I may have to sacrifice doing the job I love if I want to have a child. Neither did it cross Oatley's when she stepped onto the scene.

'I think it's important to talk about being a mum in the industry because I know senior women in our work who elected not to have children. I don't know whether they regretted it or not, but I know they felt that they couldn't do their job and have children, which is just so desperately sad. Imagine any industry where people feel the commitment to the job would be so great that they wouldn't be able to have children if they wanted them. Of course, traditionally it has never held men back.'

Having just started my career in sports journalism, I feel incredibly lucky to have had the likes of the fearless trailblazers Brown, Orvice and Oatley who have come before me. Brown has continued to break ground, always ensuring youngsters like me have a supportive network of women to go to. Oatley has balanced the demands of motherhood with her high-stakes efforts to give confidence and advice to new mums in the industry. Orvice was a fantastic mentor for many young female writers. It's thanks to these pioneers that we will be seeing more women in press boxes, newsrooms, in front of the cameras and behind microphones up and down the country.

WHAT IT COULD BE LIKE

A night watching her beloved Newcastle United prompted **Katie Mishner** *to take stock of the spectating experience for LGBTQ+ fans. There's been progress, she believes. But not nearly enough.*

Ewood Park is a two-hour drive from my house, with traffic, but it felt like so much longer as my phone, hung on a rickety satnav holder, told me I'd be arriving four minutes after kick-off. It was a mid-January Tuesday night and my first trip into the Newcastle United away end.

Like all old-fashioned stadiums, Ewood Park is the centrepiece of a residential area. Like any club at the heart of its community, the matchday takes over, no matter what day it falls on. Hence the traffic. As I drove through the Lancashire country roads, the lighting around me changed, the whole area illuminated by floodlights – a romantic sight for any football fan. Once parked up, I found my way to the ground by following a series of hurried Rovers fans whom I had spotted leaving their houses on the way. Even with a brisk walk (sometimes breaking into a jog), by the time I took my place in the away stand, I had missed Sean Longstaff's first-minute goal.

I couldn't complain too much. Blackburn Rovers had priced the midweek fixture at £10 and I was giddy to be surrounded by fellow Magpies – an exciting prospect, having moved away at the age of eighteen. Even though I've only made a dozen trips to St James' Park since, no matter where I am, wearing the black and white stripes and singing along to 'The Geordie Boot Boys' feels like home.

It all started off well. Twenty minutes in, Newcastle were 2-0 up. I was singing my heart out, and my feet weren't even that cold as the night was mild. It was everything you could want from an away day. But things turned sour quickly. When a Blackburn player was brought down, the fan next to me didn't hesitate: 'GET UP, YOU FAG,' he screamed. He said the word like it was nothing, just a casual piece of his vocabulary. Suddenly, sitting among the Newcastle United fans didn't feel like home any more.

The phrase 'the beautiful game' is synonymous with football and, of course, it is just that – undeniably beautiful. The game is lovely to look at. The luscious verdant pitch, two teams in brightly coloured kit, sometimes scintillating passing, the tactical movement of bodies, and (if you're lucky) the acrobatic goals. Its beauty transcends beyond aesthetics and it's anywhere you want it to be: kids playing in the streets with jumpers for goalposts, a player making their debut for their childhood club, and – for a Newcastle United fan – Shola Ameobi scoring at Camp Nou.

The beauty of football is what has always had me hooked. I was the first child, meaning I was my dad's first opportunity to mould a Magpie from his own DNA. Paul Mishner got way more than he bargained for. The obsession took hold of me pretty quickly. I wanted to watch, play and participate in any way I could. It has been this way for as long as I can remember. Since my dad worked away a lot, I had the luxury of new kits that included teams like Ajax, Barcelona, Roma and Spain (only if there was 'Raul 7' on the back). These kits would span far beyond the black and white stripes I'd wear on a matchday and all of them would become my day-to-day casuals. When I wasn't sporting a kit at a theme park or on Saturday's shopping trip to Whitley Bay, I'd play in yellow and blue for my local club, Tynemouth FC, with number eight on my back. I was always obsessed with scoring goals, and when I did score, I'd celebrate like Shearer, raising my hand and pointing to the sky.

As well as kits, my dad gifted me with my first visit to St James' Park. Sir Bobby Robson himself noted how important this is – it's the feeling of seeing the stadium for the first time when you walk out of the gangway. My dad's season ticket was deep in the Leazes End, below the away fans, so my mam was always concerned about the language I'd pick up. He said I was no bother, just fixated on what was happening on the pitch, refusing to engage with the conversations happening around me, my eyes just following the ball.

While my love for Newcastle and football was growing through my formative years, something else was too: I was attracted to girls. Growing up, particularly in school, you hear all sorts, and I had picked up on the fact that, according to playground folklore, girls who like football are definitely lesbians. After that, it didn't feel normal that my friend and I were arguing in the playground over who was David Beckham and who was Michael Owen rather than which one we fancied more. It certainly wasn't normal that I wanted to kiss a girl. I didn't want anyone to know about my secret, and my attachment to football felt like a dead giveaway.

All too quickly, it felt like my place in football was slipping, and I found it hard to understand. It wasn't a case of whether I was a defender or striker, just whether I belonged and whether I'd be safe. I drifted from the game that I found to be the most beautiful thing in the world, and in my early teens, when I was moving in between Middle School and High School, I really cut ties with football. I stopped playing for Tynemouth FC, stopped talking about the game, and I have very little memory of watching it. It still feels strange. It's like there is a gap in my footballing memory – several years that I have blocked out.

The side effect of this is that I find myself with a gap in my knowledge and memories. Indeed, I was having a conversation with my friend Josh, who is a Toffee. With us, conversation always finds its way to football, especially after a couple of hazy pale ales. We got on to the topic of Everton in Europe and, as he passionately talked about the events, I just couldn't remember anything he mentioned. I felt panic. It sounds daft, I know it does. My mam would routinely tell me 'it's just a game!' but it has always meant more than that; football has always been my greatest source of joy. But then it became entangled with a deeply painful internal struggle with my identity, and any memories of that period are too entrenched with feelings of self-loathing.

The good news is that I managed to find my way back. It had to start with the acceptance of myself. I am a lesbian, and my queerness is something that I now love. But I also couldn't stay away from the game, so I *had* to find my way back.

There are many moments that remind me why I love the game, but sadly there are plenty that, as a queer woman, make me feel I am unsafe. It wouldn't be football without setbacks, though – just look at Newcastle. They have not gone from strength to strength, having suffered two relegations in recent memory. It's a far cry from the entertainers I grew up with, but it feels good to support my city, my club, knowing who I am. I can now freely debate my opinion on Steve Bruce's lack of tactical nous without fear it might reveal my identity.

The most refreshing part of it is that my obsession with the entire culture has only picked up where I left it those years ago. I want to consume every single aspect of the game – following every league, reading the stories of players, groundhopping, collecting the kits and chatting about it with likeminded fans. After all, community is the truly beautiful thing about football. Listening to a group of fans stood outside the stadium, waiting for turnstiles to open, talking about what they expect from the game, recent form and their favourite memories. It's not just a physical sense of community either, as social media has opened up an entire global community, with quick access to content, meaning fans can chat more than ever. Still, every weekend you take your seat inside a stadium alongside tens of thousands of people wearing the same colours, willing the same thing to happen, singing the same song as you, muttering the same curses as you when your team is turned over in possession. It's the shared elation when the ball hits the back of the net. Football is beautiful.

And yet football is ugly too. Kick It Out reported in 2020 that 39 per cent of surveyed football fans had heard homophobic abuse in the last twelve months. That Tuesday night in Ewood Park, I became part of these statistics. To avoid homophobia on a matchday is good going; for most fans, these slurs are as deeply rooted in the matchday experience as a half-time chicken balti pie. However, the Saturday after my trip to Blackburn, it seemed as though my luck had run out: in the stands of Hillsborough, the same word was spat out at an opposition player, just four rows back from the pitch, so he probably heard it too. By the end of the month, I had had two run-ins with homophobic abuse aimed at players, from fans. It was a jarring throwback to growing up unwelcome in the only place I wanted to be, and that night at Ewood Park, surrounded by 2,200 people who I share a fierce passion with, I was unwelcome and left asking myself the same question: where do I stand within this game? If statistics are anything to go by, 6 per cent of people identify as LGBTQ+ in the UK. That means, in theory, if Wembley were full, there would be 5,000 LGBTQ+ people in the crowd. It would also mean there were 131 other LGBTQ+ Magpies there with me at Ewood Park.

While I keep coming back to the discomfort I felt in Blackburn and Sheffield, I know that I am lucky – far more so than most. The most painful homophobia I have felt in football has been an internal battle. Yet, while I've reconciled my adolescent issues with football, football has failed to address its own issues with homophobia. Throughout the UK, Europe and the wider world, the extent of homophobia in football varies from shouting at players, to sending a tweet, from slurs shouted, to a life-threatening situation. In Kick It Out's annual report for the 2019/20 season in England, it was found that abuse based on sexual orientation had increased by 95 per cent from the previous season. In 2018, the same report had found a 9 per cent increase in homophobic abuse, which means the abuse is continuously growing.

Reporting homophobia has become more accessible, and Kick It Out have their own platform that allows anyone to anonymously report abuse. This could explain the sharp increase; however, it can't be ignored that what happens in a football stadium is also a reflection of broader society. It is not a coincidence that hate crimes in football are on the rise when the UK's own Prime Minister has a long history of making discriminatory comments about gay people and ethnic minorities.

In a time of corporate social responsibility for football, which includes teams across the UK changing their corner flags and captain armbands to Pride Flags at least once a season, how is it that football is becoming more hostile towards LGBTQ+ people? Social media is undoubtedly a culprit. For all the benefits of the platforms, Twitter creates an environment that allows hatred to thrive. At least once a year on a designated anti-homophobia fixture, football clubs usually will add a rainbow flag to their profile and share messages of support to the LGBTQ+ community. During this time, you can read comments on Twitter that are far worse than the ones heard on the terrace. Twitter provides an environment where people will say whatever they want, as the platform's moderation is limited. I used to look for the abuse whenever a football club shared something relating to the LGBTQ+ community, so that I could report it. Now I will scroll past it quickly or turn my phone off, as I know exactly what vitriol is waiting in the comments section, and I know my efforts are wasted.

The problem is far more deeply rooted than the emergence of social media in football. Brighton is the unofficial gay capital of the UK, which unfortunately means the football club has become a target for abuse. In any given season, opposition fans have sung 'does your boyfriend know you're here' and 'we can see you holding hands', but this is echoed across social media too, where the comments tend to be far more aggressive and violent. It's difficult enough when thousands of people chant the same discriminatory song, but the 'retweet' feature allows more detailed abuse to be spread, abuse that does not have to fit into a verse or a rhyme.

Homophobia is not exclusive to the fans, either. In March 2020, when coronavirus shut down the world and temporarily removed fans from stadiums, homophobia was still heard on the pitch, between professional footballers.

In January 2021, Morecambe FC's defensive midfielder Yann Songo'o was sent off for alleged homophobic abuse towards a Tranmere Rovers player. This happened in the third tier of English football – in a professional football match. After investigation, the FA charged Songo'o with a six-match ban and a mandatory educational course. The player released an apology, stating he was ashamed of himself for using the slur. It seemed like a positive course of action: ignorance was being met with education, and hopefully lessons were being learned.

Sadly not. At the beginning of May 2021, a similar incident occurred in the same league. Following their match, Forest Green Rovers released a statement that alleged a Tranmere Rovers player had directed homophobic abuse at one of their players. Tranmere – who had been on the receiving end of abuse just a few months earlier – were now the perpetrators. What's more, this incident took place during the weekend of football's social media blackout, when clubs and players in English football switched off their social media accounts for the whole weekend in protest against online abuse from fans.

Are we only now learning of how frequently players use homophobic slurs on the pitch? Is it because the absence of fans leaves nowhere to hide? Or is homophobia on the rise throughout the game? It is impossible to know for sure, but it is clear that it is an issue at all levels of the game and one that is not exclusive to fans. Grassroots football has been dealing with players abusing each other for years but, unlike professional football, there is less accountability for discrimination.

Village Manchester FC describe themselves as a 'gay and inclusive football team' who compete in the third division of the Lancashire and Cheshire Amateur Football League. Founded in 1996, the club has provided a safe space for LGBTQ+ people to play football for over two decades. Given their status as an openly inclusive grassroots team, they have been on the receiving end of an unsurprising amount of abuse, which often ranges from verbal abuse to physical violence. In early 2020, the club put out a call to action to reform the FA's disciplinary procedure and offered training for referees so that they knew how to identify and deal with abuse. The club has regularly had to submit complaints and follow up incidents of abuse with the FA, but this campaign in particular was sparked after a particularly toxic match against Chadderton Park FC. The chairman of Village Manchester FC, James McNaught, stated to multiple news outlets that the homophobic abuse came from both players and supporters and took the form of insults, chants and physical abuse in the shape of dangerous tackles. The club said the referee did not know how to handle it and the abuse continued throughout the second half.

When the game has no handle on homophobia, it puts LGBTQ+ players and fans at risk. When chants are allowed to go unchallenged, they can quickly turn to violence.

Football bodies, such as the FA, frequently run campaigns to combat homophobia in the sport. However, with the rise of homophobia at football matches, in stadiums and online, I am often left wondering whether they actually mean it. On 2 December 2010, FIFA named Putin's Russia as the hosts of the 2018 World Cup. Russia is not a place known for its welcoming attitude towards LGBTQ+ people. In fact, it is prolific in its prosecution and violence towards this community. Since the decision was made, the teams that would go on to compete in the competition legalised gay marriage (in chronological order: Denmark, Uruguay, France, Brazil, England, Colombia, Germany and Australia). Change was clearly happening in the countries of the competitors, yet the hosts have continued to make the news for the wrong reasons.

In 2013, when the UK legalised same-sex marriage, Russia sanctioned an 'LGBT Propaganda Law'. In short, this law means any materials that portray a family as anything other than 'traditional' are not acceptable. It is a similar law to Section 28, which was introduced in 1988 by Margaret Thatcher's Conservative government to prevent the 'promotion of homosexuality', particularly targeting schools. Since being awarded the World Cup, the increase in hate crimes in Russia can be attributed to the LGBT Propaganda Law. The crimes are vile, too: from catfishing of vulnerable young gay men leading to brutal torture, to the emergence of anti-gay purges in Chechnya.

During the 2018 World Cup, I remember watching footage of gay fans being asked by reporters if they'd be willing to risk their lives to watch their team. Sometimes football feels like it's a life-or-death situation – especially when you support England – but, in the twenty-first century, people were legitimately putting their lives on the line to sit in a football stadium. There was an organisation called Diversity House that aimed to provide a 'safe space' for LGBTQ+ fans to watch the game in St Petersburg, but the organisation was evicted from their building on the eve of the tournament.

If Russia was not bad enough, the next country to host the World Cup will be Qatar. The country has said it will comply with FIFA's rules and that rainbow flags can be displayed, but there is no hiding the fact that homosexuality is criminalised in Qatar and punishable by a prison sentence.

It is clear that the international bodies responsible for football are not as committed to inclusion as they claim, but there are plenty of organisations taking a stand of their own. Gay Football Supporters Network, Kick It Out, Pride in Football and Football v Homophobia are a small selection of activist groups that relentlessly campaign and work to promote inclusion within the game. And, while grassroots football is not entirely safe for LGBTQ+ people, there are spaces being carved out for queer people to enjoy the game without fear of discrimination. Similar to Village Manchester FC is Stonewall FC, a football club based in London with four teams (including a 'women's & non-binary team'). Founded in 1991, Stonewall FC was born from an advert asking if likeminded people wanted to play competitive football. Three decades later, the club has a stacked trophy cabinet, including nineteen gold medals from domestic leagues and European competitions.

For those who do not want to compete in a league, there are casual groups such as Queer Space FC, who were founded in 2018 and have weekly queer kickabouts in London for self-identified queer, lesbian, bi and trans women, trans men, non-binary and intersex people. It is not just in the UK that these spaces are created, though: Dyke Soccer are on a mission to make health and wellness accessible for queer women, trans, non-binary and gender non-confirming people in America, all through the medium of football.

The importance of having a safe space to play and talk about football cannot be understated. The levels of homophobia and transphobia are enough to prevent many LGBTQ+ people from playing or attending games. While globally we may be making strides towards a more inclusive future, football seems to exist in its own timeline, with exclusion, abuse and violence ingrained in its heart. However, people in football are making an effort to demonstrate that LGBTQ+ people are welcome in football too. For instance, just weeks after I heard a fellow Magpie throw a slur at a player, I learned that Altrincham FC were going to be hosting a Football v Homophobia fixture. At the time, the Robins were competing in National League North and, as part of their regular schedule, they'd be sporting rainbow kits. It was the first time in the world that a senior football team solely modelled their kit on the LGBT Pride flag. The bold move attracted a lot of positive comments but the same old 'don't throw it in my face' comments could also be read. I decided I had to go and see this for myself.

My wounds were still fresh from Blackburn. With limited knowledge of Altrincham, I didn't know how their fans would react to this fixture, and I was once again questioning whether I was going to be safe. I walked into the stadium through an entrance on a side street. My partner, Iona, was with me, but she stood about a foot apart from me, not holding hands, not yet sure what we were walking into.

Moss Lane is a typical non-league ground. Most of the spectating platforms are concrete steps with corrugated iron roofs to shelter fans from the elements. There is one larger stand with seats above the dugouts, which looked like the most recent addition to an otherwise ageing stadium. Two food vans parked up in the ground provided refreshments and a constant scent of hot dogs. It was all very familiar, except… there were rainbows everywhere. Fans – die-hard and brand new – were wearing replicas of the one-off anti-homophobia kits.

I stood behind the goal in what I figured would be the lively part of the ground. I didn't hear a single comment made about the kits or the occasion – and, believe me, I was listening out for it. Realising that the Robins fans were not fazed by this public display of support, I settled into it. This was just another game for them.

At half-time I bought a tray of chips from one of the vans, then put my arm around Iona's waist and asked for her thoughts on the match so far.

'This,' I reflected, 'is what football could be like.'

I've come to accept that there are always going to be nights like the one in Ewood Park. Homophobia is not going to go away, and it is likely that we will continue to see it rise. I know that slurs will be thrown round on pitches, stadiums and pubs. I know that Village Manchester FC will continue to feel malice in tackles made against them on a Sunday afternoon. I will continue to read homophobic abuse on social media, and there will always be times when I do not feel like I belong in football.

But there will be more days like the one in Altrincham.

There are seats for us in Ewood Park and in our local pub. There is space for us on the pitch, whether it's the top flight of English football or a Sunday league. This game is as much ours as it is anyone else's.

GIRLS WILL BE BOYS...

***Fadumo Olow** talks to Rachel Yankey about the painful formative experience that fuelled one of the English women's game's greatest players and made her determined to change things for other young girls.*

Some people will go to any lengths to play the game they love. They will even resort to subterfuge if forced to, not that it should be necessary. Rachel Yankey demonstrated as much at the tender age of eight when she changed her name and had her head shaved to pass herself off as a boy.

'I remember there were two friends, Lawrence and Michael,' Yankey recalls. 'We figured all the people who were joining this team were boys, so we'd have to call me something different. To make me fit in.'

She decided she would be called Ray – an acronym of her full name, Rachel Aba Yankey – to sign on. But first she would need to look less like a girl, and so she took a spontaneous trip to a barber shop with her friends.

'The barber just looks at me and says, "Next customer, please." I sat in the chair and was asked, "What haircut do you want?" And I said, "I don't know, just like my mate."'

All of a sudden, she had the name, she had the look – and she was ready to play. She laughs as she looks back at how it all began for her, long before anyone could have known she would become one of the English women's game's most significant figures – indeed, the first to 120 international caps. With hindsight, she confesses, she may have done it differently. But this was an eight-year-old girl who just wanted to do something she was good at, to feel she belonged.

'I felt at home,' she says. 'I felt like nobody knew. Well, the manager knew I was a girl but no one else knew or looked at me any differently. They just saw a footballer. I never intentionally went to pretend and to trick people. But it was a hell of a lot easier. So for me playing in that team was important. I felt free. I could play, with nobody frowning, nobody looking and judging me.'

Of course, it couldn't stay that joyous and that free for ever. To her disappointment, comments were directed at her mother about her taking up the sport.

'When I was at school,' she says, 'people would say to my mum, "You know, she shouldn't be playing football because she's a girl. She should concentrate on education; girls do this and that's for boys."'

But Yankey thrived. Her skills – developed on the South Kilburn estate in north-west London where she was growing up, the daughter of a Ghanaian father and English mother – were quickly apparent and she became the team's secret weapon, leading them to their first cup final in her first season. The exhilaration quickly turned to disappointment, however.

'There was a kid on the other team who told the referee that I was a girl, so I had to leave the pitch and I couldn't play,' she says.

Behind her on our video call, the backdrop to our conversation is bare walls. There is no trophy or medal in sight, no framed shirt on her walls that might tell of the most amazing career – Arsenal and England legend and the first professional female player registered in the country, winner of seven domestic top-division titles, eleven FA Women's Cups, seven Women's Premier League Cups, one UEFA European title and 129 caps for England. There is just a football on a shelf behind her.

I notice this because our conversation has come to a halt as she recalls her humiliation at being made to leave the pitch. It is a sadness I feel too, for what happened to my footballing hero echoes what happened to more modestly talented me. Inspired by seeing Yankey play at Wembley during the London Olympic Games of 2012 when I was sixteen, I joined a women's football team. I trained all pre-season and was hugely excited for the opening game. Before the match could start, however, I was taken aside by the referee and told that FA regulations stated I could not play wearing the hijab. I was shocked. The rule changed two years later, but that was two years too late to save me from the sadness I felt – and the pain I can still feel today as I remember – as I walked off the pitch. Imagine being just eight years old and feeling that, as Rachel Yankey did.

Once the pain had settled after a few years, I returned to football, but in a different role. I felt that if football couldn't accommodate me as a young player, I would change that as a coach. It was a change that inevitably led to my role in journalism. I wanted to share the stories of people from marginalised communities and show that sports needed to be more inclusive. For me, it was a lonely, uphill battle. Fortunately for Yankey, she had an ally: Tony Chelsea was the parent of one of the children at the eight-year-old Yankey's club. As the team's manager, he decided to stand up for her at a league AGM and found himself embroiled in an equality row.

'He was saying, "This is not fair. Yeah, my best player is a girl. And she can't play. So what happens to her?" I owe him so much,' Yankey tells me. 'Because he didn't have to fight for me. He didn't have to find me a place to go. But he was so disappointed that I couldn't play football, so he found me a place. I always remembered that. If he hadn't done that – if he hadn't set up the club or hid the fact that I was a girl or found me my next club – then there would have been a lot of us, including me, that would never have gotten into football. OK, some of the boys there have not gone on to play football or continued. But we just had that sense of being in a team, feeling like we represented something. Like we really belonged.'

Yankey had not even been out of the London borough of Brent, but Tony Chelsea helped her join a club at Mill Hill and her football career took off. At sixteen years old she made her senior debut for Arsenal. A few years later, aged nineteen, she had an opportunity to join Laval Dynamites – a Canadian club that played in the American League. She seized the chance for an adventure, but there was just one drawback: the team she had joined was in Montreal, where the main language was French and she understood little.

'I'm not going to lie, I had no clue what the manager was saying,' she tells me with a laugh.

'The team talks were all in French, but football is football – you just go through some pictures and point at a few things, but you understand the game and get on with it.'

Yankey enjoyed the experience, picking up some French here and there, but in 2000 came a move to Fulham that would cement her place in women's football history and make her the first professional female footballer in England. Fulham owner Mohamed Al-Fayed had just returned from California, where he had watched the iconic 99ers' World Cup final, in which a record crowd of 90,185 saw the United States Women's national team beat the China People's Republic on penalties after a 0-0 draw, with Brandi Chastain netting the winning kick. Overnight, women's football found itself in the spotlight and Chastain's iconic celebration in her black sports bra was all over the newspapers around the world. Al-Fayed wanted similar excitement for Fulham. His investment paid off, with Fulham dominating women's football for a while. In fact, it could be said he was ahead of his time, with the women's domestic game not going professional until some years later. For Yankey, he was the trailblazer that women's football desperately needed.

'People weren't brave enough to jump on,' says Yankey. 'Because, for me, there were still some quality players back then. They just didn't have the opportunity. I credit Mohammed Al-Fayed for being brave enough to say, "I've watched this over in America, this is good." I'm just not sure everybody else was in agreement with it. Maybe that is why he's ahead of his time, but I don't know. I find it a hard pill to swallow.'

With few following Al-Fayed's lead, and TV rights and commercial investment scarce, the initiative could not be sustained and the women's club was dismantled. Yankey herself continued to excel, with spells at Birmingham Ladies and Notts County, but it was a return to Arsenal that would take her to the heights of women's football as well as bringing her new success at a grassroots level. For, though her excellence as a player is well known, her service off the pitch – equally influential in many ways – has often passed under the radar. At Arsenal she took on various coaching responsibilities, many of which included working for the development club, but it was an evening at a secondary school in Brent that sparked her interest in community work. Initially called in to hand out awards to the pupils at the school, Yankey left with her own coaching propositions.

'I had a conversation with a lady who worked for Brent Council and I just happened to talk to her about an idea for me setting up my own coaching club and going into schools, and she had a pot of funding that the council needed to use. It was a win–win situation.'

Yankey may have been an England and Arsenal legend at the peak of her career on the weekends, but during the week she was visiting schools in and around Brent trying to get young people involved in sport. The sessions didn't come without their challenges, and her community was apprehensive.

'It was really difficult to get the schools to sign up,' she says. 'Which I found really strange too. They didn't have to pay for anything. I had all the equipment.'

But gradually it all came together. From Monday to Friday she could be found driving around the London Borough of Brent during the day with a car full of football equipment; during the evenings she was at Arsenal. And as the club grew, so did the demand. Over time, Yankey had nearly 200 children taking part in her school sessions and joining her community football club. Her influence at a community level was monumental – and heavily influenced by her own experience as Ray.

'A lot of it goes back to Tony Chelsea,' she says. 'He didn't have to help me but he did because he wanted better for me. We didn't shout about what we did in the community. It was just about trying to get those kids to enjoy themselves.'

She also had an ally from the Arsenal and England teams: Mary Phillip, the first black player to captain the Lionesses, whom Yankey shared a room with on the weekends. The rest of the time, both ran community football clubs, to get young kids on their estates involved in sport. Unbeknown to the youngsters at Peckham Town and Gibbons Wreckers football clubs (where Phillip and Yankey were involved respectively), they were being trained by footballing royalty.

'Taking a minibus full of kids from Brent to Peckham was like hell, but also good fun,' Yankey says with a laugh. 'The kids loved it and now we'd taken them outside of where they live, exposed them to new things. They played against another team, but were able to say they were a team. They had their little kit and just seemed so proud.' She beams as she reflects on her minibus adventures.

Her hard work didn't go unnoticed, and over time more parents started to volunteer. Yankey's own experiences were proving invaluable.

'Growing up, what I loved most about football was that sense of community and being part of something,' she says. 'It was challenging but rewarding.'

Much of that reward lay in working in one of the most diverse communities in London. In a sport that is often criticised for its failure to be representative at an elite level, on a weekly basis Yankey was working at a grassroots level, where skill, race and class had no bearing. The space she set up aimed to be as inclusive as possible: there were no barriers or restrictions in place, and no minimum footballing ability the players had to meet; her sessions were open for all.

'There were lots of different kids from different backgrounds. We had white kids, black kids, Asian kids and kids from the Irish travelling community,' she recalls. 'When we would play other teams, they would say, "You shouldn't let the traveller community into your club – they have a bad reputation about them." But for me, they were great. You shouldn't put a restriction or a barrier for anyone to play football. I didn't believe in it. There were some fantastic footballers, and when they were here, they were amazing. I didn't care about the noise of what was going on outside.'

Having found a sense of belonging through football, Yankey is keen to pass that on to others.

'It was that sense of "this is our team",' she says, interlocking her hands. 'You know, the kids picked the name. The club was based at Gibbons recreational ground and they called it Gibbons Wreckers.' She pauses to laugh. 'You know – to wreck something? Even now, I'll be walking the dog and I'll sometimes see parents and kids that are now teenagers and they still talk about Gibbons Wreckers and smile. I think that's what football is really about and that is what makes it special.'

Yankey's inclusion in the eighteen-player squad at the London 2012 Games was almost a poetic end to her role with Gibbons Wreckers. Team GB's final group game, against Brazil, was to be played at Wembley Stadium, on her doorstep. With the help of some willing volunteers and parents, she arranged for nearly seventy children to be there.

'We bought a load of tickets to take the kids to Wembley for the Olympics,' she says, smiling at the memory. 'We try to expose them to different things and give them different experiences. I'm sure the kids have as fond memories of the Olympics as I do.'

And here again I can identify – this time with the kids. I'd also been invited to the game on a school trip, and it was my first experience of watching international football in a stadium. It was also my first time seeing Yankey play, and we both laugh as I share an anecdote about how I missed the game's only goal that day. (I've since learned never to go on a toilet break midway through a game.) For her, the experience at Wembley – by far the biggest moment for an international women's match in the UK – wasn't the fairy-tale story she had hoped it would be.

'You know, the Olympics were fantastic,' she says. 'There were highs and lows through it. The Brazil game was just low because I didn't start. For me, coming from Brent, playing at this magnificent stadium that I'd walked past since I was a kid, this was one of the games where I thought, *Please let me start.* But I didn't get an opportunity.'

She may not have started but she certainly arrived. In the sixty-third minute Eniola Aluko made way for Yankey. Her presence was instantly felt as the stadium erupted into a roar. Between 2010 and 2020, only 14 per cent of the women's national team were black, compared to 49 per cent in the men's team, and here were two black women in a much-needed spotlight. Both Yankey and Aluko have spoken out at various times about being proud of their blackness, and both were crucial in my understanding of how there can be a space for women in sport and my growth in the game. As a young black girl growing up near London, my exposure to women of colour in football was scarce, and so witnessing two of the biggest black figures in women's sport making way for one another in this historic game at Wembley had a huge impact on me. Sights like this – or like my memory of Rachel Yankey and Rio Ferdinand in their oversized football kits, with their hair braided – made sports feel so inclusive. For Yankey, it was not until after her career that she felt the weight of her role as one of the few black women in football.

'I don't think I looked at it in that way,' she says. 'I think the biggest thing for me was probably gender. I didn't really see many girls playing. So I definitely felt very different there. Rather than [because of] the colour of my skin.'

In many ways, her staging posts of Mill Hill youth club, Canada, Fulham, Arsenal and Team GB all complemented the work she was doing in between. Though she is a quiet, unassuming woman, for many of us Yankey was a role model. Someone we all hoped to emulate both on and off the pitch.

'I suppose a lot of people would come up to me and say, "You're the reason why I started playing football." A lot of black people would speak to me about football and relate to me on the football pitch. I just loved playing football. Looking back, it was pretty powerful, but when I was playing, I felt like I was just playing. I played because I enjoyed it. And I coached because I enjoyed it. I didn't ever set out to do anything or be remembered by anyone. I just enjoyed playing football. I feel grateful that people looked up to me.'

It's always amazing to hear that your biggest heroes and influences can be so grounded. For someone with such immense knowledge of the game and accolades that could probably cover every wall in her house, Yankey cuts a humble figure and speaks little of her career. Instead, it is her achievements off the pitch that she hopes she will be remembered for.

'When I got the OBE, that was special because that wasn't about me. It was about services to the grassroots game,' she says in reflection on being named in the New Year's Honours List in 2013 for her tireless work in promoting the women's game at youth level. 'You have the ability to give people opportunities and I probably had a bigger platform to affect people than others, just because of where I played and what I did.'

As our conversation draws to a close, she thinks back again to how she started out.

'Tony Chelsea wasn't a coach,' she says. 'He was just someone's dad who obviously saw his son wanted to play and said, "I'm gonna do something about it," and then created a team. I always remembered that, if he hadn't done that, there would have been a lot of us who would never have got into football. If I can help one child find a love for football like I did, then I guess that's a career worthwhile.'

Making football a more welcoming place for Rachels so that there's no need for Rays – I'd say that's perhaps her greatest achievement of all.

A BUNCH OF FIVES

We've all whiled away the hours, imagining our world-beating dream team. Here, **Jade Craddock** *plays the fantasy version of the five-a-side game.*

June and July are traditionally the months when professional footballers cast aside their boots and pitches for flip-flops and beaches. Yet, for amateur footballers, the summer is about one thing: five-a-side. Eleven-a-side may be the money-spinner and the professional pinnacle, but there is something special about the reduced format and so, for a couple of halcyon months, the small-sided game rules on pitches, astroturfs and fields everywhere, as the age-old questions reverberate: Are we playing over head height? Can the goalie come out of the area? Can outfield players go in the area? Is it throw-ins or kick-ons, corners or no corners? Is it one step for a penalty? And, most crucially, when did these bibs last get washed? This is football back to its purest form, conjuring the joy and freedom of the playground, long before the eleven-a-side game was commercialised, given a glossy makeover and fed back to us as the only legitimate format.

Though five-a-side leagues have taken off in recent years, the game still exists on the periphery, and professional five-a-side remains largely elusive (somewhat strangely perhaps, given the growth of eight-sided kwik cricket and rugby sevens – the latter even being included in the last two Olympics). But who wouldn't want to see Messi and Ronaldo, Salah and De Bruyne on a five-a-side pitch (well, aside from their opponents)? Indeed, the debates over dream five-a-sides linger, and in all likelihood that's exactly how they'll remain – dreams, at least until Messrs Ronaldo et al. get to masters' age and dig out their trainers and unwashed bibs for the occasional tournament.

So, in lieu of club and Olympic five-a-side tournaments, fans continue to conjure up their fantasy quintuplets. After all, it's easy to pick a Premier League five-a-side team, right? There'd be Petr Cech in goal. Or perhaps Peter Schmeichel. Oh, hang on, what about David Seaman… or David de Gea? It's hard to choose between even a Peter or a David, it seems. But a striker would surely be a simpler choice – it has to be Thierry Henry, doesn't it? Did someone say Alan Shearer? Sergio Aguero? What about Harry Kane?

Apparently, it's not quite as easy as just picking five names, but some fascinating possibilities for top-flight five-a-side teams emerge when you base them on a variety of parameters, as we shall see.

The Perennials

Just one appearance in the Premier League is something most of us dream of, whereas hitting the significant milestone of two, three or four hundred appearances – equating to over ten and a half full seasons – demonstrates the ability of a select few to play at the top level consistently. When it comes to creating a Premier League team based on the top appearance-makers, the following group have achieved a collective 2,881 appearances between them – over seventy-five top-flight seasons!

Gareth Barry sits top of the rankings with a total 653 outings, while Ryan Giggs comes in just behind him with 632, granting them the automatic slots in a two-man midfield, with Frank Lampard (609) and James Milner (564 and counting) just missing out. David James (572) comfortably beats Mark Schwarzer (514) to the number-one spot, while Jamie Carragher (508) edges out Phil Neville (505) and Rio Ferdinand (504) in defence. Up top, Emile Heskey (516) sees off Jermain Defoe (496) and Wayne Rooney (491).

One thing's for sure with this team: they won't let you down on a cold, wet Monday night in Stoke – or anywhere else, for that matter.

James

Carragher

Barry   Giggs

Heskey

Young Guns

You'll never win anything with kids, Alan Hansen infamously said, only to be proven completely wrong, so surely a young guns five-a-side would be worth a sneak peek. The PFA Young Player Award offers some interesting outfield options, with a team of 2010–14 winners featuring Kyle Walker, Jack Wilshere, Eden Hazard and Gareth Bale, while the most recent foursome would include Trent Alexander-Arnold, Phil Foden, Leroy Sané and Raheem Sterling – all of them pretty impressive options – but minus a goalkeeper as Mervyn Day is the only stopper to have won the award (in 1975).

Alternatively, when it comes to the youngest players ever to feature in the Premier League, a five-a-side team would line up as follows: Neil Finn (aged 17 years and 3 days), Matthew Briggs (16 years, 2 months and 7 days), Harvey Elliott (16 years and 30 days), Izzy Brown (16 years, 3 months and 27 days) and Rushian Hepburn-Murphy (16 years, 6 months and 14 days), with Aaron Lennon (16 years, 4 months and 7 days) and Jose Baxter (16 years, 6 months and 9 days) just missing out.

However, in terms of the current crop, centre-forward Antwoine Hackford was the youngest player to feature in 2020/21, at the age of 16 years, 9 months and 13 days. Shola Shoretire (17 years and 19 days) and Carney Chukwuemeka (17 years, 6 months and 29 days) were the youngest midfielders on show, while Will Fish (18 years, 3 months and 6 days) was the youngest defender. With just a handful of minutes to their names, though, looking at the young players who made a significant contribution in terms of appearances, a final line-up would include

Ki-Jana Hoever in defence (aged 18 years, 8 months and 9 days), with Mason Greenwood (18 years, 11 months and 19 days) and Bukayo Saka (19 years and 14 days) occupying the midfield. Up top would be Fábio Silva (18 years, 2 months and 2 days), while Illan Meslier (20 years, 6 months and 10 days) fills the goalkeeper berth.

Despite their age, you wouldn't bet against this quintet – and they've got a few good years to go yet.

Meslier

Hoever

Greenwood   Saka

Silva

Golden Oldies

With youth increasingly taking a front seat in the Premier League, players over thirty-five are becoming more of a rarity, and players over forty are practically extinct. But the question of whether experience trumps youth remains. So, at the other end of the scale, a five-a-side team consisting of the oldest players to ever feature in the Premier League would see John Burridge – the oldest ever Premier League player at the ripe old age of 43 years, 5 months and 11 days – line up in goal. In front of him would sit the relatively youthful Colin Cooper, the youngest in this team, at a mere 39 years, 2 months and 9 days. The midfield would see two forty-year-olds in Gordon Strachan (40 years, 2 months and 24 days) and Ryan Giggs (40 years, 5 months and 7 days), while a sprightly Teddy Sheringham would complete the line-up, aged 40 years, 8 months and 28 days.

In terms of a 2020/21 five-a-side team, it would shape up with Willy Caballero in goal as the eldest statesman, aged 38 years, 11 months and 29 days, beating 36-year-old Lukasz Fabianski to the gloves. Phil Jagielka, aged 38 years, 9 months and 6 days, would easily see off 37-year-old whipper-snapper Branislav Ivanović. Aged 36 years and 19 days, Fernandinho would continue to marshal the midfield, with his senior, Pablo Hernández (36 years, 1 month and 12 days), pulling the strings. Spring chicken Billy Sharp, at the age of just 35 years, 1 month and 9 days, would carry the baton up front, completing the line-up with a combined age of 180 years (some 87 years' advantage – or disadvantage – over the Young Guns). Scott Carson, Thiago Silva, James Milner, João Moutinho and Olivier Giroud all just miss out, but there's always next year…

Caballero

Jagielka

Fernandinho   Hernández

Sharp

Servicemen

Changing teams tends to happen as often for players as changing socks these days, yet some players comfortably settle into a club and never look back. In current times, Mark Noble is head and shoulders above any other player when it comes to long service (over 17 years and counting at West Ham), some half a decade more than his nearest contender, Séamus Coleman (over 12 years and counting at Everton). By the end of the 2020/21 season, Harry Kane was the longest-serving forward, racking up over a decade at Tottenham, while both David de Gea and Jordan Henderson narrowed in on the ten-year mark at Manchester United and Liverpool respectively, completing this line-up of loyal servants. Kevin Long, Lewis Dunk, Phil Jones, Kasper Schmeichel and Sergio Agüero just missed the cut, although perhaps they can form a quintet of their own; it would certainly beat waiting around for de Gea et al. to call time.

de Gea

Coleman

Noble   Henderson

Kane

Ever-presents
With games coming thick and fast for Premier League footballers on all fronts, playing every game in a season is an achievement, but playing every minute is a superhuman effort, not least in the jam-packed 2020/21 season. Unlike the previous season, when fifteen players achieved the feat, 2020/21 saw only seven players rack up all 3,420 minutes – of which four were goalkeepers (Hugo Lloris, Emiliano Martínez, Aaron Ramsdale and Kasper Schmeichel) and three were midfielders (Pierre-Emile Højbjerg, Tomáš Souček and James Ward-Prowse). Notably, James Ward-Prowse also featured for the entirety of the 2019/20 season, amassing 6,840 minutes, while Kasper Schmeichel went one better, having not missed a league game in three seasons – some 10,260 minutes.

But in terms of the final five, Emiliano Martínez would get the nod in goal as, of the four ever-present keepers, he kept the most clean sheets (fifteen). Stuart Dallas takes the defensive role, with 3,411 minutes under his belt. Of the three midfield options, Tomáš Souček and James Ward-Prowse would edge out Højbjerg on goals, while Ollie Watkins proved to be the most ever-present forward, playing 3,329 minutes.

With a combined 17,000 minutes between them, this five-a-side team would still be going strong after eleven days!

Martínez

Dallas

Souček   Ward-Prowse

Watkins

Marathon Men
Playing a whole Premier League season is an impressive feat in itself, but it pales in comparison to Harold Bell's 375 consecutive league appearances for Tranmere Rovers (401 including FA Cup appearances), spanning nine years from 1946 to 1955. That's the equivalent of nearly ten full Premier League seasons without missing a game! No player has come close to that record in the contemporary game, although certain players have had impressive

runs – not least Brad Friedel, who holds the record for the most consecutive Premier League appearances (310 matches between 2004 and 2012). Frank Lampard is the most ever-present outfield player by some distance, racking up 164 consecutive games. Matt Holland and Wayne Bridge totalled 115 and 113 consecutive games respectively, while Jonathan Walters completes this five-a-side team with 104 appearances. Honourable mentions, too, for the select group of players with a century of consecutive games to their name: Darren Fletcher, Joleon Lescott, Peter Crouch and Roger Johnson.

If nothing else, this team would still be going long after opposition teams hung up their boots.

Friedel

Bridge

Holland   Lampard

Walters

Hard-knocks

Sometimes a game calls for a bit of bite – a show of physical domination and rough and tumble. Some critics would be quick to point out that the elite game has developed a bit of a soft underbelly in recent decades, but this team of hard-knocks might just suggest otherwise – if they could stay on the pitch long enough to do so!

Gareth Barry and Lee Bowyer sit top of the table for total number of cards (123 and 103 respectively), but Richard Dunne, Patrick Vieira and Duncan Ferguson top the red-card charts with eight apiece and find their way into the centre-back, midfield and centre-forward berths respectively – with Ferguson carrying the dubious honour of having received the most straight red cards (six). Vinnie Jones, Roy Keane and Alan Smith, each with seven red cards, can feel themselves hard done by in missing out to Lee Cattermole (also with seven reds, but trumping midfield rival Keane by some distance, with 88 yellow cards in contrast to Keane's measly 69). Completing the line-up is Jussi Jääskeläinen, the keeper with the most red cards (four, along with Pavel Srníček) and the most yellows (24). He's certainly determined to leave his mark, and who are we to argue? In fact, this is clearly a team that wouldn't take any arguing – even, perhaps, from each other.

Jääskeläinen

Dunne

Vieira   Cattermole

Ferguson

Hey, Big Spenders
Once upon a time, Willie Groves made headlines for receiving the princely transfer fee of £100. Admittedly, this was in 1893. Ever since, transfer fees have been on an upwards trajectory, inciting a mixture of awe, bewilderment and even disgust. Following Groves, Alf Common secured the first £500-plus (and later £1,000-plus) transfer fee, David Jack the first £10,000-plus fee, and John Charles the first £50,000-plus fee, before Denis Law broke the £100,000 barrier in July 1962 when Manchester United forked out £115,000 to Torino for the frontman's services. But it was Trevor Francis's record-breaking £1,180,000 deal in February 1979 that showed the direction football was taking financially.

As the Premier League took off, the sums became more and more breathtaking, culminating in 2016 with Paul Pogba's £94-million move from Juventus to Manchester United. The French maverick slots straight into this five-a-side team of the Premier League's most expensive players. He is joined by Kepa Arrizabalaga in goal, who commanded a cool £72 million at the age of just twenty-three – a world-record transfer fee for a goalkeeper. Harry Maguire, who transferred from Leicester to Manchester United for £78 million, takes the defensive role, beating Virgil van Dijk to the spot, while Nicolas Pépé, who moved to Arsenal for £72 million (prior to Kai Havertz's similarly priced move to Chelsea in 2020), accompanies Pogba in midfield, and £76-million striker Romelu Lukaku rounds off this £392-million team.

Expensive this quintet may be, but it remains to be seen whether they would have been a match for Willie Groves, Alf Common et al.

A BUNCH OF FIVES

Arrizabalaga
Maguire
Pogba   Pépé
Lukaku

Goals, Goals, Goals
When it comes to the crunch, the most important thing in football is goals. It's great to score a worldie – a scorpion kick à la Olivier Giroud, a Beckhamesque halfway-line howitzer, or a goal that is pure poetry in motion like Dennis Bergkamp – yet it's the quantity not the quality that ends up getting the headlines (and the golden boot) come the season's finale. So here's a five-a-side team with goals from every position.

The Premier League has had a wealth of goalscoring riches, with twenty-nine players having struck a hundred times or more, but Wayne Rooney and Alan Shearer are the only two players to have topped 200 goals, with 208 and 260 respectively – Alan Shearer thus filling the striker's position in this line-up. There have been some equally notable goalscoring midfielders down the years, including Paul Scholes (107) and Ryan Giggs (109), but it is the often incongruous England midfield pairing of Steven Gerrard and Frank Lampard (with 120 and 177 goals respectively) that proves incomparable. As for defenders, while John Terry (41) and David Unsworth (38) vie for top position, it's the versatile Ashley Young (with 48 goals to his name) who triumphs. And what of the goalscoring keepers, you might wonder? There have been six gloved assassins in the Premier League, all of whom have scored a single goal, including Asmir Begović, Brad Friedel, Tim Howard, Peter Schmeichel and Alisson Becker. However, there is a standout candidate whose one goal is backed up with five assists: Paul Robinson, who completes this line-up (although whether that's in goal or up front, we'll leave the players to decide).

As a brief sidenote, a team of the milestone goalscorers in the Premier League would consist of Peter Schmeichel (the first goalkeeper to score in the Premier League), Moritz Volz (who scored the 15,000th goal) in defence, Eric Cantona and Marc Albrighton in midfield (scorers of the 100th and 20,000th goals, respectively), and Brian Deane (scorer of the first-ever Premier League goal) seeing off Mike Newell (1,000th), Les Ferdinand (10,000th) and Zlatan Ibrahimović (25,000th) up front. So it's rich pickings whichever way you play it.

Robinson

Young

Gerrard   Lampard

Shearer

Hat-trick Heroes
If there is one thing any player loves it's a hat-trick. Since Eric Cantona struck the first hat-trick in the Premier League, on 25 August 1992, more than two hundred players have achieved the feat, with just over thirty scoring four goals in a single match, and only Andrew Cole, Alan Shearer, Jermain Defoe, Dimitar Berbatov and Sergio Agüero having scored five. While Michael Owen remains the youngest hat-trick hero (at 18 years and 62 days), and Teddy Sheringham the oldest (37 years and 146 days), Sadio Mané has scored the quickest hat-trick (in 2 minutes and 56 seconds), while Salomón Rondón was the last player to score a headed hat-trick and Christian Pulisic a perfect hat-trick.

In terms of creating a five-a-side team, Sergio Agüero gets the hotly contested striker role, having notched the most hat-tricks in the Premier League (twelve), ahead of Alan Shearer (eleven), Robbie Fowler (nine), Thierry Henry, Harry Kane and Michael Owen (all eight). Raheem Sterling's four hat-tricks position him rightfully in one of the two midfield roles, with Theo Walcott seeing off Frank Lampard by virtue of having scored more recently. Finding an out-and-out defender and goalkeeper who have scored hat-tricks is tricky, so Dion Dublin (who scored three hat-tricks in the Premier League) takes the defensive role, having played there at the start of his career, while Harry Kane's only (perhaps not particularly memorable) performance in goal provides the answer between the sticks. Not that he'd be needed with the guaranteed twelve goals from his outfield teammates.

Kane
Dublin
Sterling   Walcott
Agüero

Fast and Furious

Pundits and managers often stress the importance of scoring an early goal to settle nerves, take the advantage and grab hold of a game. So if you can score a goal in 7.69 seconds (take a bow, Shane Long) that's surely all the more beneficial. And if you had a team who were all adept at scoring in fewer than fifteen seconds, you could have a 5-0 lead within 75 seconds – game over! Sadly, it doesn't quite work like that usually, but just on the off chance that miracles could happen, this is how a five-a-side team of the fastest goalscorers in Premier League history would line up.

Shane Long's 7.69-second sharp shooting secures his position up top. Ledley King wipes aside his attacking compatriots as the scorer of the second-fastest Premier League goal in 9.82 seconds and thus easily slots in at the back. Alan Shearer can count himself unlucky at missing out, despite scoring in 10.52 seconds, but Christian Eriksen (10.54) and Mark Viduka (11.90) more naturally fill the midfield positions. And if you think the team would be scratching around for a goalkeeper, think again. Asmir Begović's 13.64-second strike is topped only by the additions of Dwight Yorke, Chris Sutton, Kevin Nolan and James Beattie. Not only that but, at 91.9 metres, Begovic's goal remains the longest in history – a double whammy if ever there was one, although perhaps not quite ideal on the shorter five-a-side pitches.

Begović
King
Eriksen   Viduka
Long

Founding Footballers

Today the Premier League is one of the most globally diverse in the world, with more than fifty nationalities represented in the 2020/21 season, and more than a hundred represented across its history, including players from six continents. It wasn't quite the same story at the Premier League's inception in 1992, though, when only thirteen overseas players featured in the opening-weekend matches and just under sixty across the season as a whole. Those first thirteen players were Eric Cantona (France), Craig Forrest (Canada), Gunnar Halle (Norway), John Jensen (Denmark), Andrei Kanchelskis (Russia), Anders Limpar (Sweden), Roland Nilsson (Sweden), Ronny Rosenthal (Israel), Peter Schmeichel (Denmark), Hans Segers (Netherlands), Jan Stejskal (Czechoslovakia, as it then was), Michel Vonk (Netherlands) and Robert Warzycha (Poland). As a nod to these players having initiated the Premier League's worldwide vision, putting their countries and English football on the map, a five-a-side line-up from that inaugural season is fitting.

There are four goalkeepers to choose from, but Craig Forrest (the first player from North America to feature in the Premier League) gets the gloves. In defence, Gunnar Halle's 41 appearances and five goals from right-back trump Roland Nilsson's 32 appearances and one goal. Eric Cantona is a shoo-in for midfield, with 35 appearances and fifteen goals (including that historic first Premier League hat-trick). For the other midfield spot, John Jensen may claim the most appearances (32), but Anders Limpar's 23 appearances and two goals give him the upper hand. With six goals in 27 appearances to Andrei Kanchelskis's three goals in the same number of games, Ronny Rosenthal fills the forward berth, also becoming the first player from Asia to figure in the Premier League. This is a team of trailblazers both on and off the pitch.

Forrest
Halle
Cantona   Limpar
Rosenthal

A BUNCH OF FIVES

* * *

Debates about who should be in a Premier League five-a-side may be never-ending – after all, Edwin van der Sar, Tony Adams, Paul Scholes, David Silva and Didier Drogba (a formidable line-up in itself), as well as many other of the league's icons, haven't even had a look-in – but one thing is without doubt: a five-a-side league would be just as exciting as the traditional league, if not more so. In fact, club teams could be pretty tasty, with the likes of Ederson, Rúben Dias, Kevin De Bruyne, Phil Foden and Raheem Sterling lining up against David de Gea, Harry Maguire, Bruno Fernandes, Marcus Rashford and Edinson Cavani for the Manchester derby, while a 2021 FA Cup rematch between Leicester and Chelsea could see Kasper Schmeichel, Wesley Fofana, Youri Tielemans, James Maddison and Jamie Vardy taking on Edouard Mendy, Antonio Rüdiger, Mason Mount, Kai Havertz and Christian Pulisic.

We haven't even considered the whole question of other English leagues, let alone European club sides: how about a classic Barcelona line-up of Victor Valdés, Gerard Piqué, Andrés Iniesta, Xavi and Lionel Messi facing off against a Real Madrid line-up of Iker Casillas, Sergio Ramos, Zinedine Zidane, Cristiano Ronaldo and Raúl? Or international leagues: a Premier League side of Ederson, Virgil van Dijk, Mohamed Salah, Bruno Fernandes and Harry Kane versus a La Liga line-up of Jan Oblak, Jules Koundé, Frenkie de Jong, Lionel Messi and Karim Benzema perhaps? And, of course, international teams: a 2018 World Cup final replay with Hugo Lloris, Raphaël Varane, Kylian Mbappé, Antoine Griezmann and Olivier Giroud of France taking on a Croatian side of Danijel Subašić, Domagoj Vida, Luka Modrić, Ivan Perišić and Mario Mandžukić, maybe? The women's game deserves a whole tome on its own, with a possible WSL 2020/21 quintet of Ann-Katrin Berger, Millie Turner, Fran Kirby, Chloe Kelly and Sam Kerr, while a best-of England team could line up with the likes of Karen Bardsley, Lucy Bronze, Fara Williams, Karen Carney and Kelly Smith.

The prospects are mind-blowing, so if anyone from the Paris 2024 Olympic Committee is reading, how about a little summer five-a-side tournament? Messrs Ronaldo and Messi might even be available then – just give them plenty of time so they can get the bibs washed.

* All figures correct as of the end of the 2020/21 season. All transfer fees as per Transfermarkt.co.uk.

STADIUMS OF LIGHT

Jane Purdon *fell in love with Sunderland AFC when they won the FA Cup in 1973, but didn't get to go to Wembley because she was a girl. Finally, years later at the rebuilt, lit-up stadium, she found a resolution to the drama that drove her.*

Mine was a gendered childhood in which my brother was given a plastic gun and I was given a doll's pram, which I would turn on its side and drag about, enjoying what the sensation taught me about resistance and friction. Ballet featured for a while, as my mother, from the Birkenhead working class, was determined to give her daughter opportunities she had never had. She was right in principle, but the opportunities she chose for me bored me.

In fairness to her, we used to have something she called 'Our Saturday Afternoons', which I look back on with joy. My earliest memories of them are after we moved to Sunderland, for I recall little of my first three years on the Wirral. But for as long as I can remember, between the ages of three and seven every second Saturday she and I had the house to ourselves. She would settle in an armchair in front of the fire – one of those 1970s electric fires that had two heat-radiating bars and rotating red and yellow lights behind a plastic approximation of coal.

I had the sofa. Through the warm fug came the comfortable background murmur of the horse racing on *Grandstand* or the wrestling on

World of Sport. It was an age of three TV channels, so this was all that was on offer. We didn't really focus on the sport. We focused on the peace, the warmth, the comfort, the being-together, the long acres of time, which I now realise must have been a special blessing to my mother, after a week of running the house, cooking every meal, doing all the cleaning and the laundry. If I wish to understand where my sense of female solidarity came from, it began on those Saturday afternoons with Mum.

I always knew that the reason we had Our Saturday Afternoons was that my father and brother went away to something else. I didn't understand what this something else was but I knew it was called 'watching Sunderland' and it involved something called 'football'. If you'd asked me to define what 'football' was, I would have said it was something that my father and brother did. Beyond that, it was a mystery. I wasn't interested in finding out about it. Whatever 'football' was, it couldn't possibly top the pleasure and peace of the Saturday-afternoon fire and the murmur of the TV. And besides, 'football' was something my father and brother often returned from grim-faced. Who needed something that made you miserable?

In 1973 if you hadn't been at a football match and you weren't at home to catch the end of *Grandstand*, it was almost impossible to get the results. Mobile phones? Our Morris Traveller didn't even have a radio on which we could listen to the results. On what I now understand to be 7 April 1973, all four of us were driving in the Morris Traveller. I can't remember where we had been – perhaps to one of the North East's castles, perhaps to the Roman Wall, perhaps for a walk in the Pennines. I think that at the moment of this particular little story, we were somewhere in Sunderland, heading home, and I'm going to say that the time was early evening, say around 7.30 p.m.

And Dad did something completely out of character – out of his character, and out of the character of the times. He stopped the car, wound the window down, and started talking to a stranger. The stranger, I noticed, wore a red and white scarf. My father said to him, 'What was the score?' I didn't catch the stranger's reply, but in response to it my father and brother, and even my mother, broke into joy – smiles, laughter, happiness. I knew this meant that Sunderland had won at the football. I worked out that the talking to the stranger, and the force of reaction in the Morris Traveller, meant this wasn't any old game. Beyond that, I honestly can't remember figuring out on the back seat of the Morris Traveller what was going on. But all was to become clear over the next few weeks. The game Dad had asked the stranger about was the FA Cup semi-final, played at Hillsborough in Sheffield, and little Sunderland had beaten Arsenal 2-1.

Little Sunderland. There are many things I adore about Sunderland. Its coastline – the mile of golden sand that inspired L.S. Lowry, the arms of the harbour that reach out to the sea like an embrace. Then there's its intellectual history – many years later when working at Sunderland AFC's Academy of Light, I was delighted to learn that the path that splits the site in two was part of the ancient seven-mile track between the Anglo-Saxon monasteries of Jarrow and Monkwearmouth, and that the players running out to train were clattering in their studs over the path that Bede had walked.

Sunderland was one of Europe's artistic and intellectual power houses in the seventh and eighth centuries, and it has never been as mighty since. We Mackems know it and feel it now, and we felt it in 1973. It was then, of course, a heavy-industry town (not yet awarded city status as the consolation prize for industrial decline). Shipbuilding employed thousands, and mining employed thousands more both in Sunderland and wider County Durham. These were hard, unglamorous industries that did not make their workers rich and that sometimes killed them – rarely, but often enough for it not to be a surprise. The town felt then, as it still does, that it is regarded as second rate by those in power in the distant south.

Oh, the past is a different country. And yet in it are the seeds of our present disasters and glories. In May 1973, Britain was five months into its membership of the European Community. Irish bombs were killing and maiming in London. Millions were striking over government pay restraints. Our next family car, the Austin Allegro, had just been launched by British Leyland. And later in 1973, the oil crisis and the miners' strike would hit. The three-day week would follow. Every year changes Britain for ever, and in 1973 it certainly did.

In 1973, did we know that mining and shipbuilding – the industry my father worked in – would decline? If you'd asked us, I think we would have said Sunderland was on the down, not the up. The football club seemed to mirror the town's descent. Almost since its founding the club had been one of the greats, but in the 1950s it was revealed to have made unauthorised payments to players in breach of league rules. Fines and bans followed. A malaise set in. The club got relegated for the first time. By 1973 it had not recovered. Arguably, it still hasn't.

But then, as now, football had the power to transcend our workaday real lives, and perhaps the unexpected moments of transcendence by underdogs against all the odds have a special glory, one almost spiritual in its intense revelation of possibilities. So it was in Sunderland in the heady weeks of April and early May 1973. It is hard to remember when exactly I realised that something unique was happening. As a child, you pick up on how the grown-ups are behaving, and I remember more smiles, more bounce in steps, more happy chats.

A large clue for my seven-year-old self was that, in an age when we didn't know what branding was, the whole town voluntarily and ferociously branded itself. The clothes shops displayed only red and white clothes. Shops without the advantage of red and white merchandise showcased giant models of the Cup and red and white show-pony rosettes. Someone painted 'Haway the lads' on their car. Mams put red and white ribbons on prams. It seemed that a happy madness had overwhelmed everyone.

All Sunderland fans have stories about how they – or their dad or their grandad – did or did not get tickets for the final. I still don't know how the club's ballot for tickets worked, and I have spoken to others who have said it was shambolic. But, for my father and brother, who had been to every home match, it delivered four tickets. I think you're probably guessing what happened next, and anticipating that the rest of this piece will be about how my first football match was a Wembley Cup final.

I. Did. Not. Go.

My mother told me years later that she and Dad discussed it. Their reasoning was: a) I was too young; b) I had never shown any interest in football; c) Dad had a colleague who had been to every home match with his son, and who had come up unlucky in the ticket ballot so it felt right to offer the two spares to them.

Their reasoning was faultless. It was fair. I have never been angry about it. I've often thought with genuine good feeling about the colleague and his son. And yet, and yet. Looking at reason b), I had never shown any interest in football because it had never been offered to me. And it had never been offered to me because I was a girl. This was the first time that it dawned on me that my gender could determine my life. An unwanted toy pram could be turned on its side and dragged. A society that set different and rigid patterns of leisure for men and women was of a different order, but just as nonsensical. I recognised the absurdity of Mum and me staying at home while Dad and my brother set off for London – but I said nothing. I did what I did a lot of as a child: I watched, and I waited.

Sunderland is a long way from Wembley. Allow a minimum of five hours door-to-door whether you drive or get the train. I now can't remember if my father and brother did it there and back in a day or took two days or even three. I believe they went down on the Friday, because I vaguely recollect a feeling of pleasurable anticipation that one of the Saturday Afternoons that Mum and I enjoyed so much was going to be extended across the whole day. In those days, the FA Cup final was an extended television event on both main channels, with build-up beginning in the morning. So Mum and I assumed our positions – sofa, armchair, fire, fug – early.

Much of the build-up had a jolly, festive nature. I don't think memory deceives that there was a special edition of *It's a Knockout*, a competition involving teams of ordinary people in various humiliating and hilarious events of silly physical endeavour. Olga Korbut, who must have been passing through London, appeared in the TV studio to say that she thought Sunderland would win (God bless you, Olga). And then there were the serious pundits. Brian Clough called it for Leeds United.

Leeds United. Much has been written about the Leeds United of that time. But I am telling this story through my seven-year-old eyes, and I knew only two things about them. The first was that they played all in white, and this seemed to me to be unspeakably glamorous. It's hard for me now to say why I thought this, but perhaps it was because it was such an impractical colour for playing a sport on pitches that were in those days often churned to mud, even in the old First Division. Playing in white seemed to say 'you cannot touch us', and this led to the second thing I knew about Leeds United: they were good.

Occasionally, the joy and the cheer of the adults in the weeks before the Cup final would be interrupted – when they talked of who Sunderland would play. Leeds, I learned, were 'a division above us'. I did not know what this meant, but the solemnity of the speaker told me that it was cause for concern. More information seeped into my understanding. Leeds were very good. They were a top team. They had won the Cup the year before.

Was I worried? No. I had yet to engage emotionally with Sunderland and with football. My short journey with the game so far had been one of observation, watching fascinated as the adults behaved in ways that were most unexpected. So there I was on the Saturday, with Mum, in the living room in front of the fire, and the TV building up to the game itself. But yes, I did feel a surge of emotion when the coverage proper started. It was at seeing the people – our people – filling Wembley and making so much noise. Every inhabitant of every town that has a club that makes it to Wembley probably feels this, but try to remember the first time you saw it: the power of your tribe in their tens of thousands, holding their scarves outstretched, singing in unison. And knowing my dad and my brother were in there with them. Mum and I scanned the screen, desperate to see them.

The teams came out of the tunnel. The commentator on the version I've watched since says above the roar, 'And so they emerge into the daylight of Wembley stadium.' I love that. There's something about light and Sunderland. The Stadium of Light, built on the site of Wearmouth Colliery, was so named because miners coming up from shift talked of 'coming into the light'. I've learned other wonderful information from that commentary. Every Leeds United player was an international bar one (Trevor Cherry). No Sunderland player had ever played at Wembley bar one (Richie Pitt, who had played there as a schoolboy). You can see where the smart money lay.

I'll skip over the first thirty minutes of the game. All I have to say about it is that I watched football for the first time in my life and it didn't really make sense. I can't remember what of note happened. But I remember what happened next with absolute crystal-clear recall. In conventional football-reportage style, it went like this: Sunderland won their first corner. Billy Hughes kicked it to the far side of the goal. Vic Halom got it down, and Ian Porterfield fired it clean and clear into the goal. Wembley erupted.

Let me tell you how my seven-year-old heart experienced this. At 3.33 p.m. and 50 seconds I was a child who observed football with curiosity. Then, for a split second, there was just me and Ian Porterfield. Then he did this thing. And then I felt myself falling into a deep, deep pit. That pit was love. At 3.33 p.m. and 52 seconds, my heart had gone for ever. I was a football fan and a Sunderland fan.

At half-time, my aunt and uncle telephoned from Surrey – in 1973, one used the telephone rarely. My uncle, who was a dear friend to me all his long life, said that he was cheering for Leeds. 'You've got to cheer for Sunderland,' I said. 'Yes, that's right, Liverpool,' he said. 'Liverpool aren't even playing,' I said. I was a very literal child.

I cannot remember the play of the second half. My memory picks up about five minutes from full-time, when Wembley was full of the sound of Sunderland fans whistling. *End it, end it*, rose the collective prayer. It was the first of thousands of last-five-minutes-of-the-game agonies. And of course eventually it ended. Wembley erupted again, and I remember the sprint of our manager, Bob Stokoe. At the final whistle, he leapt off the bench and ran and ran. *He's going for Porterfield*, I thought. But Stokoe ran past every player in red and white stripes and to the man in green, Jimmy Montgomery. I felt cheated. Remember, this was the first football match I had ever watched. I didn't really understand what the goalie did. I thought it was a bit of a boring job, maybe for the slow one who couldn't kick properly. It took hearing adults, including Dad, talk in hushed voices later about how this had not been *any* goalkeeping performance. Jimmy Montgomery's double save against Trevor Cherry's header and Peter Lorimer's shot now stands as large in Sunderland legend as Porterfield's goal – perhaps larger, for it has been called the greatest double save ever.

It is a clear path from that moment to now. Dad took us all to see the team parade the Cup round Roker Park – my first time inside a football ground. Again, it was the joy, the emotion, the irrationality of the adults that caught me. I was at the beginning of my journey with football, and didn't fully understand what it was about, but I knew it was something extraordinary.

So I asked Dad if I could start coming to football too. Delighted, he said yes. There followed a few happy winters of standing on the Roker End with Dad and my brother. They ended because in 1977 Dad fell ill with motor neurone disease. He died two years later. The shadow lay across our family for years. Yet somehow, at around sixteen, I wandered back to Roker Park, perhaps to try to find Dad again. I stayed, because I was in love with football and had been since Porterfield scored. In 1985, I went to America in my gap year and saw how popular football was for girls. Later that year I set up my Cambridge college's first-ever women's football team. In 1990, I set up *Born Kicking*, a fanzine for women who love football. I managed four editions before the pressure of my law studies forced me to ditch it. I qualified as a solicitor in 1994. I never set out to be a sports lawyer but, in an extraordinary twist of fate, in 2001 I joined Sunderland AFC as their Club Secretary and Solicitor, having applied because I thought I might get a tour of the ground. I couldn't keep it together at my first game. In 2005 I joined the Premier League. In 2015 I moved to UK Sport. In 2018 I joined Women in Football.

Neither my father nor my mother saw any of this. My mother died in 1998. When I think back, she must have missed Our Saturday Afternoons – but she was to reignite our togetherness, and start a second fire burning in my heart, when in 1977 she took me to see Donald Sinden and Judi Dench in *Much Ado About Nothing* at Newcastle's Theatre Royal (although that is a whole other story).

For now, I reflect on football. And on the fact that all through my life since 1973, and to my continued astonishment, football has been ever present. I have never worked out if for nearly fifty years it has pursued me or I have pursued it. Sometimes it feels that for half a century, the two of us have been locked in an urgent, frenzied tarantella. But the metaphor of dance does not do this relationship – one of the most powerful in my life – justice. It has driven me. It has owned me. I have tried to tame it. Sometimes I have succeeded. I will never fully understand it. It will give me far less joy than I hope for, and far less joy than I firmly believe I am entitled to. Yet I will never walk away from it. For as long as there is an Ian Porterfield or a Marcus Rashford or a Lucy Bronze to create some magic – and the very essence of football is that they had their forebears and will have their successors – I don't want to walk away from it. I don't want to stop it provoking me, plaguing me, moving me, angering me, driving me.

Nick Hornby asks us whether all football fandom begins with some kind of Freudian drama in childhood. Mine's not hard to work out. Dad didn't take me to the FA Cup final when I was seven, and died when I was thirteen. We spend our lives seeking resolution of the dramas that drive us. Have I found resolution? Yes, of a kind, and very recently. In October 2020, a Women in Football board member and someone at the FA arranged for Women in Football's new logo to appear on the giant screens that adorn the outside of Wembley. Many of us at Women in Football unexpectedly found ourselves moved to tears. I was one. Not only did it mark a moment of triumph for all women in the game, it also told me a story of myself that ran something like this: 'In 1973, my dad wouldn't take me to Wembley because I was a girl. So all the paths of my life since have led to this moment, when I helped put our gender on the bugger in massive bloody lights.' Finally, after nearly fifty years, a Wembley moment in which I was truly involved had come. And there was more: in March 2021, Sunderland went to Wembley and – at the tenth time of trying since 1973 – they finally won a game there again. Sadly, neither I nor any other fans were there to see it. But my overwhelming emotion? Peace.

THE ACCIDENTAL GOALKEEPER

Julia West recalls taking the job nobody wanted – then found the fun in the role that might just encourage others to put their hands up.

I never had any intention of becoming a goalkeeper. My football journey began with me as a striker in a local senior team. But in one game, we were winning 15-1 when our keeper suffered a twisted ankle with fifteen minutes to go. The manager looked around at us, considering who to put in goal as we had used all our substitutes. Finally, she pointed at me and shouted, 'You, get over there and put that shirt and gloves on.' I was surprised but secretly relieved, as it was getting a bit uncomfortable up front. The goals just kept rolling in and I felt sorry for the opposition keeper. So there I was, accidentally promoted to goalkeeper. I had little to do in that first match, but it turned out our keeper had a broken ankle and so – after only minimal consideration, and mainly because I was the tallest player – the team's goalkeeper job was mine.

I had a revelation in those weeks of our keeper's recovery: I was pretty good at getting in the way of shots. I could use my hands well and had a reasonable first touch. Plus, I knew where keepers had difficulty with all my goals so I could almost anticipate what the striker was thinking. I enjoyed being able to see the game in front of me and having the opportunity to make a difference at this end of the pitch. Unless I made a mistake, I could appreciate the opposition's great shots. I liked challenging the striker to put one past me. When our keeper returned to full playing duty I had a stroke of luck: it transpired she had always wanted to play outfield and had only stood in goal to help out. My transition was complete.

It made me think, though. How many keepers accidentally fall into the role? Or, more importantly, how many potentially great keepers have we overlooked who have not even considered playing in goal? How does a player get inspired to become a goalkeeper? After all, it's not a glamorous role. At the recreational end of performance, there are long hours spent standing in a wet and muddy hole, the ball often gets stuck in the mud or hits a divot, and time after time you are made to look a complete fool. At academy level, you are likely to play on 3G or 4G pitches where, although your feet are dry, the ball skids very quickly off a wet surface and tests your responses. At the elite end of performance, there is real pressure to reduce your number of playing errors, and a mistake or fumble can cost a game, the cup or the league.

Goalkeeping does not get glowing references. There are always mistakes to analyse, since we are only human. Most things you read or hear about goalkeepers focus on their mistakes. Promotion around football in general relives the glory of the goal rather than the save, celebrating the scorer rather than the keeper. Goals are exciting, whereas saves are only good if it's your team and they are scoring at the other end. It can be a thankless task because all those saves give your team only the opportunity to find the winning goal; all that effort might earn your team a draw at best. Yet the best bits include those moments where you have pitted yourself against an onrushing opponent, they have pulled off a stunning move and your response is totally magic. Somehow you have redirected your entire body. Stuck out a hand or foot and successfully steered the ball away from the goal. And the great thing about all this action is that you are right at the heart of it all. You don't have to go looking for a touch on the ball. You aren't waiting for your teammates to pass you into the game. It is all right there, within eighteen yards; the action comes straight to you.

So how do we get players competing for the goalkeeper job? Are we doomed to have endless rounds of accidental keepers, relying on chance to find our next gem? Ask outfield players or coaches what a goalkeeper needs to be a good player and often they will say height. Is this all we look for in our future keepers? Yes, all keepers have an advantage when plucking the high balls out of the air before it becomes a problem, but this should not be the first or only consideration when selecting someone to play between the posts. Yes, keepers need to cultivate a commanding presence in the eighteen-yard box. But if they can use a wide range of skills and they can make effective decisions quickly, with the speed and power required to act on these, often at the last minute, then they do not have to be the biggest and tallest player on the pitch. If two goalkeepers had similar qualities and one was taller than the other, then I might agree that height is a factor. However, just as people have different strengths and abilities off the pitch, on the pitch some are better at taking high balls and commanding the aerial attack while some are better at stopping the quick hard shots in and around the box.

Creating a presence does not rely entirely on physical attributes. Of course, it comes through making great saves, handling the ball well and getting yourself to the right place very quickly, but it is also down to marshalling your defence, staying in touch with your teammates during the game, moving with the flow of the game and changing positions so you are always on the move in relation to the ball and your defence. With the right positioning, a keeper can make the goal look far away and impossible for the opposition to even consider having a shot at. It creates the impression that the goal is always covered, and a striker looking for an opportunity will be disappointed. Too often, I see keepers standing in their goal, shivering in the cold and wet of our winters, too afraid to come off their line even when the ball is not an immediate threat. The keeper looks tiny, and the goal looks big and inviting to the striker.

Good ball-handling is my number-one attribute for a goalkeeper, even in the modern game where an increasing amount of keepers' time is spent playing out with feet. If the goalkeeper can catch the ball, parry it to wide and safe areas or make strong deflections, tipping the ball over or around the posts, the opposition is less likely to score. Where possible, I prefer keepers to catch the ball to maintain possession, but making the ball safe includes steering it into a less threatening area or just spoiling its trajectory enough that the onrushing striker loses their opportunity for contact. The best keepers make ball-handling look effortless.

Quick reactions and being fast enough to respond to trouble as it develops in the game are important qualities between the posts. Quick reactions might not always look great, but if you manage to get something behind the ball you can usually block the shot. That might mean sticking out a swift hand or foot even when you are heading towards the opposite corner, or shifting your weight and momentum instantly from one direction to the other, or changing your flight mid-air in a fraction of a second. They are all part of the speedy reactions needed.

Perhaps the aspect of the role that comes under most scrutiny is aerial command: any save or clearance where the ball is shoulder height or above. Straight, hard shots bring their own problems as the modern ball moves during flight, but generally they are easier to intercept because the ball is coming towards you and there is more time to pick out the line of travel. By contrast, those fast, high balls crossed into your eighteen-yard box from the side are harder to judge. Typically, you have only a narrow margin to make contact with the ball first. Miss this and the likelihood is you will be picking the ball out of the back of the net. The calculations needed to identify interception must take into account the speed and height of the ball, the direction, whether it is in-swinging or out-swinging and how high you can jump to catch it first. All this happens before you start to consider the other players around you, every one of whom will be making similar calculations for different reasons. They are racing you to that point of contact. This can immediately put pressure on your judgement, but you really don't have time to question and second-guess yourself. If you can get in front of or higher than the attackers to touch the ball first, you will have won the tussle for now and created that all-important sense of presence. I have seen smaller goalkeepers with a bigger presence taking high balls so quickly and accurately that strikers don't realise what just happened. Successful aerial command relies on decision-making, speed and agility before height.

Distribution with hands and feet is another key aspect of the role. Where the goalkeeper holds the save, it makes sense to use hands for distribution as it is quicker than rolling the ball forwards and lining up the kick. Throwing is also often a better option after an attack as loose strikers close by might interfere with the kicking process. Unsurprisingly, there are lots of different ways to distribute the ball with the hands: throws for long or short distances, throws with power and spin to land accurately for an outfield player to control easily, loopy throws to cut out lines of attacking players, or rolling the ball out straight to a nearby outfield player's feet. Typically, girls and women are not as good at throwing for distance as boys and men – partly because girls generally have significantly less upper-body muscle mass than boys – but, in adapting our mastery of throwing, we can manipulate the technique to help us overcome this upper-body power deficit.

You would be right thinking just how much a goalkeeper has to learn and do. These skills are the generic ones, but there are also many types of dives as the ball comes in at different heights, speeds and angles. Then there are all the footwork skills. In the modern game, goalkeepers are using their feet more, creating links with their teammates. Taking back-passes involves good body positioning and a great first touch, enabling the ball to be redirected usefully and safely to a teammate. A good keeper really does need a wide range of skills and attributes.

So why does no one want the job of the goalkeeper? It just doesn't seem to be high on most people's must-try list, particularly in the women's game, where teams of all ages struggle to find goalkeepers willing to play. I have been tempted out of retirement a couple of times to play for local teams desperately needing a keeper to compete in local leagues. I have coached outfield players and managed teams in the past, and it pains me to say but one under-16 girls' side I coached fielded an under-16 boy to play in goal for a couple of years as none of the girls wanted the role. At the time, the FA age limit for mixed-team play was 16 (it is now 18) and so the next season, sadly, the team had to fold as they still did not have a female goalkeeper. When I asked why no one in the team wanted to play in goal, their responses included: 'I am too small/too short,' and 'I am not good with my hands.' Some particularly honest replies were, 'I am just too scared to dive at someone's feet,' and 'I don't want to make a mistake and let the team down.'

This last reply is understandable, as goalkeepers get a rough deal in terms of feedback from a poor game. They come under close scrutiny for errors they have made, often taking the brunt of criticism. Irritatingly this can come from players who have just admitted they don't want to play in goal. At the top level in the women's game, the level of scrutiny for keepers is even harder, yet there has been huge progress in training and match play over the past decade. This culminated in the 2019 Women's World Cup, where keepers showcased great skills and agility and were lauded by the commentators. It was the World Cup of goalkeepers. Until this tournament, whenever a keeper in the women's game made a mistake, it would be attributed to all women goalkeepers and cited as evidence that women are not great in goal. In the men's game no one claims that men are rubbish at goalkeeping when one keeper makes a mistake, but still there are calls to make the goals smaller for women. Why not make the marathon shorter for women while we are at it?!

All goalkeepers must be strong enough emotionally to withstand the relentless criticism and level of expectations everyone else has about their performance. Outfield players who make their mistakes can rectify them or they can hide within the team formation and get away with it. The goalkeeper does not have this luxury; there is nowhere to hide, and mistakes are only rectified by your teammates scoring at the other end if time and opportunity allow. In both training and matches, the keeper is often isolated from the rest of the team. Practising the varied range of skills required takes them away from the main session for significant periods of time, and it is hard to practice goalkeeping skills on your own as you really need someone to work the ball for you. The FA carried out a survey at grassroots level, asking young players why they play. The most common reasons were to have fun and be with their friends. But who can have fun when you know your mistakes will be up for public comment? Or when you don't get to be with your friends at training? Suddenly I can see why fewer young players put their hands up to become a goalkeeper.

So why do people actually choose to play in goal rather than get chosen? Well, you get to experience traditional football skills as well as ball-handling, agility and mastering the diving save. More outfield coaches are learning about the keeper's role and becoming better informed about goalkeeper training. The coaching courses we attend have goalkeeper content and there are now more specialist goalkeeping coaches, like me. We help our goalkeepers develop complex and athletic movement skills – and have lots of fun while doing so. Some of the motor movements you carry out are similar to Parkour or gymnastics moves, and the classic image is of a keeper in full flight, smoothly and effortlessly soaring to the top left-hand corner of the goal. (I have a picture like this on my office wall!) As a goalkeeper you have an opportunity to develop assertiveness and effective communication skills, repositioning your defensive unit to reduce the number of saves you need to make. You get to practise and refine mental strength and resilience. If you are playing with a supportive coach and team, outfield players will acknowledge their part in defeats and you can all strive together towards success. Some of my teammates would pick the ball out of the net so that I wouldn't always have to do it, which was a lovely gesture and allowed us to share a quick word of encouragement and focus. When my coach and teammates picked up on my successes rather than my mistakes it was a special moment and served to remind me that I was good at my role. Positive perceptions of competency also enhance self-confidence, which in turn has a good effect on performance.

Finally, the last couple of reasons that you need to consider becoming a goalkeeper are the best two reasons, and they make all the training worthwhile. Firstly, you are not expected to actually make the penalty saves. Not at all. Scientifically speaking, the acceleration of the ball from the penalty spot to the goal line takes significantly less time than a person can physically see the cue, make the decision and react to the ball. Even when testing goalkeeper anticipation and pre-shot cue detection, the ball is still too fast. Yet penalty saves do happen. Everyone gets very excited about one penalty save from the goalkeeper and you are made to feel like a king or queen for a day, with all previous mistakes forgiven. The feeling is sweet and dreamy. You are the power step to start the dive, you become the streak across the goal. It is your moment of glory.

The final reason you need to become a goalkeeper is that the keeper gets the best view on the pitch. No more surprises from behind; you face play for the entire match. You watch your team pass, move and strike. You move with them. You spot the attack and the sneaky strikers early because they are in front of you. You can plan your defence and refine the plan at a moment's notice. All the action happens right in front of you.

The modern game has undergone a marked change for goalkeepers over the years, with rule and role changes. Today's keeper adopts the sweeper role, playing more with feet and getting involved in the overall game frequently. Goalkeeper distribution and positioning are even more important to counteract the faster pace of the modern game. For all these changes, the number-one message to the number-one player is still 'keep the ball out of the back of the net.' There are more coaches including goalkeeping in their sessions, and there are more dedicated goalkeeper coaches who know what it is like alone in that eighteen-yard box where eighteen yards can feel like eighteen miles. But oh, that buzz. That moment when it all comes together. That silent challenge to the striker: 'Want to try? Fancy your chances?' Even if there is no save to make, you have forced the opposition to acknowledge you. It is a powerful feeling. As for those magnificent saves… I cherish mine even now.

How could you possibly not put your hand up to be the goalkeeper now?

A CULTURE STILL CRYING OUT FOR CHANGE

Katie Whyatt *reflects on the barbs in person and online trolling she has been forced to endure growing up as a female fan supporting Bradford City and in her job as a women's football reporter. Here she calls for football to hold itself accountable for the climate it has created.*

It's difficult, sometimes, to reflect on my existence in football: it feels at once political and apolitical. So often, I played football as the only girl, and operated not with a chip on my shoulder but a constant, underlying awareness that I was, as a result, a representative of all my kind. A mistake would not be mine alone but would mean that girls could not, and should not, play football. They were not as strong, as fast, as agile, and they could not control the ball as expertly. The worry that I was not supposed to be there, and was spoiling everyone else's fun, lingered until I was into my late teens and had discovered England's Lionesses. The summer of their World Cup bronze medal, in 2015, marked the first time that I could play publicly without the feeling of eyes on me. I felt free.

Yet I always was, to a point. My earliest forays into football were instigated, and sustained by, women. My mum took me to my first football training sessions. It was at an auntie's suggestion that we bought our first season tickets for Bradford City – my twin brother and I were nine – and she and my mum would take us each fortnight. Eventually, my brother drifted away and our party became all-female. I share the most exhilarating and draining moments of my life as a football supporter with women. My mum queued with me for pictures and autographs, drove me to my first press conferences in the university holidays, bought the kits each year and knew which name and number to get on the back.

She has leapt just as wholeheartedly into my move to covering women's football. She will follow the TV coverage of the games I'm covering, texting me her views. She travelled to Nice to watch England in the 2019 World Cup and ended up staying in the same hotel as Steph Houghton's family and bumping into the Lionesses at the airport. Her response to Chelsea Women reaching the Champions League final was to open a bottle of champagne to 'celebrate with Emma' Hayes.

Before going to Valley Parade, we would meet before kick-off, at my grandma's house, and she would follow the game on the radio. She cared because we cared. She would read all the match reports and interviews in the local newspaper. And every so often, she would supply us with a gem along the lines of: 'Dagenham and Redbridge? Are they playing two teams?'

It is odd to think that all you have ever known, and all you can ever be, is political. Even raised largely on a diet of men's football, I never really knew football without women. But to exist in a sport that has constantly disregarded and actively undermined women is in itself a form of protest – a fact I had not really considered until I interviewed the former England and Arsenal Women forward Lianne Sanderson. As a gay woman of colour, she felt that the Twitter trolls who clogged up her messages daily only pursued her in the hope that she would, eventually, stop. To continue was to defy them and to make a statement that gay women of colour belong in football.

For every woman to stay in football, dodging myriad obstacles on the way, is to do the same. Maybe it always will be until we reach total equality.

It is not always easy to feel safe, let alone represented, as a woman at a football match. The murder of Sarah Everard prompted a national conversation about female safety that startled men, who could not believe the lengths women had to go to. Many of us reflected on leaving grounds and press conferences hours after full time to be greeted by eerily empty streets and rapidly descending darkness, or covering women's games in remote stadiums outside of main cities, poorly lit and with no public transport links or Ubers, or train journeys crammed with drunk football fans chanting luridly.

Then there is the irony of football clubs rushing to hand out free sanitary products while failing to provide any sanitary bins. It is a curious existence: you are all too visible when you want to blend in, and ignored when you need to be seen.

It does not help that women are so often made to feel 'lucky' to even be allowed there in the first place, and that football culture can seem to operate with its own rules and power balances that outsiders are frowned upon for questioning. Women are viewed as too far removed from the masculinity that has traditionally dominated football culture to ever fit in but, at the same time, are challenged and targeted when they dare to deviate from gender norms.

I celebrated my sixteenth birthday by going to watch Bradford play Huddersfield Town in the League Cup. Wearing a pink vest, a female Town fan on the front row was gesticulating vehemently and chanting at the top of her lungs.

The shout tore through the away end: 'Who's the fatty in the pink?'

I squirmed. Those next to me joined in, chuckling as they went. I didn't. I was worried about how she felt to be bodyshamed in front of a whole football stadium. And not only bodyshamed, but shamed for singing, for waving her arms, for being passionate and emotional – all the things that male football fans are permitted to be, if not lauded for. Implicitly, the away end policed her actions, and policed what a woman was allowed to be in a football stadium. There, but not visible. There, but not engaged. There, but not loud and uninhibited. And they used her body to do so.

Antagonism between home and away fans is such an accepted part of football culture that it blurs the line between discrimination and acceptance. Was this the latter? Was this woman just treated as any opposition fan would have been? I have seen excitable male fans jeered and booed too. But this was not the same. I've remembered that night, and I wonder if she does.

* * *

I hesitate to use the word 'lucky' to describe my experience with trolls. In this context, it's a word I feel ambivalent towards at best. I am not – should not be – 'lucky' that I have avoided the worst abuse reserved for women with far higher profiles than me. To call me lucky – what purpose does that serve other than to normalise the death and rape threats that have formed part of Alex Scott's and Karen Carney's experiences as pundits? Am I the exception to the rule?

Perhaps, in refusing to wear that badge, I'm failing to see just how prevalent this level of abuse is for scores and scores of women. More damagingly – and most crucially if we're to see any kind of change – perhaps I'm overlooking how the climates we've cultivated in sport and wider society are not only disadvantageous to women but actively hostile.

My first week at the *Daily Telegraph* involved covering the rape and death threat directed at Karen Carney in October 2018. That was my first news story. By my own admission, I did not reflect on the significance of that at the time: I was learning how to prosecute breaking news, who to call, how to submit a Met Police media enquiry.

And truthfully, it felt closer to a one-off than to anything that risked becoming commonplace. Women in football are hardened to the more unimaginative jibes; it may come as a surprise to some Twitter users, given their undoubted wit, but they are not the first people to order me back into the kitchen or to make a joke about whether I am on my period. Carney's message was doubtless more extreme, and far rarer at that point. None of us realised how that story would set the tone for women in football – particularly women of colour – for the next several years.

Ignoring online abuse is easier for me because it is rare that I ever feel in danger. The trolls have stayed resolutely in the virtual world; my address has never been leaked online. I've never been threatened or needed to call the police. The old adage that trolls crave attention has always made me reluctant to give any of them oxygen, and I worry – rightly or wrongly – about inflicting mob justice on people who themselves might be vulnerable.

The majority of it isn't rational or reasonable enough to be worth losing sleep over. Put simply, I don't. There is no reasoned debate to be had around someone who has never met me ordering me to 'get a proper job' or chiding that 'this is the problem with women reporting on football' because they feel inexplicably threatened by a sport that poses no risk to the men's game. Those messages are frustrating more than anything. None of it is ever new. None of it is ever funny. There are reasons – which none of these men ever seem eager to acknowledge – that the women's game has vastly inferior attendances, and it is because men banned the sport at the height of its popularity.

For the entirety of my time at the *Telegraph*, I got so much criticism that it just became white noise. It will be immortalised below the line for anyone who feels especially compelled to look, and I just have. You can click on any of the pieces I did during my time there and invariably there is something.

'I could also write articles that no one is interested in – give me a job!'

'How much longer is this going to continue?' someone had replied to my exclusive interview with the world-record women's signing – a scoop for the newspaper.

'Truly cringeworthy!' reads one comment below a column on women footballers and their periods.

'I really, really want to know why you write a lengthy article that no one reads.'

From the World Cup final, I wrote a piece on Megan Rapinoe and the impact of her dizzying, dominant summer. A user had dived through my Twitter account and found that I had jokingly promoted the piece as a 'love letter to Megan Rapinoe'. Therefore, I was a lesbian and had written the whole thing in a fevered coital frenzy.

'Calling oneself a "Women's Football Reporter" clearly excuses you the need to write anything balanced, or even factual,' went one reply. Women in sport, as we well know, either are sleeping with everyone or are thinking about sleeping with everyone. If they'd looked further, they would have also found I'd talked about writing a love letter to the London Underground, presumably also to sleep my way to the top.

It feels strange to look back on those comments, because I didn't see half of them at the time. I cannot lie: I feel empty, like I've been gutted. I felt the same when, at the World Cup, someone sent me a picture of my by-line photo and told me I was so ugly that I must be a virgin. I feel angry, too, and I feel sorry for my younger self. Looking back, it was a lot to fall solely on a 21-year-old's shoulders every single day. No one had warned me that any of that would ever happen. No one really discussed it with me. The only thing that saved me was that I stopped looking. And I did so because I knew what they would write even before they did.

Then there was the letter. It was an advertisement from the sports section trailing my feature for the next day, 'Why men's coaches are flocking to the women's game'. The sender had written: 'Because they failed to make the grade in real football.' Next to my photograph, they had added: 'Don't let the wind blow you over, dear. And mind that your glasses don't fall off when you head the ball.'

I uploaded that to Twitter with the caption: 'More relieved than anything else that whoever sent this felt that the point was sooooo urgent that they used a second-class stamp to send me a newspaper clipping from 27 DAYS AGO. 70p for a first-class stamp. For 9p more you could have sent me one with Harry Potter's face on.'

The post went viral, liked more than a thousand times. What no one knew was why I found it so easy to jest: because I was emotionally numb. I was being treated for severe depression at the time. That day, I'd been to see a counsellor two hours from where I lived. I came home, alone, to find that letter. It didn't register to me as a violation because I had nothing left to give. It was just another thing to add to the desperately growing list of bad things. I couldn't be moved by it. So I laughed.

A CULTURE STILL CRYING OUT FOR CHANGE

I look back now and I think whoever authored that letter was lucky. Lucky that my depression had taken me to that place of utter indifference and emotional inertia. What if I had leaned the other way? What might the outcome have been then? Anyone else might have been totally cut to shreds.

Listing everything in full, it feels absurd that I even considered calling myself 'lucky' at the start of this piece.

* * *

In April 2021, the singer-songwriter Billie Eilish told *Vogue* that she did not know 'one girl or woman who hasn't had a weird experience or a really bad experience' with men. It garnered headlines across the world, and comments tinged with disbelief. I was more stunned that anyone could be surprised. I am certain that all women will feel the same. Online, men have commented on my body and sent me lewd messages. The first time, I was twenty. I'd been to the end-of-season awards at Bradford City. I'd uploaded a photo of myself and the two players with whom I was sharing a table. What I was wearing does not matter. Nor does how I was posing, or the angle of the shot, or who I was with, or any other possible straw anyone might want to clutch to somehow excuse what happened next.

The following day, over several hours, the comments crept in. Each one was about my breasts and nipples.

I sat on my bed in tears. I felt so utterly powerless and overwhelmed with anger. I felt violated. How dare they? What did they expect my reaction would be? Why was it that, at twenty, I was supposed to swallow down my hurt and to humour men more than twice my age? Why was the onus on me? Why was it always on women? As Eilish put it: 'Young women [are] expected to know and do everything and be everyone's mom when we're, like, fifteen.'

Something similar had happened to me in the flesh barely a year earlier. Bradford had played Millwall in the play-off final, and my mum, auntie and I were the only women on our particular coach travelling to London. It was a boisterous one: there were offensive chants, fuelled by the beers cracked open well before noon. It is hard to challenge that behaviour because – again – as a woman in football you are so often made to feel like an uninvited guest. That you are the intruder, and you must grin and bear it and play by their rules.

This is why I didn't say anything when I was sexually harassed that day.

My age did not matter, but I mention it only to give context to Eilish's words. I was nineteen and, once more, in the face of men decades older than me, I was as compliant and silent as society generally teaches young women to be. I wasn't a regular on that coach; I felt that it was 'their' day out more than mine. Men go to football matches and get drunk. Those are the conventions, and I should have known better. This was their space, not mine, and I had to be obliging and silent.

But they should have known better. Instead, I – a teenager – was burdened with everything that encounter meant.

I'd got up to go to the toilet at the back of the coach. Eight men, from their twenties to late fifties, bent out of their seats and insinuated that I wouldn't be able to aim if I didn't have a penis. They laughed – loudly, rollickingly – about how flat-chested I was. I tried to hurry down the aisle but I felt like their words had clung to me. I felt dirty, and like I needed to scrub them off. It is hard to explain how powerless you feel when men try to take ownership of your body. The term 'skin crawls' is exactly how it feels.

But girls learn early to get used to it. I wasn't at all surprised by Ofsted's announcement that sexual harassment in schools and colleges had become 'normalised'. I remember my first time, and the emptiness that lined my stomach as I walked the corridors alone until it made sense. I don't think it ever did. The solution was rarely to confront boys but to train girls to police their bodies. We had rules about skirt length – no shorter than two inches above the knee – before skirts were banned altogether because they were 'distracting to male pupils and teachers'. It is not only laughably rape-apologist but also setting an insultingly low bar to teenage boys to suggest they cannot control their sexuality. Girls were taught that they must shrink to stay safe. Everything was explained away as 'that's what teenage boys are like'.

A CULTURE STILL CRYING OUT FOR CHANGE

If we so robustly protect boys from consequence – when that is the climate in which we're raising teenage boys – can we be surprised when they grow up to be so intolerant of women sharing any space, and with little idea of how to reflect on their own behaviour? That they go online and can abuse without consequence, just as they have done all their lives?

It is right that we demand more from social media companies. It is harder to admit that we need to do more ourselves: as a society, as parents, as media, as educators. Maybe my existence in football – political or otherwise – will contribute to the right fight. But women – and specifically the next generation of young female journalists – should not carry all the responsibility to change the world. This is not their battle to fight alone and nor are the flaws theirs. Football must be accountable for the culture that it has created, reflected and enabled. Only then can women truly feel safe, welcomed and embraced, as they have always deserved to be.

GIANFRANCO WHO?

The name Zola has a huge literary cachet. But it was a book featuring the Chelsea player of that name, rather than the French novelist, that inspired **Renuka Odedra** *and dared her to dream.*

I have always been a bookworm. Reading offered a form of escapism, and my favourite class at school was English, especially when the teacher would read a book to us. While some of the kids in my class rolled their eyes and yawned, wishing the hands of the clock could move faster, I would be immersed in another world. *Beaver Towers* by Nigel Hinton, or any Jacqueline Wilson book, and then, as I grew up, the brilliant world of the *Noughts & Crosses* series by Malorie Blackman.

One morning my neighbour was going to the library with her kids and asked my mum if we would like to come along. My sister and I eagerly looked for even the slightest nod from Mum, who finally said yes, and off we went. An hour later I was waddling back down the hill with a bag full of heavy books, unaware that one book would spark my curiosity for football and a player called Gianfranco Zola.

We loved to pick through the library's sale box, where books were going for as little as 10p or 15p, seeing which front covers piqued our interest. Coming home after those trips, we would tip our haul onto the living-room floor, and my mum would roll her eyes, doubting whether we would even read them all. As I looked through my treasure trove from that day's pickings, one book stood out: *Cool!*, a sad and slightly depressing story, especially for a children's book. A child having a car accident and falling into a coma was not exactly the sort of uplifting subject you think a young person would want to read about, but the front cover was… well, cool. And reading *Cool!* left me with a lot of questions – not least, who was Gianfranco Zola? 'Well,' I concluded, 'he must be important because he is pretty much the hero of the book.'

Football was always a part of my life because it was a part of my brother's life. The theme tune for *Match of the Day* was seared into my brain because of the number of times I heard it on the television. Then there were the football sticker packs and cards. For my whole neighbourhood – and I have found this to be true for a lot of working-class kids growing up – Match Attax and Shoot Out cards were a must-have commodity. These cards were sold in your local corner shop, and featured the current year's Premier League cohort. Each player was awarded a star rating, which was where it got really competitive in the school playground. Like configuring a shady deal, the boys would gather in the corner at playtime to swap their doubles and boast about their five-star players: Andriy Shevchenko, Cristiano Ronaldo and Cesc Fàbregas. The first time I bought a packet – just to join in with my cousins – my brother glared as the shiny Fàbregas card came out of my pack. I think he is still secretly jealous to this day.

Apart from broadcasted games, my brother talking about it, and Shoot Out cards, football did not play a big part in my life until I read *Cool!* by Michael Morpurgo. The author's name was familiar to me because of his coveted titles like *War Horse* and *Kensuke's Kingdom*. Yet what drew me in was the cover: a Westie, a boy in hospital with tubes in his nose, a football, and a Zola shirt. It was a fairly short book and had pictures, so I dived in, despite having no idea who Zola was. Naturally, I asked my brother all my questions: 'Who was Zola? … Who did he play for? … Were Chelsea a good team?'

I don't remember his answer to that last question, but I would imagine it was 'no'. All – and I mean *all* – my cousins supported Manchester United. Sir Alex Ferguson was at the top of his managerial game, with a wealth of talent like Wayne Rooney, Paul Scholes and David Beckham at the club, so success was normal and expected from United fans. As a kid who could pick which football club they wanted to support, Manchester United had the allure. But I was always a maverick. I usually wanted to go against the grain, sometimes to annoy people but mostly because why follow the crowd, right? That is just boring. So, when I picked up *Cool!*, it sparked the start of falling in love with a team from west London, miles away from the terraced houses in Highfields, Leicester.

My siblings and I were never taken to football matches as kids. We were what hacks like to call 'armchair fans'. A stigma is often attached to the fans who do not support their local side or have not been to the stadium to see them play live, but not everyone has that opportunity. When Leicester City won the Premier League title in 2016, I could not have been prouder. My home city was finally on the map. People knew the name of Leicester, all because of this underdog team who played their way to the pinnacle of English football. And, oh my, was there some beautiful football played. But countless people asked me why I didn't support my local team. Well, here is the thing: cricket was king in my Indian household. That may be stereotypical, but it is true in this case. One memory that I hold dear is when my late grandfather would walk to the kitchen every half-hour or so to grab a cup of tea during the 2003 cricket World Cup final between India and Australia. Imagine a small living room packed with three families, the adults securing seats on the one sofa in front of the television. My cousins and I would take our place on the floor, snacks at the ready, waiting for the action to unfold in front of us. First- and second-generation immigrants all rooting for their motherland in that moment. The name of players like Virender Sehwag, Rahul Dravid and Sachin Tendulkar in the Indian team that day conjure memories of watching cricket as a child. But, in this match, victory was not to be. The wickets tumbled faster than my cousin, sister and I could run to the mandir (temple) in another room to say a quick little prayer. Prayer could not even save the horror to come. India lost and it was heartbreaking for us all.

The beauty of being a second-generation British Indian in Leicester was that my siblings and I got to choose which football team we would support. That is a big choice to make. I did not have parents who were Leicester City fans, so there was no baton to pick up and run with. Instead, I could choose my own baton, and that was liberating. No one could have predicted that picking out *Cool!* from the library's sale box would be how I chose my football team and career, but Zola was a hero figure in the book and later I would find out he was also a hero on the pitch for Chelsea. That's when I decided they would be the club for me. Besides, I knew Chelsea were forging a rivalry with Manchester United at the time, and what better way to annoy my siblings and cousins?

The Chelsea side that brings happiest memories for me is the one that José Mourinho first took charge of in 2004. That season, I immersed myself in the art of football, and suddenly the ruckus of the football commentary, with all its alien names, started sounding like poetry. Players like Frank Lampard, Michael Essien, Didier Drogba and Arjen Robben, whose names all soon became so familiar, were magical on the pitch, and it was a delight following them all season long and gloating about how well my team were doing. Football, I discovered, brought me joy.

As I grew up, I understood that Chelsea's owner, Roman Abramovich, was pumping money into the club and building the side into a real superpower in the Premier League. That meant you were almost frowned upon for supporting the club, and there was no shortage of criticism: 'They have just bought all their titles… You can't even keep a manager for more than a couple of years… They're not a proper football club, though, are they? … The fans are all glory-hunters.' This was only amplified by the larger-than-life Mourinho, whose ego was clear to see. He talked a big game, but it was all justified by the number of trophies he added to the Chelsea cabinet in his first season alone. He was hated by rival fans and adored by the Blues faithful, and for a while Chelsea played the role of the villainous club. As a fan, it was honestly fun to be part of. Although, for me, it was all about what was happening on the pitch: the excitement with each pass, goal and celebration.

I had been following the club for some time when the Champions League final of 2012 arrived. It was the one trophy we had dreamed about our team lifting. How I would have loved to be in Munich that night, but the tension that came with each passing moment pulsated to me and every other single Chelsea fan across the globe. This was especially true with the last kick of the game.

It all came down to penalties. Bayern Munich's Bastian Schweinsteiger missed his penalty, meaning we had the chance to finish the game. Would we be cheeky enough to win a European title in the German side's own back yard? Didier Drogba walked up to the spot and pulled up his socks... This was it. Cool as you like, ignoring Neuer's antics and the sea of red shirts behind the goal, Drogba slotted home. They had done it! The big-eared trophy was ours at last. What sticks in my memory is how some Chelsea players dispersed, slid through the grass to random parts of the pitch and had a moment to themselves. All their resilience and hard work, right up until the clock stopped, that is what won Chelsea the trophy that day.

It is not a surprise that when I reminisce about the past, football evokes happy memories. It was joy among chaos for the kids like me from a working-class background, with parents who would work mainly manual-labour jobs all week while we were at school. Whether on the television or having a kickabout in the playground and streets, football was our way of getting away from it all. Football stayed with me as the years went by, and soon enough I was at college and applying for universities. Life pulled all my childhood friends into adulthood, where the daunting questions arrived: What do you want to do? What do you want to be?

For a long time, I denied my passion for both writing (which derived from my love for reading) and football. Looking at the football media on television, listening to commentators on the radio and reading by-lines in the national newspapers – nobody looked and sounded like me or had a name like mine. I convinced myself that I did not belong in sports journalism. The football media industry was for white, middle-class and privately educated men. Even the women who did get a foot in the door were white women, so how was a woman from a South Asian background ever going to be given a chance? And so I stopped daring to entertain my dream of becoming a football journalist.

One pivotal moment changed this for me when I dropped out of Manchester Metropolitan University after less than a month. I hated the course and did not want to force myself to endure another week of it, let alone three more years. I was scrambling to see if I could join another course close to home, when a lecturer at the University of Derby tried to help me figure out whether media and communications or journalism was right for me. I told him I thought it would be best to explore the more theorised side of media and avoid the practical part, and he asked me who I admired in sports journalism. Jacqui Oatley and Reshmin Chowdhury were the first two names that immediately came to mind. Jacqui for the reason that she was a football commentator and I still thought football commentary was poetry at its best, encapsulating the excitement of football, in what I would later learn is a highly skilful job. Reshmin because she was – and still is – one of the very few women from a diverse ethnic background to report on football on UK television. She was the 'if you can see it, you can be it' factor for me, which is so powerful for marginalised groups. In that moment, it hit me that I was running away from what I really wanted to pursue, and I realised that I wanted to give myself the chance to achieve my dream.

It is sad that the thought I did not belong in the industry even crossed my mind. Yet, it is not uncommon for women like me. If I am completely honest, this niggling worry and dark cloud still passes over me from time to time. Am I good enough to be a sports journalist? Will I be accepted and respected as a South Asian woman in football? But I should not be scared that the colour of my skin or gender is an issue. No one should grow up feeling like this and shutting down their dreams even before they have had the time to realise them. It is this that keeps me going and fighting for my place in sports journalism. My dream is to be a respected sports journalist and to commentate on a football match for a national broadcaster one day. Can I not be afforded the chance to accomplish my dreams, the same as a white man?

Little did I know that pursuing my dream would take me back to football and Zola, but one evening while covering Leicester City at the King Power Stadium for my local hospital radio station, I saw the man himself. Turning around to get out of the long queue for a cup of tea in the media suite, I found myself face to face with *the* Gianfranco Zola. He was there as a TV pundit for the Leicester City v Chelsea game. I sat at a table with my co-commentator for the match and kept glancing over towards him and secretly beaming on the inside. Kick-off was approaching and so Zola left just as swiftly as he entered – and, looking at my watch, I realised I'd better make my way to the press box too. Alas I didn't get to speak to him, but life has a funny way of working, and it all came full circle for me in the most wonderful way possible in that moment: I was doing what I love, at a football stadium where there just happened to be the little Italian maestro himself.

The funny thing is I do not remember watching much of Zola play at Chelsea. He arrived at the club in 1996 – the year I was born – and left in 2003. I caught him playing at the tail-end of his Chelsea career. Watching footage of his wizardry on the pitch now makes me sad that I didn't get to follow his career a little more as a youngster. He was a gift to the game, just as the book he featured in was a gift to me. I would love to meet him properly one day and tell him how that book led to a pathway for me to dare to dream.

For a British South Asian woman, it took one book and Gianfranco Zola to find her love for football. And, in the mother tongue of the man himself, *il resto è storia*.

IS THIS THE REAL LIFE...?

Glamour, glory and glitches – **Alison Bender** *recalls how she helped set up, then presented, Real Madrid TV.*

I shuffle into position, squinting into the bright lights and tighten my hand around the microphone. My hand quivers, and I squeeze tighter to steady myself. Towering above me is the Santiago Bernabéu, the most majestic football stadium I have ever seen, its bright white exterior glowing against the inky Madrid sky on this balmy August evening. I don't know it now, but in a decade from now the image of this stadium will almost reduce me to tears of bittersweet nostalgia. This stadium will feel like a second home, although right now it feels totally foreign to me.

'*Diez... nueve... ocho... siete,*' I hear in my ear. I nod.

Everything about this evening feels exotic – from the Spanish chatter in my earpiece and the warm breeze on my face, to the red carpet soft beneath my skyscraper heels and my hair slicked back in a tight bun. Tuxedo suit on, like a matador, I'm ready for action.

Suddenly the noise levels rise – fans shouting and limbs waving – and I see why: David Beckham is walking across the red carpet, long locks flowing, a dazzling smile. He looks as comfortable as I feel nervous. He gets closer and closer until he's right next to me and I can smell his aftershave. Cameras are on every angle of us. It's the film premiere of

Goal! and we are live across the globe on Real Madrid's club channel. I should be excited but I'm too nervous to enjoy the moment.

'Focus, Alison,' I tell myself.

The hard plastic earpiece that sits firmly in my ear is my only link to the gallery, the room they call the 'central nervous system' of television, where all the production staff work. The only problem is that what I'm hearing is completely alien to me, as I don't speak a word of Spanish.

This moment feels like the culmination of all my years of hard work and hustling: making tea, running tapes, writing scripts, rolling autocue, setting my alarm for 3 a.m. to work a nightshift, studying journalism after my shift. Finally, someone is trusting me to do it for real and is paying me for doing what I've been dreaming of since I was a child. It feels huge. With the words '*En directo!*' in my ear, we are live.

I feel like I am exactly where I am supposed to be. Like a player when he crosses the white line, or a dancer on a stage, in front of a camera feels like it is my natural habitat. The adrenalin helps me perform; I find it both uplifting and intoxicating but it somehow allows me to centre myself. It's highly addictive, and is perhaps one of the reasons I love this job as much as I do. Once that red light goes on, I am in my element – like an exam I've prepared for, everything flows out of me and time disappears.

'Look at this reception!' I offer with a smile. 'Fans everywhere, just trying to get a glimpse of you. And now you are an actor – is this a step into Hollywood?'

'No, no, I'm a footballer...' he laughs. And we're off, chatting away and joking.

Before I knew it, I was high-fiving with the crew and drinking Estrella on plastic chairs outside the stadium. We'd done it, and it had gone without a hitch. Job done.

The year was 2005 and I was twenty-seven years old, living my best life. Somehow I'd landed one of the most incredible jobs in the world. I was in charge of launching a brand-new TV channel for Real Madrid at one of the most exciting times in the club's history.

They call it the Galáctico era, though it's a word I never used as it was banned from the channel and our club president, Florentino Pérez, detested it. We had Raúl, Roberto Carlos, Zidane, Ronaldo (the Brazilian one), Owen, Guti, Casillas – some of the most talented footballers on the planet – and it was my job to watch them train and play. Everywhere you looked, there was a footballing great. I couldn't quite believe my luck. At the same time I was so out of my depth, but this had always been my dream and so I had to make it work.

Rewind to the 1980s. I'm ten years old and I've just told my teacher I want to be a TV presenter. She laughs politely and puts it in the same bucket as 'ballerina' or 'footballer', I'm sure. But I'm deadly serious. I've been thinking about it constantly and write about it in my diary often. I've since framed one of those diary entries and it hangs proudly in my bathroom to remind me what happens if you want something badly enough.

A few years later, I am picking degree courses and universities and I suggest my presenting idea again. (By now I've had some experience too: every Friday night I work for free at my local hospital radio station. I visit the wards, asking old people what they want to listen to for my request show. It's a grim job and the wards smell of bedpans being changed, but I know it's a means to an end. I'm taken aback when one little old lady replies: 'Nothing, dear. I just want to die.') I'm doing everything I can to follow this dream and no one is taking me seriously. My teacher scoffs in one of our so-called career lessons: 'You need to do a proper degree. There's not a card in the box to cover this. You have to pick something else!' But I am adamant this is my calling – a strange choice for someone who is actually pretty shy, but I feel it burning away inside me and I won't stop until I get there.

Despite teachers doing everything they could to put me off, I followed my dream, studied hard, and straight after university I landed my dream job at a rolling news channel. CNBC Europe was in a towering building on Fleet Street by St Paul's Cathedral. I felt so grown-up getting the Tube into the city every day, passing suited and booted commuters and heading up to floor ten in the lift. It was a high-brow business news channel and my grasp of politics and business was poor, but I was being given a chance and so I worked ridiculously hard, learning off so many brilliant minds. I read the *Financial Times* every day, which was a big leap for someone who had not even read a newspaper at university.

This was in 1999. To put the era into context, I remember my boss telling us he had a brand-new phone that allowed him to read the papers on his commute. We were all awestruck; this felt like the height of technology.

That's where I found my first female role model, Maria Bartiromo, the first woman on the Stock Exchange floor. 'The money honey', as she was known (which sounds laughably sexist now but at the time felt like a valid compliment), was smart and attractive but didn't rely on her looks; it was all about content for her, and she worked her arse off. I wanted to be just like her. I watched the way she spoke, moved, presented and dressed. She was the reason I slogged away reading those boring newspapers: if I studied hard enough, I could be just like her.

I started on the bottom rung of the ladder at that channel, as a broadcast assistant, and worked my way up – cutting tape and rolling autocue, writing scripts and eventually producing shows in the gallery (which was, and still is, the most exciting part of TV: screens everywhere and a constant frenzy of excitement and adrenalin). Later, I ended up running the news desk, which involved forward-planning, booking and pre-interviewing guests – the perfect foundation for what lay ahead of me.

I worked there for about six years before deciding I felt ready to try my hand at presenting. I was told I lacked gravitas and didn't appear old enough, so I took myself to the City and bought some stiff-collared shirts and sat on set every night after my shift practising lowering my tones.

Those years were a blur. I worked the breakfast show, so my alarm would sound at 2 a.m. and I'd head into the office. I was supposed to use the day for sleep, but I had to get presenting experience, so when I finished my producing shift at CNBC I'd head off to do presenting jobs in the day, grasping whatever I could get my hands on. I did Shopping TV, quiz channels, The Community Channel, film-review shows, fashion TV – anything and everything I could to put a showreel together and do those all-important repetitions. I spent every other bit of time I had scouring the papers for opportunities and applying for jobs.

The audition for Real Madrid TV was just another application process; it was like many I'd had in that period – just another opportunity to get more on-camera experience. I had no idea what it might lead to or that it would end up being the most important audition of my life.

I remember it like it was yesterday: a small room in a TV studio just off Carnaby Street in London. The room was full of experienced hosts and presenters – some of them household names – and I was sure I had no chance. A couple of weeks before, we'd all been sent a script to learn. It was unthinkable to imagine we were supposed to learn two sides of A4, but that's exactly what I'd done. I pored over that script for hours and hours, learned it as if it was my part in a play. I think about that a lot now; opportunity is often disguised as hard work. That one single audition changed my whole career – my whole life, really.

I remember the moment I received the news, sitting on Clapham Common, drinking beers in the sun with my mate when my phone rang. Not only did they tell me I had got the job, but they also asked if I could be in Spain the following week. Those next few days were a whirlwind. I quit my job (with a very understanding boss who realised this was an opportunity not to be passed up), packed my suitcase and bought a one-way ticket to Madrid. It was the craziest, most impulsive thing I've done in my whole life.

I arrived at the Hotel Plaza de España, my new home in Madrid, with a huge suitcase of all my belongings. Before I had time to feel anxious or homesick, I was rushing to a local tapas bar to meet my team – the people who would be my new family for the foreseeable future. It was a rustic little place with wine barrels scattered around as tables with high stools, and cute little mosaic tiles on the wall. A huge hunk of jamón sat on the counter, and the beers arrived in little goblets. There were six of us, all under thirty. I decided I liked them almost immediately. We were all from different parts of the country and had little in common other than the fact that we'd be launching this channel together.

There was Dan, a cheeky chap who adored football. Claire was straight out of university but had a maturity about her. She'd played football for Doncaster Belles and clearly loved the game. Joel was bilingual and well travelled. Eric was French and sophisticated. He smoked like a chimney and rode a scooter. Then there was strong, independent Charlie, whose beauty hit me the second I entered the room. She was a fitness fanatic and took me on runs so long I felt like heaving my guts out. I'd never known physical drive like that in my life before.

How on earth had they chosen us lot? Most of us didn't speak the language and half of us had never presented a football show. To add to that, it became clear quite quickly that nobody had told them I had been hired as the producer in charge of overseeing the launch: I was their boss! But as the beers went down and the night ran away from us, soon I didn't care if I was in charge or not. We were a team, and we were going to make this work together.

'Is this for real?' Joel laughed. 'What if it's a social experiment? What if it's a reality TV show and there is no channel?' I knew what he meant – where was the production team? Where were the journalists? The script-writers? Who would make the graphics? We'd soon find out.

The site for Real Madrid TV, or RMTV, was in the middle of nowhere on a big industrial estate with a Spanish-language cinema and not a lot else. To get there you'd have to run the gauntlet: after a train and a tram, you'd walk across fields and dirt tracks, winding your way to the site. I had no idea places like this existed in Madrid. My pale English skin wasn't used to the harsh sun and I'd turn up red as a beetroot and delighted the studios were air-conditioned.

The studios were massive – the most impressive TV studios I have ever seen and about ten times the size of CNBC. They were in a huge warehouse like a hangar, with ceilings covered in lights and cameras, and three glossy, well-lit sets. There were make-up rooms with lightbulbs around the mirror. I stood there, staring at the jackets arranged in colour order across the rail by the stylists, and felt like I was in Hollywood. Like the whole Real Madrid brand, it oozed class. Even now, looking back on my whole career in TV, I'm not sure I'll ever feel so excited again.

My boss, Michael, gave us our brief: 'You have a month before we go on air, maybe less. We actually don't have a transmission date yet, but one day soon we'll press the button and we'll be live across the globe! The channel is yours; you can do whatever you want with it, but perhaps at the start just copy the Spanish version and go from there.'

Michael dealt in clichés and inspirational quotes, but he was exactly the kind of person we needed to believe we could achieve this. He was like Gene Wilder's Willy Wonka, arriving at opportune moments to tell us about some exciting new idea, waving his hands around in the bright blue Madrid sky as if he was visualising whatever he was talking about, and then disappearing as quickly as he'd appeared. With this job it felt like I really had won the golden ticket, even if I had seemed like an unlikely candidate.

Shortly after arriving at the set, I was thrust into a small meeting room with no windows. I surveyed the room; everyone was chain smoking. 'But I don't speak Spanish,' I protested. For the first time in my life, I couldn't chat my way out of it. There were two banks of computers, and every now and again someone would pick up a metal microphone. '*Uno, dos... uno, dos*,' and then they'd start recording, cigarette in the other hand. There seemed to be very little preparation but, right before my eyes, TV was being made as if it was a very normal thing.

I guessed this was a production meeting, but I couldn't understand a word that was being said. The tall bearded man who was speaking, Felix, would look over to me every now and again and smile or nod, and I would nod back. I have no idea why I stayed in that room for the whole forty minutes because none of it meant anything. I was scared and frustrated.

'So you understand a bit of what we said, right?' asked Felix, looking at me seriously.

'No,' I said, slightly welling up, 'I don't speak a *word* of Spanish.'

Thankfully Joel filled me in, and day by day our mission became more and more apparent. We were told we would have a whole production team of Spanish journalists and technical staff but the final shows would be broadcast in English. That meant the production people rolling video (VT), counting in our ear and putting up graphics would all be Spanish-speaking. It was time to learn the language, fast. We started putting together a glossary of words we would need in order to do our job.

It was very strange working in Spain with Spanish people yet creating an English product. I found it far more of a struggle to learn the language than I could have ever imagined. I used to chat with David Beckham about how bad we both were, and when he joked we should learn together I had secret fantasies that we'd become language pals and spark up some kind of special friendship! Of course this was never going to happen, but we were both a little misplaced and this one small thing connected us and made me feel I had something in common with this superstar. He would always treat me kindly with a soft smile, or kick a ball at me in training to acknowledge me. It meant a lot in those early days when everything else around me seemed confusing and foreign.

The club sent me to Spanish lessons, so my brain was always working; there was no down time. My knowledge of Spanish football was growing too because, if I wasn't working, I was reading – articles, autobiographies, learning tactics and memorising stats. I joke that I put myself through 'a degree in football', but the more I learned the more I wanted to know. I wanted to understand everything, to know the history of the club, the game and every competition. I took meticulous notes from the managers and pushed myself every day. This job felt different to any other job I'd had before: where every other job had felt like a stepping stone, in Real Madrid and football, I felt I'd found my destination. I guess I was falling in love with it.

We really were living the dream. The channel was 'our channel' so we could make it about anything we wanted. We decided it would be a mixture of news shows, training-ground reports, debate shows and lifestyle shows. We even had travel shows as we travelled across Spain and Europe for matches. It was the stuff of fantasies: I was creating my very own TV channel in one of the most beautiful countries in the world.

As our launch date loomed, though, I was afraid. I didn't feel we were ready. For months we had been presenting a show to no one. Now our boss said he was ready to press the button, but I wasn't so sure.

Everyone gathered in the studio to watch our launch. Eric was down at the training ground, giving updates. Dan and Claire were presenting the later news show, so they had done some interviews and put together our VTs on the big game ahead and our new signings. Joel had done a load of translation and voicing packages, and Charlie had been in Austria reporting from our pre-season camp. Our thirty-minute news programme was ready, and I was sat on the set with make-up fussing around me.

There was a camera on a long jib that swung around the enormous studio as the opening titles rolled. The music rumbled. Jesus, the director, shouted in my ear and I knew I was in vision but only from a distance. I could see the jib sweeping closer and closer to me, so I did some pretend paper-shuffling, something I'd copied from other newsreaders, trying to make it look as convincing as possible. I wrote a word or two on my script to make it look more realistic, but what on earth is a presenter doing writing down anything one second before they are due to talk? I just did what I'd seen others do. And then suddenly I could see my face in the monitor. I smiled: 'Hello, you're watching Real Madrid TV live from the Spanish capital. I'm Alison Bender.' It felt great. Everything looked so professional, from the set and graphics to my make-up and clothes.

As the show progressed, I realised I was either over or under time as I could hear the PA shouting numbers in my ear. It was petrifying. And at one point I called for a graphic to appear but no one understood my cue. 'If we can just take a look at the top of the table,' I said. But nothing happened. I ended up having to use the Spanish word *clasificación* for the director to realise that I wanted to cut to the league table.

It was a steep learning curve, but we'd done it. Fortunately back then there was no social media, so we had freedom to be experimental without too much criticism, and we were lucky to be able to grow.

The shows were one thing, but then there was the football itself. It became patently obvious very quickly that I wasn't a trained football journalist; I was a TV producer. I'd worked in a huge corporate with team meetings and daily debriefs, and I'd been part of a huge production team with very clear guidelines, but here I had never felt so alone. Entering the Bernabéu, I'd swipe my card through the turnstiles and jump into the lift. Journalists would chat to one another speaking over me; they belonged here. In those early days I spent more time looking around the press box than at the football, learning how I should be doing things. I didn't know shorthand and could barely touch type, so everything I did made me feel like an outsider. There was no one I could ask and no spare time, so it was all about learning on the job and getting by.

My time at Real Madrid TV was magical but also a rollercoaster. People came and went – managers, players, colleagues, but I was always doing what I love, presenting live TV, and I was in my absolute element. We lived in the sunshine and would travel to training sessions to watch the Galácticos train every day. It was a wonder to watch so many incredible players up-close in action. They played in a beautiful stadium, and the training complex was light years ahead of most clubs in those days.

The travel was incredible too. I ate paella in four-metre frying pans in Valencia, picked sweet fresh oranges off the trees in Seville, trod the streets of Pamplona where the bulls raged towards the ring, and felt sand between my toes in a seafood restaurant in Barcelona. I lay in crisp white sheets in some of the most glamorous hotels I'd ever seen and stepped off planes to exploding lightbulbs and fan frenzy. I led the life of a superstar, even though I was just borrowing it. I would often stand in front of the hotel mirror, staring in disbelief at where I had found myself.

After a few months of living in a hotel, I decided it was time to throw down some roots. I wandered the streets of Madrid, looking for rental signs, scribbling down numbers and checking out new areas. I pounded every cobble, discovering new cafés and neighbourhoods, walking miles every day. I crossed through Retiro Park into the posh business districts, where the well-heeled would pop out of their offices for a red wine in a wafer-thin glass and sip gazpacho in the shade of an olive tree. I crossed La Latina, where tattooed teenagers hung out in cheap bars drinking *Tinto de Verano* (a combination of red wine and lemonade). I walked down a street with gold poetry on the floor and practised my Spanish and sat in Hemingway's favourite haunts, absorbing the history and the culture. And then I found it: the perfect apartment slap-bang in the centre of Madrid in an area called Sol, where everyone gathers on New Year to eat twelve grapes as the clock chimes. I lived right behind that clock in an apartment on the eighth floor with a stunning view of Madrid. It was through two charming courtyards, a welcome respite from the blazing sunshine. The first was painted mint green and had laundry hanging in strings across it. The second was rose pink and was filled with the constant sound of Spanish chatter and tinny TV sets blaring out of the windows as the sun cast beautiful shadows around it.

I loved Madrid and the feel of the cobbled stones under my wedged sandals as I walked across Plaza Mayor to work, or stopping for a fresh orange juice as I read through a Spanish newspaper walking through the arches, and it quickly started to feel like home. I loved the people, the job – everything about it, really – and I couldn't see myself ever leaving. Football had become my life and it didn't get much better than working for Real Madrid at that magical time in its history. If I wasn't at home or the training ground, I was at my other 'home', the Santiago Bernabéu, to me the most beautiful stadium in the world. I watched so many glorious games there, including one where a shy, humble Zinedine Zidane was hauled onto the pitch by David Beckham to receive a standing ovation at his last home game as a player. Most matches were late kick-offs but you'd always catch those last glorious rays for the first half of the game during golden hour, squinting into the sunshine. The second half would usually be under a magnificent sunset, watching mesmerising football.

Matches and travel were the highlight, but the daily routine was long. I'd roll out of bed bleary-eyed around 6 a.m., usually with a hangover or at least recovering from a late night, and head to the studios for hair and make-up. I'd recite my lines and step onto set to record my lifestyle show, swivelling from camera to camera and doing re-takes until it was perfect. I'd then head off to the training ground, a forty-minute journey that made me car-sick every single time, probably as I was always learning lines. As I stepped out of the car, I'd welcome the players arriving and take my place on the balcony to watch them train, notepad in hand in the bright Madrid sun. After training there was a press conference and an opportunity for interviews, and this was just the start of my day. I'd head back to the studio, write, produce and read a news show and then finish the day with my journalist chat show, *Extra Time*, that ran until the early evening. It was relentless but I loved it, and it was teaching me so much.

I could have stayed in that job a lifetime and yet, before I knew it, it was all over. After less than two years in the job – albeit two years that felt like a lifetime – I was uttering my final words on my show, tears rolling down my face and flicking my hair across my eyes to make sure no one saw me cry. It sounds daft, as I wasn't saying goodbye to a fifty-year career, but it felt like my time had been cut short and I was so sad to leave it. Yet opportunities arise without thought for when you are ready, and this opportunity was one not to be passed up.

I'd been doing a piece to camera at Highbury (which tells you how long ago it was) as Real Madrid faced Arsenal in the Champions League. I could see a man watching me out of the corner of my eye. He came over and said he thought I'd be perfect for Sky Sports. I was pretty blown away, as Sky Sports felt like a big deal for a young, junior reporter in my first football-presenting gig, but he promised to make an introduction. That introduction led to a job offer that was too tough to resist – and one I was told was a one-time-only offer. I'd be anchoring Sky Sports News and also working at Chelsea TV after I sat an audition there. I knew I had to go. I remember Andy Melvin, the head of Sky Sports, telling me, 'It's not as cosy or comfortable here in the Premier League. It's not all glamour like you have in Madrid. The journalists here are tough to crack, but if you can crack them then you'll have a successful career.' I was scared and conflicted, but it felt like I had no choice but to go. I felt like I was letting my team down, as I was the first one to leave and we'd been on this amazing journey together. I was sad, and I knew I'd never have a job this good again, yet something was pulling me back to England.

The history of Real Madrid had seeped its way into my body, and I supported the club and everything that came with it. I'd enjoyed so many precious moments here and there had been so much sacrifice. I felt such sadness at leaving the club and vowed to continue watching every single game, and even now when I think about my time at Real Madrid I feel such emotion. But that was it, I was leaving Madrid – my morning fresh orange juice in the courtyard, my apartment, the bar where you take off your shoes and socks and stand in the sand, my friends, the incredible football – I was leaving it all.

I never learned Spanish with David Beckham like he joked we would. I never stayed to win the league like I hoped we would. But many of those players I would meet again, and the experiences would be the bedrock of a long career in football that I never knew I'd have. As my taxi drove past the Bernabéu on my way to the airport, I took one final glimpse at the stadium – the place where it had all started, the place where I fell in love with football.

MUMS UNITED

Christina Philippou *reflects on the trials, tribulations and sheer fun of setting up a football club for a group often forgotten by the game.*

FIFA often refer to the 'football family' and emphasise the importance of inclusivity and diversity. We've seen acceleration towards this goal in practice, with the US national team's lawsuit for equal pay, the FA losing their chairman as a result of racist non-inclusive comments, and a large number of clubs and leagues supporting Black Lives Matter. There are now role models and pathways for young girls, disability athletes, black coaches, and even increasingly popular walking football for those of a certain age/injury level. Yet the member of the football family who is consistently forgotten is also the one most closely linked with the term 'family': mothers.

It's not all bad news. FIFA bringing in a global maternity policy for athletes, in late 2020, is a reminder of just how far the football family has come since the days when women were banned from playing. Famous athlete mums who have shared their frustration at their 'slow progress' in returning to the game postnatally have helped shed a light on the darkness of childbirth. (Although, seriously, Alex Morgan? At 184 days post-birth, I was lucky to be able to drag myself to the local shop and back without collapsing.) Tired, broken and overwhelmed – even before adding in paid work and pandemics – mothers are marginalised both outside and within the football family.

Onslow Mums FC started, as a lot of these things do, with a random throwaway comment. At a book club one evening, Anna Kessel's *Eat, Sweat, Play* – a book on why more women don't do team sports and why they should – inspired a drunken 'Yes, why *don't* we play team sports? Chris, you play team sports – shall we sort out at game?' A shrug, some loud cheers worthy of a rowdy crowd in a capacity-filled stadium, and a mums' football WhatsApp group was born.

It is true there is a dearth of options for women interested in playing competitive or team sport in their thirties and forties. While there are multiple veterans teams and turn-up-and-play leagues available for men, the FA rules around mixed football (loosely translated as 'women, piss off now you are eighteen') make it almost impossible for women to get involved given the small number of women players in that age category: the numbers just don't exist for leagues, and women are effectively excluded from playing casual football with men if there are qualified refs or FA-involved organisers.

Back to the WhatsApp group that I had expected, as with most drunken ideas, to go no further. Something unexpected happened: by Monday morning, the group – ten of us initially – had more than fifty members, and the clamours to start something were echoing round the community. Cue the usual admin challenges associated with grassroots sports: agree a time and date to suit as many people as possible, find a pitch, work out funding and pricing, and source equipment. It was impossible to get a pitch on a weekday evening (the most popular choice among the members), so we settled on a Sunday-evening slot at the local sports club. I hunted around my garden for size-5 balls, borrowed bibs from the local dads' kickabout team, and decided on a price that would cover pitch hire and an equipment kitty. Deep breaths required.

Our first session found me pacing and chewing my lip and hoping we would have at least eight along to get some sort of a match going and cover most of the pitch costs. I needn't have worried; more than twenty turned up. A quick show of hands at the start revealed only one had ever played football before, and that at school a few decades back. Five years of coaching the under-6s came in handy as I started the session with a very basic 'this is how you kick a ball' explanation. That session, out of all of them, has seared itself in my brain. As someone who grew up surrounded by football – both my mum and stepmum are die-hard fans, and I always played with my dad and brothers when we could – the concept of not knowing the first thing about kicking a ball was shocking to me. One mum spelled this out as 'I was never taught how to throw, how to catch or how to kick at school or elsewhere, but people automatically assume that everybody knows how to do this and so I have always been labelled as being bad at throwing, catching, and kicking.' (Spoiler alert: she's not.) It's a simple point, but one often forgotten in 'families' where anything football is second nature.

Laws of the game had to be explained. I found myself drawing diagrams and creating videos to talk through rules and regulations that were so entrenched in my brain I never realised they were actually rules and regulations. Forget the offside rule (which, perhaps because it's often used as the definitive 'women know nothing about football' test, was the one best known and understood among the group); these women needed to learn the difference between a throw-in and a corner, or between a corner and a goal-kick, and what a kick-off was. There was also the issue of terminology – blank stares greeted me as I instructed the mums to 'stand goal-side', pass the ball 'square' or 'down the wing', or 'cross it in' – and so a football jargon glossary got created.

Finally, play could commence – and the mums were brilliant. Given that many of them 'hated football', 'hated sport' or were just battling with fitness, they threw themselves into the warm-up skills and subsequent matches with an enthusiasm and relish I have not witnessed in a lifetime of watching, playing and coaching. It was the raw epitome of beauty. 'People come out and play football without fear… Everyone supports everyone else and the atmosphere is great,' as one mum put it, perfectly expressing what I witness on a weekly basis.

As the team was set up for mums (although we have, in the spirit of inclusivity, welcomed non-mums too and so renamed ourselves Onslow

Ladies), we take a 'turn up and play' approach to ensure maximum involvement. The group members who are yet to attend have all cited reasons linked to childcare: 'extracting myself from the kids', 'personal family circumstances' and 'childcare arrangements are all that stops me'. Many research surveys – including those highlighted by Sport England and This Girl Can campaigns – have recognised childcare (and guilt linked to it) as a key deterrent for mums getting involved in sport, so we work around this by not having monthly payments or other barriers but by allowing members to pay per session. More than 10 per cent of our members attend 'when I can' (i.e. less than once a month), with only a third making it almost every week, and this flexibility has been key to ensuring the sustainability of the project. We also place a continued emphasis on the casual nature so that no one feels intimidated as the more regular attendees' skills improve in leaps and bounds.

The biggest emphasis, however, is on fun. The change for many from being someone who 'never had any confidence in team sports, was never picked at school and therefore assumed I was just no good at all' to someone who 'would never have thought I'd start football in my forties!' is a common theme. The laughter reverberates around the pitch as mums of all shapes try to grapple with this round thing at their feet. So important is fun that the team rules include 'saying "sorry" is not allowed' and 'try to keep squealing to a minimum', while goal celebrations are mandatory (apart from when FA rules prohibit them due to Covid).

Community spirit has been fostered too: mums on the school run now reminisce about events on the pitch on Sunday night. 'It's really great to be part of such a supportive group who are all enjoying playing football and encouraging each other to have a go at new skills and get better. If only sport had been like this at school I might have got involved in team sports years ago,' said one mum, while 'sense of community/belonging' came top in our last two annual member surveys as a benefit of joining the team.

The comedy has helped. We've seen phenomenally impressive yoga-move saves, incredible (if often unintentional) turns and flicks, and a particularly hip-displacing 'do not try this at home' twerking defensive block. There was one move that sent me running to the Laws of the Game: a player chested the ball and kept running with it balanced on her ample bosom. Aside from the defender challenging for the ball, the rest of us stopped and watched in awe as the ball refused the calls of gravity for second after excruciating slow-motion second.

The positive effects of this project have not just been felt by the women involved but also by the wider community as starkly as the cliché 'team spirit' encapsulates. As one local dad put it, 'I used to have to argue over the remote, but now we get to watch football as a family and that is simply awesome.' More women are now watching the game as playing has increased their understanding and interest. One mum came into the pub during the 2019 women's World Cup, laughing, 'I just had the most surreal conversation with my mother. I told her that I had to hang up as I had to go to the pub to watch football with my football team. First time I've ever rendered her speechless.'

We've seen an effect on family play too: the local recreation ground – once filled with dads playing with their sons, for the most part – now sees a lot more women involved in impromptu kickabouts, and a third of our members said their daughters are now playing football as a result of watching their mums play and enjoy it. Nearly half of our members say they never used to have kickabouts with their family but now do, with comments on this including 'the kids love it when we play together' and 'we've always enjoyed kickabouts but now I'm more competitive!' Additionally, the local football clubs have seen a vast increase in girls playing from the under-10s down (and the creation of more teams in each age group as a result). One mum noted the importance of 'role modelling the enjoyment of sports for my kids', while another said presenting herself as a 'positive model for my daughter's football journey' was one of the benefits of joining the team. But it's not just about girls: although lots of members had sons already playing, 'kudos with my young boys' and 'playing sport with my sons' were also some of the benefits cited.

Health effects of team sports can never be underplayed. With this particular demographic, it is even more important as so many fall into the quagmire that is motherhood, where everybody takes priority over you. 'It's brilliant and great to have some "me time" away from the kids and work' is a common sentiment among the group. 'It's bloody brilliant to have an excuse to get out of the house for an hour or so on the Sunday to do something just for *me*,' said one mum. Making exercise fun means plenty of our members now have an opportunity to get involved in exercise where they 'might not have bothered before'. As one mum remarked, 'I love the team spirit and getting to run about the pitch, building up fitness without noticing too much that I'm running!' Another noted that, 'Football has gone from having no role in my life whatsoever to being the highlight of my week. It gives me a reason for staying fit and healthy the rest of the week, and it's something I look forward to all week.' A third said, 'It has switched my focus from doing exercise to get fit, to having fun playing a game while also getting fit.' There are many more members' comments revolving around fitness and confidence in some way, but the common theme is that football has inspired them to 'improved fitness confidence post-babies!'

The mental health aspects – especially in view of what a joy the 2020/21 season turned out to be – have also been great. 'It's a major part of my week, has boosted my self-esteem (I'm not as terrible at team sport as I thought) and motivates me to improve,' noted one mum, while another said, 'It's really the funnest time of the week! I come away feeling good in mind, body and spirit. And the buzz lives on in the WhatsApp group the other six days.' Unsurprisingly, given the juggling of home-schooling and work (and that's for the lucky ones), mental health was the most talked-about issue in our 2020 member survey and was summed up by one mum as: 'I always get home in a better mood than when I leave it, which is good for all the family as well as me!'

Now let's pander to stereotypes and talk shopping. Administrative logistics over kit highlighted how poorly supplied the female market is. I don't know why I was surprised, considering global kit manufacturers' propensity to ignore women in the market, but hours spent wading through the internet in search of a non-exorbitant team shirt supplier brought too many responses to name that involved the phrase 'unisex kit'. To clarify (and the fact that this needs clarification is infuriating): there is no such thing as a unisex kit when it comes to adults. 'Unisex' simply means 'male' – a lesson learned from decades of playing in ill-fitting kit that was too tight around the chest area but tent-like around the waist. We finally found a supplier who only did short-sleeved kit, but by that point we were close to settling for 'slim-fit unisex kit' (read: still tent-like but more sleek modern dome than old-fashioned flapping triangular tent). That the sizing required almost everyone to settle one size up from what they usually wore felt less painful after the drama of finding kit in the first place.

Then there is the football itself. Yes, we have emphasised teamwork and fun. Yes, we have giggled and come close to wetting ourselves (thanks to incontinence being one of the wonderful side effects of childbirth) on a large number of occasions. And yes, we have refused to take ourselves seriously when it comes to mistakes. However, there has also been mass improvement in skill level during the couple of years we have been running. While 'being slightly less scared when I get the ball' and 'improved accuracy' are easily addressed, there has been great progress too in spatial awareness and ability to control the ball. As our players have become more comfortable on the ball, they naturally look up as they run, which means they no longer look like hunched chickens but graceful footballers.

When Covid hit and the first lockdown ground football to a halt, the group continued to support and entertain each other. Balls were distributed to those who didn't have any at home, videos from the FA were shared, and challenges set. Members sent each other footage of themselves practising skills and attempting everything from balancing footballs to Cruyff Turns, alongside images of their kids doing the same. 'It really kept me sane, just being able to do some of the challenges in the kitchen during down time,' said one of our members who works for the NHS. The constant in-and-out of lockdown in 2020/21 tried our patience and sawed at every last nerve but, even then, the idea of football helped: 'I felt so low all weekend when lockdown 2 was announced on the Saturday, but forced myself out the house to go to football and afterwards felt like I could handle it and it'd be OK. Partly because I'd had so much fun and partly because we were all feeling similar and like we're in this together.' And as the lockdowns continued, we took the opportunity to hold an online awards ceremony to celebrate our season-and-a-bit of 'mums' football'. From the runner-up for Best Goalscorer (who had genuinely struggled to dribble when she first joined), to the winner of the Players' Player award (whose constant support and meticulous scorekeeping kept us endlessly amused), to the hardest award to vote for: Most Improved (who struggled to hold back tears when I dropped off her award), there were a lot more worthy mums than trophy funds allowed.

Today the members keep on coming. When I ask new joiners how they heard about us, the answer is inevitably, 'I've heard so many of the mums raving about it on the school run and I thought, *If they can do it then so can I.*' And yes, they can, although it should come with a health warning, as one of our new joiners' partner despaired, 'What have you done to my wife? She was doing lunges on the school run this morning and when I asked her what she was doing, she said she was stretching in preparation for football on Sunday!'

A tour is next on the list, although finding similar clubs to ours is hard because there aren't many. Since we started, we have won a community sport award and I've spoken to community directors at a number of clubs and federations about the project. Their response is similar and can be summarised as 'we want mums, but can't seem to get them to come along.' In order to spread more of this around the country/globe, we need to concentrate on the barriers. 'I was nervous about joining,' said one of our mums, 'as previous experiences of joining sports teams as an adult (I tried netball and hockey a few years ago) weren't great, as my lack of experience and subsequent mistakes proved to be frustrating to the skilled players.' Similarly, instead of having fliers showing fit-looking women running at the camera – as a local 'all welcome' team does – I'd advocate targeted, relatable advertising such as that adopted by a similar club showing what could be a grandmother modelling their kit. 'Anyone welcome' should mean *anyone*, not just fit people or those who have played before.

Of course, the comments from third parties have not always been supportive, and I still overhear snide remarks about aspects of the mums' control, passing, shooting and dribbling. But these comments are both increasingly rare and drowned out not only by the mums themselves (with their improved confidence) but by the kids and partners who have also indirectly formed part of this journey. One mum's remark that 'I always hated group sports at school and hadn't played any since I left at sixteen. It was a great surprise that I really, really enjoyed football on a Sunday. I would encourage others to give it a go as it's genuinely enhanced my life,' articulates this journey better than I ever could. And, if nothing else, more than seventy members and a weekly turnout of more than twenty for a group of tired and overworked mums on a Sunday night is testament to the importance of projects like this to support and encourage all members of the football family, not just the ones we are used to seeing and idolising.

AT THE COURT
OF ST JAMES

From shameful snubs by male journalists to the story of the player who ended up in A&E after an overdose of Viagra, **Louise Taylor** *has seen and heard it all as a national newspaper football writer in Newcastle. Here, she shares the lows and the highs covering one of the English game's great soap-opera clubs.*

It is the early 1990s and final-year Durham University students are filing through a tight passageway inside the city's Three Tuns hotel before taking turns to receive careers advice in a borrowed backroom.

Two chairs occupying a quiet corner between the bar and a staircase have been commandeered by Newcastle United's goalkeeper and a young female journalist, freelancing for the *Sunday Times*.

Even by the standards of the era just before corporatised 'media training' took hold and started draining too much originality and controversy from so many interviews with footballers, Mike Hooper is unusually open, honest and... well, human. He tells me about the pressures of keeping goal for Newcastle and the day his car was stolen in Liverpool while he played golf.

After a while a tall, trim, briskly efficient-looking older man walks past, his arms full of files. It's Mr Hudson, the careers advisor, who, a decade earlier, had diplomatically advised a third-year law student to 'grow up' when she told him of her plan to become a football journalist, and, more specifically, the north-east football correspondent of either the *Observer* or the *Sunday Times*.

Mr Hudson doesn't recognise me as he walks past, but he shoots Hooper a second, slightly startled, glance. Driving back down the A1 to my new house in a village south of Darlington, I turn the music up loud and squeeze the accelerator a little harder.

The crazy career decision made one night in 1983 when a twenty-year-old football-obsessed Sunderland supporter sat in a small, shared, ground-floor television room inside Durham University's Trevelyan College and watched Julie Welch's brilliant *Those Glory Glory Days* had somehow become reality. Life felt good.

Be careful what you wish for…

* * *

The invitation to the North East Football Writers' annual dinner was welcome but, to someone who had spent the previous six years attending loads of that type of thing in the course of her junior football reporting role at *The Times* in London, also pretty routine. Then the phone rang. The man on the other end seemed embarrassed. He was terribly sorry but I was de-invited. The other locally based national newspaper reporters didn't want a woman there and were adamant it was a male-only do. I spent the night at home alone but contacted the national FWA – as a member, I'd attended several previous national dinners at London's Royal Lancaster Hotel – and they made it clear to the north-east branch that a woman could not be excluded.

A reluctant admittance to the fold followed, but conversations often died as I approached and there were a few 'stitch-ups'. The day Kenny Dalglish was sacked as Newcastle's manager, he asked a colleague to relay the message that he would meet us all in a Tyneside pub for an off-the-record debrief. Judging by the whispering going on at an unrelated press conference that afternoon, it was clear something was going on but, not for the first time, the party invite never arrived. Shortly afterwards there was a half-hearted apology. Dalglish – taciturn in press conferences, generous and emotionally intelligent once the tape recorders were switched off – had apparently enquired where I was and some of the 'chaps' felt slightly uncomfortable.

One of them later told me I must have a very thick skin. I didn't, but I was partly in denial, partly naive, loved football, adored writing and remained extremely determined to make it work. During a youth spent mainly in southern England but also featuring two interludes in Lebanon and Egypt, I'd romanticised both the North East and the realities of football journalism. If a small part of my subconscious said it was all a ghastly mistake, I ignored it. Anyway, it was surely destiny; there had to be a reason that as a twelve-year-old, I'd filled a school exercise book with a Watford v Sunderland match after my father took me to Vicarage Road. Besides, what else was there to do? Law didn't appeal, my parallel fantasy of becoming a Middle East correspondent foundered on a struggle to learn Arabic, I had a contract with the *Sunday Times* and page leads flowed.

Above all, the football was fantastic. The move from London was made in time to be at Grimsby's Blundell Park to witness the joyous pitch invasion from the away end as Kevin Keegan's Newcastle won promotion to the promised land. To say they switched the recently formed Premier League's lights on is no exaggeration. The story of Special K, his entertainers and their agonising forfeiture of a twelve-point lead over Manchester United at the top of the 1995/96 table has been told many times but, looking back, it all seems part of a charmed, increasingly distant world.

There were the daily Keegan press conferences at Maiden Castle, the Durham University Sports Ground that Newcastle then shared with students and where literally hundreds of fans routinely turned up to watch Les Ferdinand, Andy Cole, Peter Beardsley, Rob Lee et al. strut their training-ground stuff. David Ginola – who offered me red wine as I interviewed him in the lobby of the then pre-eminent Gosforth Park Hotel – could not believe how 'amateur' it all was and found it hard to compute that lunch arrived via the daily sandwich runs to Marks & Spencer undertaken by Keegan's sidekick, Terry McDermott. These days the Gosforth Park is a faded three-star member of the Britannia hotels stable, and sports scientists and dieticians swarm all over Newcastle's high-security training ground, aiming to create that vital extra percentage of fitness that might, somehow, keep the team in top tier.

If the idea of a journalist drinking wine – or even water – with an interviewee without a club PR minder or agent in sight has become almost unthinkable, the same goes for the moment, in January 1995, when Keegan stood at the top of a short flight of steps to the right of main reception at St James' Park and argued the toss with angry fans. He had just sold Andy Cole to Manchester United and, for the first time, the Toon Army's adoration for the man many believed capable of walking on the Tyne no longer seemed exactly unconditional. Keegan talked them round in much the same way he banished doubt from the dressing room.

'We never practised set pieces. Kevin said he found dead-ball routines boring,' said Rob Lee. 'But he always made you feel ten feet tall.'

John Beresford, the left-back, recalled Keegan standing up in the dressing room shortly before kick-off, scanning the team sheet in his hands and saying: 'Jesus, if we're not 2-0 up against this lot after five minutes we're doing something wrong.' By way of emphasising his point, Newcastle's manager proceeded to screw that bit of paper up into a ball, hurl it into a bin and motion his players towards the tunnel.

Their talent-studded, improvisation-rich brand of tactical anarchy took The Entertainers a very long way, but then in February 1996 Faustino Asprilla stepped off a plane at Newcastle airport and walked through a snowstorm wearing an oversize fur coat. It wasn't the maverick Colombian's fault, but Keegan had imbalanced his team. As the Tyneside gossip grapevine thrilled to tales of gunshots heard during a party at Asprilla's rented Ponteland mini mansion, and club staff despaired of the striker ever turning up for training on time, Sir Alex Ferguson's Manchester United ghosted up on the blindside and snatched the title. Keegan's days on Tyneside were numbered but there was still time for him to make Alan Shearer the world's most expensive footballer by bringing the Gosforth-bred England striker 'home' from Blackburn for £15 million.

The kindly and supportive London-based editor who had feared exchanging the Thames for the Tyne might involve 'falling off the edge of the journalistic world' had been overly pessimistic. Back in the late 1990s the North East emerged as a key football-reporting hub, with the task of chronicling the colour and chaos of its on- and off-field events often as challenging as the toughest of those English Comprehension tests favoured by secondary school teachers in the 1970s.

At Newcastle, Dalglish succeeded Keegan but, although Asprilla would score a Champions League hat-trick against Louis van Gaal's Barcelona at an electrically charged St James' Park, Dalglish's key attacking signing, Jon Dahl Tomasson, failed to rack up the goals demanded by the Gallowgate End. Tomasson, currently managing Malmo, went on to star for AC Milan and Denmark, winning the Champions League and scoring goals galore for clubs in six countries but, at that time, English football was far too elemental for his specific talents. Midway through an interview, Tomasson took hold of my notebook and pen before sketching out a mini tactics board full of Xs and little circles as he explained precisely where he needed to be played and when teammates should be making decoy runs. The Dane's cause was hampered by the injury to Shearer, which prevented him playing off Newcastle's number nine, but, as the Leeds United striker Patrick Bamford puts it: 'Grass isn't always greener on the other side; it's greener where you water it.'

Unfortunately for Shearer, Dalglish's successor, Ruud Gullit, evidently failed to get that particular memo. Indeed, the former AC Milan and Holland star had no sooner swaggered into Toon than he parked his tanks on Shearer's front lawn and the north-east football media found themselves reporting on an internecine civil war. As the stand-off between the local hero and their swashbuckling new manager intensified, Newcastle fans were torn. The city has always loved its bling, and the former Chelsea manager was glamour personified. They adored the pictures of Gullit gracefully vaulting a fence at Newcastle's new training base at Chester-le-Street's Riverside County Cricket Ground as he took a shortcut into training, and there was a brisk trade in tribute dreadlocked wigs repurposed from kitchen mop heads. At one point, every other fan inside St James' seemed to have one on their head, and the excitement reached fever pitch when Gullit – who commuted daily from Amsterdam on KLM – introduced a fresh pair of legs, flying into Newcastle airport with his fiancée Estelle Cruyff ahead of a joint shopping trip to the Gateshead Metrocentre. Such a jaunt – complete with trailing cameramen – would probably have provoked little more than mild interest elsewhere, but, although a conurbation, there remains a lingering village-style element to life in Tyne and Wear. It was more pronounced in Gullit's day yet, even now, almost everyone not only knows someone who knows someone who plays for Newcastle but can also tell you an anecdote about them. The young Newcastle footballer who took Viagra out of curiosity and required hospital treatment when his erection failed to subside did not remain anonymous for long.

Given this 'goldfish bowl' habitat, there was no concealing the growing stand-off between Gullit and Shearer, with the former erroneously believing the latter to be past it and, in a significant miscalculation, also sidelining his close friend Rob Lee. At the time, arguably only Manchester United's Roy Keane was a more influential central midfielder than the often-underrated Lee, and Newcastle's football deteriorated accordingly. To a Sunday newspaper reporter it was the equivalent of striking gold, but Gullit exuded sufficient self-confidence to take the criticism in his elegant stride.

'I've been reading the papers and seeing what the sharks are writing about me,' he commented as we met, somewhat awkwardly, at the halfway point of a training-ground staircase. 'And you are a bad shark. I think you're shark number one!'

If Gullit was losing the off-pitch PR war, Peter Reid's Sunderland were infinitely more adept than any journalist at showing their studs and, on a late-August night of apocalyptic rain in 1999, Niall Quinn, Kevin Phillips and company weathered the storm, ending Gullit's reign with a 2-1 win at St James' Park. Before kick-off the press room was packed and steamy, and the arrival of a Shearer-less team sheet brought a rare consensus: it was a suicide note. In the event, Shearer stepped off the bench in the seventy-third minute, but it was too little, too late. There would be no truce with Gullit until 2016, when he and Shearer were reunited on BBC punditry duty; today the pair are best of friends, with the Dutchman possibly best remembered on Tyneside for his refusal to accept a pay-off from Freddy Shepherd, Newcastle's late chairman.

Shepherd divided opinion, but his legacy is the magnificently modernised, genuinely citadel-like St James' Park. I always got on well with Freddy, enjoyed his Geordie humour and will never forget the Sunday afternoon when I called him for a quote about something or other and was greeted by a barrage of expletives. At a loss to fathom out how I'd upset him, I called back and received the explanation that he was in his car and a speed camera had flashed as he answered the phone.

Newcastle's former owner, Sir John Hall, was always a gentleman to deal with; although the less said about a drunken lunch for Sunday reporters hosted by his son, Douglas, the better. A major topic of conversation centred on the respective attractiveness of the players' wives and their breast sizes.

Happily, the late Sir Bobby Robson's installation as Newcastle's manager raised the tone. The former England manager could be ruthless but, crucially, he retained enormous generosity of spirit. Adept at disguising his ego, appreciating life's shades of grey, and making game-changing triple substitutions, Robson not only led the team back into Europe but made Newcastle a classier club. He also restored Shearer to former glories, camouflaging the half a yard of pace he had forfeited to serious injuries by, among other things, encouraging him to rethink his movement and play on the half-turn rather than spending so much time with his back to goal.

It was during Robson's tenure that, due to a combination of editorial cuts and a difficult working relationship with a new deputy sports editor, I lost my contract and began freelancing for the *Guardian* and *Sunday Telegraph*. To my considerable surprise, Sir Bobby phoned to commiserate and offered to help by giving me an 'exclusive' interview for the *Sunday*

Telegraph. Considering the furore the previous 'one on one' we had done provoked, it was a wonderful gesture.

At the time of our first exclusive, I was struggling to survive at the *Sunday Times* and, when Robson questioned David Beckham's suitability to captain England before musing that Kieron Dyer 'needed to learn to respect women', it felt like a 'there is a God' moment. Even so, I tried to write the piece sensitively and in context, but it emerged from the editing process in full 'Robson slams Becks' front-page mode. I still remember the shock of seeing the story in print at the newsagents with the offending headline partly, and rather incongruously, disguised by the promotional free packet of garden seeds stuck to each copy of the paper. Sir Bobby imploded – although by the end of a telling-off at St James' Park we were friends again – and the sports editor eventually agreed the piece's presentation had been unnecessarily macho. Creditably, he wrote Robson a letter apologising and received a polite reply expressing sympathy 'with your predicament'.

When I subsequently wrote something in the *Sunday Telegraph* that upset him, he sought to upbraid me in Newcastle's now-weekly pre-match press conferences. Except I wasn't there and a frustrated Sir Bobby addressed the packed room, exclaiming, 'Where's the stupid tart?' The next day Newcastle played at Middlesbrough, and colleagues delighted in revealing that Robson had said 'something bad' but, when pressed, came over all faux coy and said they 'didn't like to repeat it'. In the end it took a television journalist – much more accustomed to working alongside women and regarding them as fellow humans – to explain.

After the game – a 2-2 draw, if memory serves – I stood at the stop of a staircase Robson would have to descend with the aim of hijacking him. As the club's press officer endeavoured to avert such an encounter, the man himself arrived: 'Of course she needs to speak to me,' he said. 'I've called her a stupid tart!' It was all, typically, resolved amicably, with Robson laughing when reminded that it wasn't really the sort of language befitting a knight of the realm.

Bar one or two fleeting highlights, Newcastle have arguably been on a downward trajectory ever since the day, in August 2004, they sacked

Sir Bobby. His 'crime' was merely finishing fifth the previous season and 'only' reaching the semi-finals of the UEFA Cup. He was succeeded by Graeme Souness, who strode into Toon and quickly branded the club a 'banana republic'. Lowlights of Souness's time in office included a breakdown in relations with the admittedly combustible Craig Bellamy – in marked contrast to the skilful way Robson handled the Wales striker after chairs were thrown in a private lounge at Newcastle airport following a row between his assistant, John Carver, and Bellamy over car parking – and the surreal sight of two Newcastle teammates, Kieron Dyer and Lee Bowyer, fighting each other on the St James' Park pitch during a match against Aston Villa in 2005. Small wonder Michael Owen's wife, Louise, was spied crying on the same turf after her husband signed from Real Madrid for £16 million later that year.

Even Owen's arrival could not quite save Souness, and in came the late Glenn Roeder, promoted from running the academy and freshly recovered from the brain tumour that, while West Ham's manager, almost cost him his life. It was thanks to Roeder that I finally saw Newcastle win a trophy: the Intertoto Cup in 2007. At a time when women football reporters were rarer than today and could still be given a rough time by certain 'old-school' male colleagues, I appreciated Roeder's subtle support, particularly his occasional phone calls to pass on information he suspected I might otherwise be excluded from. Such generosity did not always go down well in the press box.

'We've talked about it and we can't think of a single reason why he likes you,' one colleague informed me. 'We just can't fathom it.'

Sam Allardyce, Roeder's successor, most certainly did not like me but, as a Shepherd appointee, he did not last long before being replaced by Newcastle's brash new owner, Mike Ashley.

Cue Keegan's second managerial incarnation on Tyneside, an interlude destined to conclude at an industrial tribunal after his crossing of swords with the club's most unlikely director of football, Dennis Wise, and the latter's acquisition of Xisco, a little-known Spanish striker, without the manager's consent. While Keegan walked out, Xisco scored one goal in the course of his five-year, £50,000-a-week contract.

Next came a lurch from the sublime to the ridiculous. Joe-Kinnear-as-Newcastle-manager was a figure no television drama script-writer would have dared dream up. Mercifully I was absent – on a Champions League trip with Chelsea at Romania's Cluj – for Kinnear's C-word-punctuated diatribe against north-east journalists and the *Mirror*'s Simon Bird in particular, but there was little doubt the club had reached a new nadir.

Within months, Kinnear underwent triple heart-bypass surgery, leaving Chris Hughton holding the fort until the night of 31 March 2009. I was just about to leave the press room at Nottingham Forest's City Ground after covering an England Under-21 game, when a voice on the television set in the corner reported rumours that Alan Shearer was poised to take over at St James' Park. The vast majority of my long drive home up the A1 was spent on the phone, checking the story was true and then dictating copy to the long-suffering night sports editor. Much as I believed my contact's confirmation, the awareness that the story would be dominating the 1 April edition of the paper was not conducive to a good night's sleep.

By now I was the *Guardian*'s north-east football correspondent and, although I had some good friends and allies in the press room (the *Newcastle Evening Chronicle*'s former football correspondent Alan Oliver foremost among them), the initiation period was tough. While reporters from other parts of the country were invariably friendly, supportive and refreshingly normal, a couple of influential reporters (happily no longer in the role) within the north-east dailies pack made life tricky. If they had vaguely tolerated me as a Sunday reporter and then a freelance, they believed the more formal *Guardian* role should have gone to one of their pals. It all dictated that for the first four years – from 2007 to 2011 – I was invariably blanked when I walked into north-east press rooms or conferences. It never happened in other parts of the country, and some local daily colleagues did speak if we met individually, but it was – apparently – all part of 'the treatment' then dished out to newcomers, regardless of gender. One tabloid reporter who had moved up from the south was privately sympathetic and explained: 'You're getting "the treatment"; it happened to me for the first six months, then you're in and you'll all be best mates.'

It's important to stress that an influx of new faces and new attitudes dictates the north-east reporting landscape is transformed beyond recognition and infinitely more welcoming these days. But back then the 'staff men', as they called themselves, could make things uncomfortable for an outsider or anyone perceived as a bit different. The danger of being 'stitched up' was ever present. In 2007 Joey Barton, then a Newcastle player, was arrested on suspicion of assault during a night out in Liverpool. Having received a tip-off that something had happened, I phoned Newcastle's press officer for confirmation but he declined to help, saying he knew nothing about it. It meant that, legally, the *Guardian* could not run the story. With every other north-east reporter having received confirmation of the arrest, I was not exactly popular with the sports editor the next day. Some time later the press officer apologised, explaining he knew it was wrong but he had wanted to 'keep the others happy'.

By the time Hughton was, harshly, sacked and replaced by Alan Pardew, 'the treatment' was mercifully ending, but there seemed little hope of Mike Ashley – the sports retail tycoon who bought Newcastle from Hall and Shepherd in 2007 and swiftly started regretting it – succeeding in selling the club. If managers came and went (as a banner unfurled by Aston Villa fans when Shearer's Newcastle were relegated at Villa Park in 2009 put it: 'Who's your new Messiah: Ant or Dec?'), so too did takeover stories. A Malaysian consortium, a Nigerian consortium, two or three local Tyneside businessmen/property developers, an alliance of US-based financiers, a big-money bid from the UAE and another from Singapore were all, variously, reputedly close to buying Ashley out. None actually happened, but these stories appeared with such bewildering frequency, they were eventually dubbed 'fake-overs' by increasingly sceptical reporters and supporters. Most purported 'bids' lacked substance (it is amazing what some individuals and companies will do to see their names in the sort of headlines that might convince others they are worth lending money to) until a deadly Saudi Arabian-fronted takeover offered Newcastle fans a crash course in geopolitics.

Along the 'fake-over'-strewn road between Pardew's installation and the day when it became essential for north-east football reporters to brush up on the 'Cold War' between Saudi and Qatar, Jamal Khashoggi's grisly murder in Istanbul and the intricacies of the Premier League's overseas television rights deal with Doha's beIN Sports, Newcastle's managerial churn continued apace. Admittedly there was a brief interlude of quasi-stability when the team finished fifth in the Premier League, Pardew was anointed Manager of the Year, Yohan Cabaye controlled midfield, Demba Ba and Papiss Cissé scored vital goals and Hatem Ben Arfa bewitched fans. Being Newcastle, it did not last, but at least there was a run to the Europa League's last eight and a narrow defeat to Benfica in April 2013 to enjoy before everything fell apart.

The first part of the journey to Lisbon for the first leg of that European quarter-final involved a short bus transfer from a private terminal at Newcastle airport to the chartered plane that would transport the team, media and sponsors to Portugal. Getting to the aircraft entailed the bus crossing the main runway and, as we approached it, red 'STOP' lights began flashing on the vehicle's dashboard and a stilted voice commanding that the brakes be applied, urgently, crackled over the intercom. Within seconds, a rapidly accelerating, Dubai-bound Boeing 777 hurtled past.

'Wow, you wouldn't want to be hit by that,' said someone as it disappeared high into the Tyneside sky.

'The Emirates flight has taken off early today,' said the driver nonchalantly. 'I thought we had a few more minutes.'

Pardew probably imagined he would have longer in the north-east sun but, as Newcastle fans became increasingly – if erroneously – convinced he was Ashley's 'puppet', results dipped and his relationship with the owner deteriorated. In May 2014 an anonymous fans' website 'Sack Pardew' had been established and the toxicity inside St James' Park was such that the manager was forced to retreat deep into his dug-out as wave upon wave of abuse crashed through the ground during a 3-0 end-of-season home win against relegated Cardiff. Pardew, though, was nothing if not streetwise, and managed to leave on his own terms, taking over at Crystal Palace in January 2015. His interim successor, John Carver, did not lack confidence.

'I still think I'm the best coach in the Premier League,' Carver informed a roomful of somewhat startled reporters, straight-faced, after losing eight matches in succession. It was a minor miracle the team remained in the top tier that season.

Steve McClaren promised brighter days and better passing but lasted nine months, handing the baton to Rafael Benítez with Newcastle nineteenth and ten games remaining. Why, outsiders wondered, did Benítez – a Champions League winner at Liverpool and most recently in charge at Real Madrid – want anything to do with Ashley and Newcastle? The answer probably lay in the Spaniard's brief stint in charge of Chelsea, when, following a narrow defeat to Pardew's team at St James' Park, there was a certain spark in his eyes as he scanned the stadium's vaulting architecture during a strangely wistful post-match media debrief. One, well-documented, part of Benítez is logical, detached and dispassionately analytical, but he is also a football romantic and, in the spring of 2016, he was ready to fall in love with Newcastle.

To say such feelings were reciprocated fails to do justice to the bond between manager and public. When Benítez narrowly, gallantly, failed to prevent relegation, there were fears he would leave. Surely the Championship was no place for a world-class coach? Newcastle were already doomed by the time they beat Tottenham 5-1 at home on the season's final day, but a full house of 52,000 still chanted 'Rafa Benítez – we want you to stay' on a continuous, extremely loud loop from start to finish. He could hardly say no, and a swift return to the top division quickly ensued, followed by two seasons of solid survival and chess-like political machinations with Ashley. The relationship between this pair of enigmatic control freaks was always destined to end in tears but, while Benítez remained in post, hope no longer seemed a stranger on Tyneside.

I was in France, reporting on the 2019 Women's World Cup and squeezed into a packed train heading to Le Havre, when the long-dreaded text message arrived: after waiting for a takeover that never came and eventually abandoning hope of Ashley committing the investment required to finance a push for Europe, Benítez had left Newcastle.

Fast-forward a month and, at approximately the same time as Britain's new Prime Minister stood outside 10 Downing Street outlining a radical prescription for change, Newcastle United's new manager unveiled a bold manifesto of his own. If Boris Johnson cannot possibly have envisaged quite what the next couple of pandemic-hit years would hold in store, Steve Bruce presumably had more than an inkling of the supporter hostility and relegation perils ahead, but he still proved powerless to say no.

'I always remember Sir Bobby Robson saying to me: "If you ever get the chance, go to Newcastle. You take it because anyone who cracks it will be an absolute king up there,"' Steve McClaren says, explaining the irresistible magnetism at play.

Along with too many predecessors to mention, both Sir Bobby and McClaren had overlooked Gallowgate's grim history as the public execution site known as 'Gallows Hole'. In 1650 twenty-two people – including fifteen 'witches' – met their end there on one summer's day alone. The noose was not finally removed until 1844, just three decades before the first ball was kicked on the St James' Park pitch and a new breed of boardroom and press room executioners began lining up their track-suited victims.

'I knew taking the job was a big risk, a big gamble,' acknowledges McClaren. 'But I thought, *High risk, high reward*.'

Like many before him, he soon learned that, at Newcastle, success is a flame that managers sometimes touch but rarely hold.

ALL INCLUSIVE

Football had largely passed **Tracy Light** *by. Then her family circumstances led her to become a champion of disability football and a campaigner for levelling the playing field to make it a game for all.*

Bill Shankly, the former Liverpool manager, so I am told, is famously quoted for suggesting football mattered more than life and death. If you know a little bit about football, then I am sure you know the quote I'm referring to. I didn't until someone mentioned it, but that's because I'm relatively new to all this in the scheme of things.

Clearly football does not (and never will) matter more than life and death itself, and that has never been more apparent than in 2021, more than a year into a global pandemic that has affected so many lives in so many ways. But to many of us – me included – football really does matter, and in ways that some people may not always fully appreciate.

Take my sixteen-year-old son, Thomas, who happens to have Down's syndrome, who lives and breathes football, as a player, a spectator, a fan, a FIFA Xbox player, and a student of the game. For him, football is much more than just a game. It provides him with the building blocks for a happy and fulfilling life. It's the key to his mental and physical health and wellbeing. It allows him to be fully involved and immersed in a community who accept him without bias or exclusion. It provides him with social contact that may otherwise be missing in his life, and offers him joy, hope and aspiration. And, if all goes to plan, it will provide the basis of his future studies at college, leading to a career in football, because he aspires to be a coach.

Take my husband, who was diagnosed with Parkinson's disease aged just forty-five. With exercise recognised as one of the best ways to manage the disease, he started a football team for others with the condition, where all are welcome irrespective of their age, ability or gender. Playing football regularly provides the team with a huge dopamine boost, and so football for them is – quite literally – their medicine, both mentally and physically.

Take my youngest son, who has some additional needs and difficulties coming from his adoption, and for whom inclusive football has been an excellent way to build his confidence when a mainstream team would have been too much pressure for him. He has been able to be involved and, as well as developing his skills, be part of a team and make friends. He has also learned so much about others of all abilities, and at training he shows great empathy and understanding. This has transferred into other settings too, and at home he is a great companion to his older brother, choosing to play football together whenever they can.

And then there's me: an unexpected champion of disability football, with a vision of how things can and should be run to make the game more inclusive. With some amazing role models and mentors, I am determined to redress the inequalities that exist in football and to help really make it a level playing field for all to play, enjoy, learn and benefit from the game. I believe football can – with the right support, backing and understanding – provide far greater opportunities and life chances for those who want to get involved but may not be given the opportunity. There are clubs, coaches, charities, volunteers and support staff across the country doing some amazing work around inclusive football, but there is still such a long way to go. The journey so far has been both enlightening and frustrating, but there is a great deal of hope for a positive shift in thinking.

* * *

He was six when he looked back at me, his grin huge. The achievement was his: a goal. He was totally elated. Yet again, I was filled with immense pride and hope. Nothing else mattered for that moment in time. All the struggles, the injustice, the knock-backs, the lack of opportunity, the limited belief and perceptions of many, the frustrations, the fears for the future – they had all gone, at least for a while.

Over the next ten years these precious moments on the football pitch continued, each time giving us hope and bursts of happiness. Slowly but surely, I found myself with a passion for a game I'd once had little time for, and my interest continued to grow. By the time Thomas was sixteen, his love for football was all-encompassing, and I had become involved in football in a way I could have never imagined.

I often wondered how on earth – as a 51-year-old director of my own marketing business and with limited historical interest in football – I had become the secretary for a countywide inclusive football league, was an FA Level 1-qualified coach (albeit by the skin of my teeth), and was now coordinating the inclusive section at our local football club, St Albans City Youth FC. (Now in its sixteenth year, this section provides opportunities to more than sixty inclusive players.) I had become totally immersed in the game. It is a game that has brought so much positivity and inspiration to so many – including my family – and, without it, things could have been very different for us.

The first football Thomas had was a small sponge ball. Even before he could sit up properly, we used to roll it to him and, as he grew, there was always a ball for him to chase and try to kick. He had been delayed in his walking, and a football was one of the big 'keys' to encouraging him to walk – along with me singing the Peter Kay song '(Is this the way to) Amarillo' to get him to march along! His love for football had begun; my singing was work in progress.

My love for football at this point was lukewarm. I had spent many hours as a child watching my dad referee local matches and had often heard him being shouted at, which was hard to understand at a young age. I had listened to my grandad, an avid Spurs fan, watching the tickertape results on a very old TV every Saturday, but I never really grasped what 'the Pools' were, apart from I knew that a man came to the door every week to collect some money. I sometimes kicked a football about with friends, but both my sister and I were keen netballers and played in a local netball team. Football was not really an option for girls during the late 1970s and early 1980s. I am convinced we would have got involved had it been available to us, though, and I know the absence of football for girls at that time is a source of great frustration and even sadness for several of my female friends who would have pursued their football given the opportunity.

When Thomas was six, many of his peers were joining junior football teams. Even then, I knew how much he would enjoy and benefit from being part of a football team. The search was on for a training session that Thomas could join. He was strong and determined, but he struggled with mobility, had coordination difficulties, a speech and language delay and was much slower at running than most of his peers. He also had a tendency to run off or plonk himself down in the middle of the pitch when tired or fed up. Unfortunately, even at that age, there were very few options in our local area for children who had any kind of disability or additional needs to join a club and learn to play football, and it became apparent that many coaches, frustratingly, did not really know how a child with Down's syndrome would fit into their mainstream football training group.

Despite these knock-backs, I wanted to make sure he did not lose his confidence, that he developed his football skills and had fun. I always saw football for Thomas as a route to connecting with others in many different and positive ways, but the teams – even at that young age – were competitive and often not accessible to all. I often found myself wondering how people could say that football was a 'beautiful game' when it was often disheartening, sometimes selective and regularly far from inclusive. I constantly fell in and out of love with it. As much as it was an amazing sport, at the same time it could be harsh and cruel.

I have always been passionate that the younger you are, the better it is to get into sport, and so we continued to pursue several options. Eventually we were lucky to hear of a local club running inclusive football sessions for younger players as well as their established adult sessions. Thomas joined and – with the help of dedicated volunteers who 'got it' – things went well. At times, when he was in the 'I'm going to sit here in the middle of the pitch' mode, I used to pick him up and run with him to kick the ball into the net. He thought this was hilarious, and I came home from football training exhausted while he was still lively, but it was fun. Each time he went to training he improved, he got a little bit more coordinated, grew in confidence and had a great time.

Unfortunately, this team folded after a couple of years because volunteers moved on and the whole thing was dependent on someone else taking it on. Although not unique, I believe it is most prevalent in pan-disability sport, where a shortage of willing volunteers exacerbates the availability of already limited inclusive options. We had a year without football training, but Thomas's school had started a football team during this time, and he went to the training regularly and gave 100 per cent each week. However, he never got to play in a match, despite much enthusiasm – not even for five minutes – since, even at the age of nine or ten, it was all about winning. He was disheartened, but we kept things moving and he started to go to a local mainstream FA Skills session after school. Despite the countless pushy parents believing their child was the next Lionel Messi – and some of the kids believing it too – the attitude and aptitude of the coaches was brilliant. They gently pushed him to improve his skills, he was included fully, and he was genuinely happy. The other kids soon learned that he was a capable player but just needed a little more time, and overall they were accepting and pleased to see him (the odd mini-Messi aside).

Watford FC's Community Trust offered holiday courses and they too were always extremely welcoming of Thomas joining their mainstream groups. The coaches were great at making minor adjustments to help accommodate him, and their attitude was always so positive. He was also invited along to the many inclusive football events they were running, including playing on the pitch at Vicarage Road and community days to meet the first team – all such fantastic, memorable days.

Luckily, after a while, we found another club who were keen to grow their under-12s inclusive team, and Thomas joined St Albans City Youth FC. At the time, this was the only football club in our local area that was offering 'inclusive' football opportunities for this age group. This is remarkable, considering the number of grassroots clubs in the area. Again, dedicated volunteers quietly ran a fantastic training session for pan-disability players of all abilities, and it was amazing to find out that the two main coaches were in fact inclusive players who had worked their way up the player pathway to become Level 1 coaches. Thomas was happy to be part of a team, have the social interaction and be able to play football on the pitch once again, just like his peers. He was immediately accepted into the team and made friends, and things went from strength to strength. I became involved as a parent-volunteer and started to learn more about how few opportunities there were for youth pan-disability players to not only train but also be able to play either competitive or friendly matches and tournaments just like their peers.

* * *

Ever since he was born, we have always been strong advocates of ensuring Thomas was involved in mainstream life and activities. With a few minor adjustments, a bit of support and the right attitude from those around him, he has generally been included and accepted. From his first nursery place, through his primary and secondary schools, his education has always been a mainstream setting. The same goes for most of his interest and hobbies: we tended to steer away from some groups in preference for mainstream and inclusive settings. This was our preference, but every individual is different and what works for one child and their family does not always work for others. After all, life should be about having choice, where everyone accepts diversity and difference. But with football, even from an early age, his participation had primarily revolved around being part of a pan-disability team. More recently I have seen mainstream teams providing opportunities for those with additional needs who wish to engage in sport. Again, it is about providing the choice and the opportunities and support to meet the needs of each individual player. Yet I was always surprised to see there were limited opportunities to play against other inclusive teams, either in a grassroots league or tournament of some kind – a basic rite of passage for any young footballer, you would think.

In the early stages of Thomas starting to train with St Albans, I was part of a committee of some fantastic individuals all running inclusive teams, who set up a community group called Herts Youth Inclusive Football. Our goal was to provide more opportunities for inclusive players of all abilities to play matches, get involved in football and have fun. There were still only a handful of clubs running an inclusive football section in our large county of Hertfordshire, but we set up tournaments for existing teams to play matches regularly, as well as football festivals and skills days to encourage more individuals to get involved in inclusive football. Our plan was simple: to grow the inclusive game, to encourage more players to join in, to try to support more local clubs to set up an inclusive section, and to create pathways for further player development.

A fantastic partnership with Watford FC CSE Trust created several opportunities for the players to attend tournaments, matchdays and other special events locally and nationally. Thomas was part of the team representing Watford FC Community Trust Inclusive and played at AFC Bournemouth's Vitality Stadium, travelling on a luxury coach with tables and tinted windows all adding to the excitement of these trips. It gave all the players such a boost. He also played at various Premiership clubs' inclusive tournaments and regular events at Watford FC's Training Dome.

These would be amazing experiences for any child, but for our players it was particularly poignant to see those often excluded or on the periphery of football being offered such opportunities. I always noted how Thomas's confidence grew more and more from being involved. It was something exciting to talk about, and the positivity that flowed from it carried on into school the following week and saw his schoolwork improve. Football time and stickers were often used as a reward to complete schoolwork, and conversations to develop his speech and language were often centred on football.

When he was eleven, he was lucky enough to be invited by Watford FC to be a player mascot at Wembley for the 2016 FA Cup semi-final against Crystal Palace. It was an incredible experience that made him a superstar at school for being on live TV, watched by many millions globally. He was about to start mainstream secondary school, so the timing was perfect. Understandably nervous about going to secondary school, we said to him, 'If you can walk out onto that pitch in front of 80,000 fans, then you will be fine going to school with 1,000 other pupils.' Yet another confidence boost linked to the football. Soon after the game we also received a letter from the FA, commending him for his compassion and kindness on the day because he had looked after another young mascot who was having a panic attack.

The confidence boost worked, and football became an important part of enjoying secondary school. Football at lunchtime was a reward for good work, although it became quite an obsession at times and a few occasions of bouncing the ball in the corridor were not appreciated! Unsurprisingly, PE was one of his favourite lessons – provided it involved a ball. Maths lessons often used league tables as a tool to teach addition and subtraction, and English or speech and language would often be centred on a favourite player, around Watford FC, a Manchester United game he had watched or a match or tournament that he had played in that weekend.

* * *

Through the hard work of everyone involved with Herts Youth Inclusive Football, I began to see what football really meant to so many inclusive players of all abilities and ages. Nothing was taken for granted and any opportunity was grabbed with a ton of enthusiasm. Behind the scenes, everyone involved – including coaches, referees and volunteers – demonstrated an unwavering commitment to ensuring matches were safe and the different ages and abilities of every individual were considered. Small adaptions were made depending on the players: for instance, giving a player who needed it more time to react or be on the ball or adjusting teams' players or numbers to rebalance the game. These small changes made a considerable difference and all the players showed great progress in their football development. There were also young adults still keen to continue their football and it was always apparent how the opportunities for those reaching the transition to adult football were restricted, especially for those who were not ready to move up to adult inclusive football but their age determined they should.

Herts Youth Inclusive Football carried on evolving and the number of inclusive teams and players in the area grew. We were on our way to achieving one of our goals! But we did not stop there. In 2020, through a partnership with Hertfordshire FA and Watford FC CSE Trust, an Inclusive FA Level 1 training course was held for some of the inclusive players who had been seeking to gain this qualification. The course was held at Watford FC's training ground and delivered by excellent, inclusive tutors. I was fortunate to be on the course with the inclusive players, and it was these players who helped me get through it! The course created an often-absent pathway to possible employment in football for these players and enabled them to pass on their knowledge and understanding of inclusive football to others playing and working in football. This is such a valuable tool – to be able to fully understand inclusive players' needs, adapt accordingly and to coach their progression – and should be encouraged throughout football.

On the final evening of the course, just a few days before the first lockdown, I was also able to watch my husband's team play, who happened to be in the Training Dome at the same time. They are a truly inspirational group of players, of all ages and abilities, all with early-onset Parkinson's disease but all fully committed to improving their fitness and alleviating their symptoms. I saw first-hand why he had called his team Fighting Fit Football. Using the game to fight a disease, both mentally and physically, and supporting each other through it as a team shows just how powerful football can be.

It is often said that you never truly appreciate the things you have around you until they are gone. This has never been truer than during the Covid pandemic, which caused unprecedented disruption to all our lives, including to the game that brings us so much. During each of the lockdowns, the cancellation of grassroots football was a difficult and frustrating experience, and many of the players we know struggled without the regular social interaction and camaraderie of their teams. Local clubs and their committed bands of volunteers did their best to run regular online quizzes and chats and to check in on each other. When professional football resumed during the first lockdown, Thomas became a TV-side referee and pundit (as well as football quiz expert!), watching many games and often spotting discretions before the referee did. We started calling for 'TAR' – Thomas Assistant Referee – to adjudicate on any contentious moments in a game, and I began to fully realise just how much he knows about football's rules, formations, players, tactics – the lot!

During these challenging times (while often being in goal as my two boys played around me), I reflected even more on the importance of inclusive football and how there is still so much work to do to provide opportunities for players of all abilities with the chance to be part of a team, play football, have fun and develop. There are pathways for players looking to go further with their football, but they are still limited. For instance, there are the English FA pathways for Cerebral Palsy, Blind, Partially Sighted, Deaf and Powerchair football. However, there are no English FA pathways for anyone with a learning disability, and it is estimated that over 80 per cent of inclusive players are left without anywhere to progress. That is many thousands of players across the country who are being overlooked. There is the fantastic Special Olympics, but to be on this pathway there is a specific criterion for intellectual abilities. Overall, the opportunities are often restricted and limited across all the pathways.

In UK education for over-16s, there are a growing number of football and education academies for boys, but they are only for 'elite' players and only for those who are ready to study A Levels. Yet there is a huge demand to study sport from individuals who are not necessarily 'elite' (however that is determined) and who would bring a lot to the game but may need a little extra support to do so. This is short-sighted in so many ways. Not forgetting girls, who should also be offered an 'elite' and inclusive option, but why are there so few academies for them too? Still such a long way to go.

There has never been a more crucial or poignant time to harness the power of football to help improve mental health and physical wellbeing of those most in need. Yet there are still too many barriers for many youngsters and adults to be able to join a football team and just play. There are not enough inclusive teams available or enough backing – financial or otherwise – to encourage the development of inclusive football. It relies too heavily on committed volunteers, many of whom are often themselves busy parents and carers of children and who have taken the initiative to set up and run teams. The development of inclusive players fortunate enough to find a team is often limited by the lack of competitive or even friendly games available to them and a finite number of player pathways. And then there is the lack of player academies for anyone other than mainly 'elite' boys' teams.

The journey continues, and I have found myself sketching out how an inclusive football and educational academy could work for boys and girls – basically the same as an 'elite' academy but with some reasonable adjustments. I do not think it's that much of an ask and I know it would make a huge difference to so many. Individuals of all abilities should be given a voice about how they want their football to develop, which means they need more choice and less attitudinal barriers to achieving this. The more opportunities that are created for inclusive players of all abilities, the more it will be able to evolve. And as momentum builds, the deeper the passion for it will be, driving others to offer more and for it to be more inclusive from the top down, equal to other sections in clubs rather than just something that runs on the side.

Football has a huge impact on so many people. It is more than just a bunch of players kicking a ball around – and, yes, it is more than just winning. Football creates opportunities to connect, to express yourself in a safe space, to gain confidence, to learn new skills, to make new friends, to develop communication skills and to stay fit, healthy and happy.

And when supported with the right attitude and understanding, the possibilities are endless for everyone of all abilities.

Although each individual player is different, the desire to be included in football is the same for everyone, yet the playing field is unlevel for inclusive football. But I believe a change will come – and when it does, football will be all the better for it.

Dedicated to everyone who gives their time, understanding and support to inclusive football.

CONTRIBUTORS

KEHINDE ADEOGUN is an employment lawyer and has always loved football, taken part in playing, coaching, managing and reporting. She is now forging a new career as a registered intermediary. Her sister Taiwo is a freelance researcher, caregiver to their mother and a trainee horticulturist. She too has always been involved in football, from playing to travelling around the world following and documenting the African women's game.

ISABELLE LATIFA BARKER is a sports journalist, mainly covering football. She graduated in journalism from Nottingham Trent University in July 2019. She began writing for *The Sun* in August 2019 after winning the first Vikki Orvice scholarship and with it a two-year contract at the paper. Isabelle is a Fulham supporter and regularly features on the Fulhamish podcast as well as TalkSport, BBC Asian Network, BBC Radio 5 Live and Times Radio.

KATE BATTERSBY began work as a secretary with MI6, after which she moved to ITV's *World of Sport*. She was the first (and, to date, the only) female Chief Sportswriter in Fleet Street, and has been freelance since 2003. She has always been hopeless at sport.

ALISON BENDER is a freelance football presenter and reporter. Her work in football has taken her all over the world: anchoring, making documentaries, interviewing managers and players, and reporting pitch side. Alison appears regularly on radio, TV and podcasts. She lives in Richmond, Surrey, with her husband and two children.

JADE CRADDOCK has a PhD in English Literature and works as a freelance copyeditor and proofreader on fiction, non-fiction, football programmes and annuals. She is also a book reviewer and contributes articles and author interviews to a number of outlets. Her football claim to fame is playing against a young Karen Carney, but sadly her own football success peaked at county cup level rather than World Cup.

HAYLEY DAVINSON is a freelance content marketer and a board member of the Fulham Supporters Trust, heading up their drive to promote more involvement from female fans at Fulham and helping grow the support of the FFC Women's team. She also co-writes a monthly newsletter titled 'Books & Humanity'.

MOLLY HUDSON is a sports journalist, mainly covering football, with a specialism in and passion for the growth of the women's game. She began writing for *The Times* in 2017 and has since coved the Premier League, Champions League and women's World Cup. She was shortlisted for Football Journalist of the Year in 2019 and highly commended in Young Sports Writer 2020 at the Sports Journalists' Association awards.

CONTRIBUTORS

 **TRACY LIGHT** is a director of her own marketing company and has, in the past ten years, brought together her work, life experiences and knowledge to champion inclusive football. Leading the Inclusive Football Section at one of the largest grassroots clubs in the country and Secretary of an Inclusive Football League, Tracy is passionate about Sport for All.

 **KATIE MISHNER** is a football writer who grew up in Newcastle and found a second home in Sheffield. A lifelong Newcastle United fan, Katie has always been infatuated with football. She has written for a variety of outlets and covered the FIFA Women's World Cup 2016 and UEFA Women's Euros 2017.

 **RENUKA ODEDRA** is a freelance journalist and writer from Leicester. She has written for Eurosport, *VICE UK*, *Resurgence & Ecologist* and more. She has also broadcast for BBC local radio and BBC Sport. In 2018 she was the recipient of a Print Futures Award by the Printing Charity.

 **FADUMO OLOW** is the sports social media editor for the *Telegraph*. As an ambassador for the Youth Sports Trust, her first passion is youth work, and she has worked with various charities on engaging young people in the community and providing training on social activism and anti-racism work. She is a co-founder of the I Think She's Offside podcast, which focuses on bringing underrepresented conversations in sports to life.

 **CHRISTINA PHILIPPOU** is a forensic accounting lecturer who also teaches sport finance (including for the Premier League's Elite Academy Manager programme) and researches financial education of footballers, football finance and sport corruption. She has three children and, in her limited spare time, she is a grassroots youth and community football coach.

 **JANE PURDON** joined Women in Football as CEO in 2018, having previously worked for Sunderland AFC, the Premier League, and UK Sport, and is also Independent Chair of the Professional Game Academy Audit Company. She is studying for a Creative Writing MFA at Manchester Metropolitan University.

 **ALI RAMPLING** is a communications assistant, football freelancer and Ipswich Town fan who has written for The Athletic, Eurosport, *When Saturday Comes*, the *Manchester Evening News* and 90min.com. She was also voted Witnesham Wasps Under-10s Most Improved Player of the Year 2006/07 but doesn't like to bang on about it.

 **LOUISE TAYLOR** has been the *Guardian's* north-east football correspondent since 2007 and also reports on women's football. She previously spent ten years in a similar role for the *Sunday Times*. A Durham University Law graduate turned Thomson Regional newspapers trainee, her earlier career encompassed stints in Peterborough and London with *Match* magazine and *The Times*.

 **JULIE WELCH** was brought up in Loughton, Essex, and educated at Bristol University and the *Observer* sports department, where she was an award-winning football reporter. As well as working for most national newspapers, she wrote the acclaimed film, *Those Glory Glory Days*, about her childhood passion for the Spurs double-winning side of 1960/61. Her books include *The Biography of Tottenham Hotspur* and *The Fleet Street Girls*.

CONTRIBUTORS

 **JULIA WEST** is a goalkeeper coach who has a lot to say about the position, sometimes resulting in a different perspective on the game. Many of her keepers are now playing at good levels throughout the game and this is testament to the open-mindedness of her coaching philosophy.

 **CASSIE WHITTELL** is a former magazine editor and publishing operations director who now works for a Premier League/Women's Super League football club as regional talent club manager. A lifelong Liverpool FC fan, she's happiest spending time watching as much football as she can fit into the day, reading, and playing with her rescue cat, Alfie.

 **KATIE WHYATT** is a UK-based women's football correspondent for The Athletic. She was previously the women's football reporter for the *Daily Telegraph*, where she was the first full-time women's football reporter on a national paper. She was named the 2020 Young Sports Journalist of the Year by the Sports Journalists' Association.

 **SUZANNE WRACK** is a women's football writer for the *Guardian*. She won best colour piece at the AIPS awards in 2019 for her investigation into abuses suffered by the Afghanistan women's national team. She has been shortlisted for Football Journalist of the Year at the Sports Journalists' Association awards and Writer of the Year at the Football Supporters' Association awards twice.

ACKNOWLEDGEMENTS

By Ian Ridley, *founder of Floodlit Dreams publishing and curator of Football, She Wrote.*

In the months after my talented, treasured wife Vikki Orvice died from cancer on 6 February 2019, aged fifty-six, I thought long and hard about what fitting initiatives might honour her life and further her legacy. Many things occurred to me, because she was involved in so many things and deserved to be remembered for so many things.

Vikki – the first woman to become a staff football writer for a tabloid newspaper when she was hired by *The Sun* in 1995 – was a founder of Women in Football (WIF) and a board member, as well as vice-chair of the Football Writers' Association. She loved the game and she loved writing.

And so I decided through Floodlit Dreams, and in collaboration with WIF, to create the Vikki Orvice Book Prize. We had some remarkable entries, the winner – chosen by an eminent five-person judging panel – being Susie Petruccelli for her honest and touching memoir chronicling her love for football, *Raised A Warrior*, which was published in 2020.

It sowed a seed with me. What about all those other entries? There were a lot of great ideas among them, plenty of fine pieces of writing. They deserved a home.

The result is this remarkable, unique anthology of twenty pieces giving an overdue voice, certainly when it comes to books on football,

ACKNOWLEDGEMENTS

to more women. Ten of them, as established and experienced writers, were commissioned; ten chosen from an intriguingly diverse entry list of submissions for a competition that Floodlit Dreams set up with WIF.

It is why I must first thank the marvellous organisation that is WIF, in particular their chair Ebru Köksal and chief executive Jane Purdon. I have come to see personally, as Vikki always spoke of, just how people can work together to make a difference when talents and efforts are harnessed to reach a common goal. Vikki was fierce in her belief that women should help other women and I have been determined to carry on the work that she was so passionate about as a champion and mentor.

My thanks to the editor of this anthology, Charlotte Atyeo, a quite superb publishing professional, and my partner at Floodlit Dreams in Seth Burkett. Steve Leard produced yet another stunning cover and Alex Ridley, Vikki's stepdaughter, acted as picture editor. I am grateful to Jen O'Neill, editor of *She Kicks,* who helped Charlotte and me to decide on the ten new writers.

Above all, my gratitude goes to all the contributors for a cracking collection of diverse reads. I hope they feel as proud of this book as I do. They certainly should. I think between us all we have created something that Vikki – an English Literature graduate and a very discerning reader – would certainly have applauded.

ALSO BY FLOODLIT DREAMS

ADDED TIME
Surviving Cancer, Death Threats and the Premier League
Mark Halsey with Ian Ridley

THE BOY IN BRAZIL
Living, Learning and Loving in the Land of Football
Seth Burkett

A DAZZLING DARKNESS
The Darren Barker Story
Darren Barker with Ian Ridley

THE SOCCER SYNDROME
English Football's Golden Age
John Moynihan
(Foreword by Patrick Barclay)
(Afterword by Leo Moynihan)

THE HITLER TROPHY
Golf and the Olympic Games
Alan Fraser

FOOTBALL'S COMING OUT
Life as a Gay Fan and Player
Neil Beasley with Seth Burkett

RAISED A WARRIOR
One Woman's Soccer Odyssey
Susie Petruccelli

THE BREATH OF SADNESS
On Love, Grief and Cricket
Ian Ridley

TITANS OF THE TEARDROP ISLE
A Season as a Pro Footballer in Sri Lanka
Seth Burkett

www.floodlitdreams.com